VIRGINITY REVISITED:
CONFIGURATIONS OF THE UNPOSSESSED BODY

PHOENIX

Journal of the Classical Association of Canada
Revue de la Société canadienne des études classiques
Supplementary Volume XLIV / Studies in Gender Volume I

Studies in Gender
Editors
Alison Keith *Univeristy of Toronto*
Ingrid Holmberg *University of Victoria*

EDITED BY BONNIE MacLACHLAN AND
JUDITH FLETCHER

Virginity Revisited: Configurations of the Unpossessed Body

UNIVERSITY OF TORONTO PRESS
Toronto Buffalo London

© University of Toronto Press Incorporated 2007
Toronto Buffalo London
Printed in Canada

ISBN 978-0-8020-9013-3

Printed on acid-free paper

Library and Archives Canada Cataloguing in Publication

Virginity revisited : configurations of the unpossessed body / edited
by Bonnie MacLachlan and Judith Fletcher.

(Phoenix. Supplementary volumes. Studies in gender)
Includes bibliographical references and index.
ISBN-13: 978-0-8020-9013-3
ISBN-10: 0-8020-9013-3

1. Virginity – Social aspects.   I. MacLachlan, Bonnie, 1944–
II. Fletcher, Judith   III. Series: Phoenix. Supplementary volume
(Toronto, Ont.) Studies in Gender

BL325.V55V57 2007   306.73'2   C2006-904477-5

University of Toronto Press acknowledges the financial assistance to its publishing
program of the Canada Council for the Arts and the Ontario Arts Council.

University of Toronto Press acknowledges the financial support for its publishing
activities of the Government of Canada through the Book Publishing Industry
Development Program (BPIDP).

This volume is dedicated to the memory of Jenny Franchot

CONTENTS

Contributors ix

Introduction 3
BONNIE MacLACHLAN

1. The Invention of Virginity on Olympus 13
ELEANOR IRWIN

2. The Virgin Choruses of Aeschylus 24
JUDITH FLETCHER

3. The Hippocratic *Parthenos* in Sickness and Health 40
ANN ELLIS HANSON

4. Why Were the Vestals Virgins? Or the Chastity of Women and the Safety of the Roman State 66
HOLT N. PARKER

5. 'Only Virgins Can Give Birth to Christ': The Virgin Mary and the Problem of Female Authority in Late Antiquity 100
KATE COOPER

6. *Virgo Fortis*: Images of the Crucified Virgin Saint in Medieval Art 116
ILSE FRIESEN

7. Amplification of the Virgin: Play and Empowerment in Walter of Wimborne's *Marie Carmina* 128
JENIFER SUTHERLAND

8. Christ from the Head of Jupiter: An Epistemological Note on
   Huet's Treatment of the Virgin Birth   149
   THOMAS LENNON

9. 'Sew and snip, and patch together a genius':
   Quilting a Virginal Identity in Margaret Atwood's *Alias Grace*   156
   ANNE GEDDES BAILEY

Works Cited   177

Index   197

CONTRIBUTORS

Anne Geddes Bailey is External Relations Coordinator in the Faculty of Arts at the University of Alberta. Her research specialty is contemporary and postmodern Canadian fiction. She is the author of *Timothy Findley and the Aesthetics of Fascism* and co-editor of *Paying Attention: Critical Essays on Timothy Findley*.

Kate Cooper is Senior Lecturer in Early Christianity and Director of the Centre for Late Antiquity at the University of Manchester. Her current research focuses on gender and the family during the Christianization of the Roman Empire and post-Roman period. She is the author of *The Virgin and the Bride: Idealized Womanhood in Late Antiquity* and co-editor, with Julia Hillner, of *Religion, Dynasty, and Patronage in a Christian Capital: Rome, 350–750* (forthcoming).

Judith Fletcher is Associate Professor of Archaeology and Classical Studies, and Women's Studies Coordinator at Wilfrid Laurier University. Her research interests include the representation of women's speech in Greek drama. She has published articles on Greek tragedy and comedy, epic poetry, and the theme of the Underworld in contemporary fiction. She is co-editor, with Alan Sommerstein, of *Horkos: The Oath in Greek Society* (forthcoming).

Ilse Friesen is Professor Emerita of Art History at Wilfrid Laurier University. Her publications include *The Female Crucifix: Images of St Wilgefortis since the Middle Ages*; *Albrecht Dürer: 114 Famous Prints: Woodcuts and Copper Engravings in the Graphic Collection of the Monastery of Stams, Tyrol*; and *Earth, Hell and Heaven in the Art of William Kurelek*.

Ann Ellis Hanson is the author of some one hundred articles in the field of papyrology and of Greek and Roman medicine. She was a MacArthur fellow from 1992 to 1997. She currently teaches in the Classics Department of Yale University and is working on an edition of the gynecological treatises of the Hippocratic Corpus for the Loeb Classical Library.

Eleanor Irwin was a member of the Division of Humanities, University of Toronto at Scarborough, for thirty-three years (1968–2001). She is author of *Greek Colour Terminology*. Her interest in virginity developed from teaching courses on classical mythology and women in the ancient Greek and Roman world. In retirement she tends plants, both literal and literary, teaches occasional courses, and considers how the decision not to marry may have contributed to the scholarly success of women classicists such as Sarah Fielding, Kathleen Freeman, and Queen Elizabeth I.

Thomas Lennon is Professor of Philosophy at the University of Western Ontario. His area of specialization is the history of early modern philosophy. He has published half a dozen books and scores of articles dealing in particular with such figures as Descartes, Malebranche, Bayle, Locke, Berkeley, and Hume.

Bonnie MacLachlan is Associate Professor in the Department of Classical Studies at the University of Western Ontario. She specializes in Greek lyric poetry and in ancient religion. She is the author of *The Age of Grace: Charis in Early Greek Poetry* and co-editor, with Robert Wallace, of *Harmonia Mundi*.

Holt N. Parker is a Professor of Classics at the University of Cincinnati. He applies anthropological, literary, linguistic, and historical theory to the study of ancient texts, working in the area of gender studies, ancient religion, Augustan poetry, Roman comedy, and ancient medicine.

Jenifer Sutherland has a PhD from the Centre for Medieval Studies at the University of Toronto. She is presently teaching at Branksome Hall in Toronto and writing about the medieval institution of confession and the modern institution of psychoanalysis.

VIRGINITY REVISITED

Introduction

BONNIE MacLACHLAN

Comus, in Milton's poem of the same name, attempts to persuade the Lady to forfeit her virginity. His rhetoric is summarily dismissed by her, and she responds with serious high praise of the 'doctrine' of virginity:

Thou hast nor ear, nor soul to apprehend
The sublime notion, and high mystery,
That must be utter'd to unfold the sage
And serious doctrine of Virginity.   *Comus* 784–7

As a doctrine, virginity has been a cultural artifact. For much of human history, it has been held in high esteem for young women approaching marriage: virginity has been an essential quality for determining their market value. Once virginity was lost, a nubile woman's worth was greatly diminished. All this has changed recently, of course, but the sexual permissiveness that many North American youth have enjoyed in the last three or four decades is now being challenged by other young people who are reclaiming the value of sexual renunciation. 'Athletes for Abstinence,' 'True Love Waits,' and new age monasticism are attracting growing numbers of adherents. Space has even been found for women wishing to regain lost virginity. Elizabeth Abbott, in *A History of Celibacy* (1999), describes the movement known as 'BAVAM!' (Born Again Virgins of America). Self-identifying as 'recovering sluts,' these women have mounted a much-visited website, publish a newsletter, and sell T-shirts. The movement was founded by a twenty-five-year old landscape gardener who is, as Abbot reports, dedicated to restoring the moral fibre that she believes America was built upon. If people reassert power over their bodies and gain self-respect, she contends, they will thereby be freed to show real respect for others.

Despite cultural variations in the understanding of virginity, it is clear that in all cases virginity is closely allied with power. Consider, for example, the *ius primae noctis*, which ensured submission of the bride and her family to the lord of the manor, the priest, and so on who assumed this right. But what if virginity is retained? Mastery over one's passions, praised by Aristotle as *autarkeia* and practised by the Born Again Virgins of America, offers enhanced self-esteem. When others – would-be seducers like Comus, or parents eager to marry off a daughter – are thwarted in their aims by a woman zealously guarding her virginity, there ensues a power struggle for control of the woman's body. This in turn becomes symbolic of something much bigger. Narratives of the Christian martyrs are full of such power struggles; the virgin martyr's body becomes the site for a political contest between the fledgling church and Roman imperial power.

Autonomy and the power that accompanied virginity had potential of another sort. Remaining 'intact' before engaging in sexual activity reserved the full force of erotic energy for this anticipated event. This is the program for 'True Love Waits.' The same understanding of the force of reserved energy lay behind an ancient Greek festival in honour of Hera, wife of Zeus. During an annual festival at Nauplion, Hera's virginity was restored by the bathing of her statue in the spring known as Kanathos, ensuring renewed potency in the sexual encounter between the primary divine couple.

Similar ritual or mythical accounts from ancient Greece suggest that not only Hera, but Athena, Aphrodite, Artemis, and even Demeter participated in a process which they shared with other Indo-European goddesses and heroines, replenishing the reservoir of their power because they possessed the ability to return to the state of being sexually intact – to revisit virginity. Mythical examples from other Indo-European traditions have been compiled by M.R. Dexter;[1] among these females is Madhavi, a heroine in the Indic epic *Mahabharata*. Madhavi marries three kings in succession, bearing a son to each then recovering her virginity and her potency as bride. The Scandinavian goddess Gefjon bears several sons for her giant husband but remains a virgin. Inheriting the powers of these women is of course the mother of Christ, Mary, ever Virgin.

Dexter distinguishes two types of potency released from the energy reservoir of the virgin female: the type that is outwardly directed, serving men in a patriarchy, and that which is retained in the female, leaving her independent of male control. The link between virginity and power was the topic of a conference held at the University of Western Ontario in November 1998. The object of the conference was to study various ways in which the choice of sexual renunciation, particularly when made by women, conferred autonomy and power on themselves and on others. This book consists of revised versions of some of these papers, along with others inspired by the conference. They span nearly four millennia, from Bronze Age Greece to the twentieth century.

The celibate choice was made by independent women such as Elizabeth I or Joan of Arc, who repudiated liaisons with men, preferring the power released by personal independence. In the recent movie *Elizabeth* (1998), directed by Shekhar Kapur, the young Tudor queen is shown bedding her lover but later opting to reclaim her independence. In the film she reconstructs her identity as a virgin, modelling herself after the Virgin Mary, and in so doing capitalizes upon both Mary's maternal authority and her virginal autonomy. Elizabeth's sixteenth-century public recognized the potential of a woman's youthful and celibate body to be invested with political power. Portraits of her, painted during her lifetime, took pains to portray her as a nubile but chaste young girl even when she was sixty years old.

At the centre of the attention paid to Mary, the most famous virgin in the European tradition, is an arresting paradox – postpartum virginity. Since the fourth century, the veneration of the Virgin Mary has focused on her ability, like Madhavi or Gefjon, to be a virgin mother. This veneration was founded upon a belief in Mary's own untainted birth from the womb of Anna, together with lifelong virginity, guaranteeing her independence from contaminated mortals. Mary neither carried forward original sin nor engaged in the sinful activity of having sex with a man. As an iconographic motif, the image of Mary standing on a globe that rests upon a serpent has conveyed to the Christian world the unambiguous association of power – temporal and spiritual – with virginity. Early defenders of Mary's sexual purity had to struggle to accommodate references in the Gospels to Jesus's brothers and sisters. Keeping intact the virginal body of Mary was vital for the survival of the Christian cult, which was anxious to negotiate space in the Roman Empire. The connection between female chastity and the success of an institution would have been understood by every Roman: the very survival of Rome and its empire was predicated upon the virginity of its Vestal priestesses, the subject of Holt Parker's essay in this volume.

In late antiquity until the early modern period the figure of the Virgin Mother Mary served as a social icon. Onto her pure and 'closed' body a variety of projections could be cast by different historical, social, and gendered constituencies, including ascetics and householders, intellectuals and mystics, civic and church leaders, and the ordinary man and woman. Kate Cooper of Manchester University, one of the two keynote speakers at the conference in 1998, has written extensively in recent years about virgins and the Virgin

Mary as social icons in the early centuries of the Christian church. In this volume she provides a compelling example of women in late antiquity making creative use of the power of virginity as a symbol that would meet their own social ends. While previous studies of early Christian virgins have tended to focus upon virginal women as pawns in a game played by men – often bishops – Cooper argues that we need to learn to read for the signs of women's own agency in the game of forging a sexual identity.

During the fourth and fifth centuries CE the cult of Mary developed into one of the main axes of Christian devotion, not least because from dynasty to dynasty the women of the reigning Roman imperial family, and later barbarian abbesses and queens, saw in Mary an image of female authority – both maternal and vulnerable – with which they could claim identity. That the Virgin Mother was a figure of paradox meant that she was in some ways difficult and elusive as an object of *imitatio* and identification, but at the same time it added enormously to her power, in the eyes both of her imitators and of their audiences.

The flexibility of this construct of Mary meant that men too could benefit from her as an icon. The contemplation of her images in the medieval period actually became a means of liberating human potential for both men and women. An example of this is the thirteenth-century Franciscan Walter of Wimborne, who composed *Marie Carmina*, a poetic reflection upon the Virgin. Jenifer Sutherland's essay explores the empowerment described by Wimborne in light of Piaget's work on the importance to ego development of a child's imaginative play with dolls. The Virgin functioned for him as a kind of soul-doll, representing in turn sister, daughter, mother, beloved, and dominatrix, permitting Wimborne to explore and ultimately to gain control over a range of potential life experiences. Mary's virginal body presented itself to him – like those of the sexually chaste prophetesses of the Greek and Roman world – as a direct conduit to divinity.

Men could also reflect upon Mary's virginity at an intellectual level, taking advantage of its flexible parameters. A debate between two theological perceptions of her perpetual virginity is the subject of Tom Lennon's paper. From the work of the seventeenth-century thinker Pierre-Daniel Huet, who launched a vigorous epistemological attack against Cartesianism, Lennon exposes a contemporary debate in France over the evidence for Mary's virgin birth: was there evidence for her *physical* virginity, or was the truth claim based on something else? Physical evidence is set against dogma, traditional belief. For Huet, Mary's virginity is a *fiat*, the result of public conviction, of assigning to her the social category of the virginal state, and the status of this conferral is elevated to theological proof.

It is not without some degree of irony that the foundation of the veneration of Mary as Virgin Mother derives from the Septuagint translation of the Hebrew *almah* as *parthenos*, 'virgin.' The text in question is the prophecy found in Isaiah 7.14, that an *almah* would conceive and bear a son and call his name Immanuel. The Greek *parthenos* rendered by the Septuagint does not cover the entire range of meanings of the Hebrew word; *almah* ('young woman') could refer equally to young widows, concubines, or prostitutes. Although the range of meanings for *parthenos* was more restricted, it was still a term with much more elasticity than the English 'virgin.' *Parthenos* was a term applied usually to an unmarried young woman, but on occasion it could denote a young mother, as has been pointed out by Giulia Sissa[2] and by Ann Hanson in this volume and elsewhere.[3] In a similar vein, Dexter contributes the detail that the Scandinavian Gefjon remained a *maer* (Old Norse for 'unmarried maiden') while bearing sons. *Almah*, *parthenos*, *maer*, the Latin *virgo*, and even the English 'virgin' (applied to Mary and Elizabeth I, for example) denote not a physical state but a social one, a relational one, one that evokes the qualities of social autonomy and potency.

Virginity as a socially constructed category is treated historically by Eleanor Irwin and Ann Hanson in their essays. Irwin attempts to historicize the construction of the divine virgins of the Greek pantheon – Artemis, Athena, Hestia, and Hecate – situating the independence they enjoyed as a consequence of their virginity in patriarchal Athens. Ann Hanson's approach is also a historical one, working with Greek and Roman medical texts. She focuses on the liminal position of the virginal young woman: neither child nor woman, the *parthenos* is poised on the edge, preparing to make the transition from one social category to the other. Failing to do this, not to engage in married sexual activity, was to refuse to make the transition. According to most of the medical writers, remaining physically and socially intact beyond menarche was dangerous: it set the young girl up for various pathologies and death.

The wide-ranging belief that there is particular potency residing on the margins of the familiar has been the subject of several studies; perhaps best known is Mary Douglas's *Purity and Danger*.[4] This power is experienced as a threat to the social order, but when harnessed by ritual or physical intervention it can be converted for the common good. Virginal young women, on the margins between childhood and womanhood, carried this power. Judith Fletcher, in her study of the gendered discourse of virgin choruses in the tragedies of Aeschylus, illustrates just how they were feared and despised because their bodies were charged with an energy that was disruptive, destructive. Their speech is politically charged, and the potentially dangerous voices of the virgin choruses in *Seven against Thebes*, *Suppliant Women*, and *Eumenides* are modified in order for the young women to direct their powers for the civic good. The transgressive nature of women with ambiguous sexual status was admired by Athenians when contained, and feared when not.

The Vestal Virgins were women whose bodies were consecrated to the Roman state. Taking a vow of chastity for the duration of their service from childhood until late adulthood, they reserved their fecundity for the welfare of Rome. (This is consistent with Dexter's identification of the reservoir of energy in the virginal female that could serve patriarchy.) If accused of violating her vow of chastity, the Vestal became a social pariah and was buried alive. She was interred within the walls of the city, however, so that she could continue to release her powers as a scapegoat, a *pharmakos*. Like the energy in the voices of virgin choruses on the tragic stage, the autonomy of the Vestals – conferred by their virginity – meant that their bodies could serve the state as saviours; their destructive potential could be converted to good through ritual means. Holt Parker's essay in this volume explores this potential, reading the 'fallen' Vestal not only as *pharmakos* but also as *prodigium* and *devotio*. Parker draws his analysis from the anthropology of magic.

Although a social category, virginity's physicality could not be ignored. In a young woman the virginal body was sexually charged but resistant. This resistance itself accounts for her attractiveness to men, for whom possession of the intact woman becomes a quest. In Greek myths this was true both for Artemis and the nymphs who followed her in the wild; it was also true for the 'cool' virgin Athena and even the stay-at-home Hestia. In the case of these mythical virgins male desire was satisfied by divine rape. The desire to possess the virgin is the subject of Anne Bailey's chapter on the Canadian historical novel *Alias Grace* by Margaret Atwood. The reader of this story, like the novel's doctor/investigator Simon Jordan, is attracted to the figure of Grace Marks and wants to 'know' her sexual status. Ultimately, Grace keeps to herself her inner core, remaining tantalizingly untouchable, unknowable, virginally intact.

Jenny Franchot, in whose memory this book is dedicated, presented a keynote address at the conference in October 1998, less than a week before her untimely death. Her paper grew out of her work on the nineteenth-century Protestant fascination with the celibates of the Roman church.[5] Cloistered convents in the nineteenth century gave rise to suspicion about the interior life of nuns. The secrecy of their life, together with their refusal to engage in the economy of marriage and reproduction, created anxiety and rage in outsiders. This 'radical aloneness,' a resistance to being exteriorized and known, provoked outrage. Convents found themselves besieged by ransacking Protestant mobs. Nuns who emerged from the cloisters were stoned; the Ursuline convent just outside Boston was burned to the ground and graves in the convent cemetery were opened to examine the bodily remains. The unknowable, unpossessed bodies of the women behind the walls were forced into the open to reveal – unlike Grace Marks in *Alias Grace* – their secrets.

In her conference presentation, Jenny Franchot reviewed the Protestant exposé of the activities of nuns in the Hôtel-Dieu convent in Montreal, recorded in a book written by a woman called Maria Monk in 1836, the same year the Ursuline convent in Boston was burned.[6] The book claimed that via underground tunnels connecting the Hôtel-Dieu convent to a neighbouring monastic community, priests and nuns violated their vows of chastity. Babies who were born to the women were thrown into lime pits, Monk claimed. Monk depicted herself on the cover of her book as a nun, holding a baby, attesting to the fascination of her reading public with what they chose to abhor, the cloistered body, here – once again unlike Grace Marks – with its secret 'exposed.'

When the celibate choice is successful in fending off male sexual intervention, traditional gendered expectations no longer apply. Among the virginal goddesses of the Greek pantheon, Athena as sexually independent was free to embody the city of Athens. Since birth she wore the armour that signalled this identity, a protected and protecting figure. (These ideas are explored in detail in Eleanor Irwin's essay.) Her masculine attire did not prevent Athena from participating in activities routinely assigned to women, activities such as wool-working and weaving; her androgyny was central to her performance. This was true for the Vestal Virgins, a Roman incarnation of many of the features of Athena. As Holt Parker makes clear in his paper, the Vestals were robed as married women, tended the hearth like daughters in a Roman household, but enjoyed the legal status of males. Their freedom from possession by fathers or husbands liberated them from the conduct expected of married women, and – like Athena – they were thus enabled to represent the state itself. This same exemption applied to the maiden choruses in Aeschylus's tragedies, as Judith Fletcher points out: acting for the good of the city, they shed their roles as women and spoke in public like men.

Gender transformation and transvestism fill the tales of the early Christian martyrs. Young women, rejecting the role of bride and mother, disguised themselves as men to facilitate their mobility in the Roman world, or were actually physically masculinized in the process of engaging in an independent life that professed a direct connection to divinity.[7] Social androgyny in the Roman Christian world may be accounted for by the pervading practice of asceticism, which permitted women to sidestep their obligation to become mothers and transmit property, since there was less demand for producing heirs. Instead, they were able to present themselves as independent agents. The practice of ignoring these traditional constraints placed upon women was fuelled by the narratives found in the *Apocryphal Acts*, in which virginal heroines – like those of the ancient Greek romances – became the object of both male and female devotion. Both sexes when reading these early Christian narratives identified with the nubile but independent heroines, who were fiercely loyal not to their families but to apostolic authority. For men, erotic desire was transformed into spiritual constancy, akin to the heroines' attachment to the male apostles. For women readers the identification was more direct. The popularity of the *vitae* of these ascetic women is reflected in the fact that four such lives were copied on vellum by a seventh-century scribe who, short of writing material, created a palimpsest, scraping a copy of the Gospel in order to give priority to these stories.[8]

Even in the medieval period, stories of the masculinized Christian virgin continued to flourish. Effeminate portraits of the crucified Christ opened the door for the legend of the bearded female saint Wilgefortis, whose name is quite likely an adaptation of *Virgo fortis*, 'powerful Virgin.' Ilse Friesen's essay on Wilgefortis demonstrates the deep and complex implications of gender ambiguity contained in the body of the virgin. The virgin's body did not make the progression towards full femininity as defined by her society, but the arresting of this development released new powers. Wilgefortis for the English became Saint Uncumber, patron of women wishing to become 'unencumbered' by oppressive husbands. She was also called upon to assist with afflictions that ranged from sexual dilemmas and infertility to warfare and floods.

The story of Joan of Arc, one of the best-known virgins in European history, is not represented in this volume. Nonetheless, her narrative is woven through most of the aspects of virginity treated in the essays. Joan was born in a rural French village at Domremy in Champagne in 1412. In the wars fought between the Duke of Burgundy and the French King Charles, Domremy remained loyal to Charles, and Joan the warrior championed Charles's cause, although she was ultimately betrayed by him. Joan's biography and the legends that grew from it exemplify elements from the cultural construction of virginity with which we are now familiar. Joan was uneducated and illiterate, but witnesses at her rehabilitation trial, twenty years after her death, testified to her piety and skill at sewing and spinning. Textile working has long been an index of chastity. Roman tombstones honouring good wives bore the inscription *lanam fecit, domum servavit* ('she made the wool, she preserved the home'). Jules Bastien-LePage painted Joan of Arc (1879) as a simple peasant girl looking off into the distance, her distaff behind her. Overhead float images of Joan in armour and two angels, harbingers of her future sainthood. This can be compared with Dante Gabriel Rossetti's *The Girlhood of the Virgin Mary* (1849), which depicts the young Mary working at her embroidery. Both Joan and Mary Virgin can be compared with the Greek goddess Athena, virgin warrior and patron of weaving and other feminine handicrafts.

Like Athena, Joan of Arc was an armed warrior. As Marina Warner has pointed out in her study of Joan,[9] one of the aspects of her behaviour that upset her inquisitors most deeply was her self-representation as an androgyne, insisting upon wearing men's clothing, which she declared had been prescribed by St Michael in a vision. This was an outward sign of her violation of the norm. In other ways, too, her body did not conform. She was said not to menstruate, a condition perhaps incurred by her fasting. Her amenorrhea contributed, in popular belief, to her exceptional strength. By renouncing sex she released inner force. Her flesh did not acquire the spongy softness of the mature woman, and she, like the Greek *parthenos* who resisted the taming brought about by sexual activity, remained in a permanently liminal stage. She chose for herself the title 'La Pucelle,' a word with many of the same connotations as *parthenos*.

Joan's body was, like that of Grace Marks or the Ursulines, an enigma. Her refusal to enter full womanhood led to doubts about her natural gender. After her death, her body was removed from the funeral pyre partly consumed by the flames and displayed to her doubters. When they were satisfied that she was indeed female, her body was returned to be burned completely. Her suit of armour, however, would remain the physical symbol of her privacy concealed. The armour had been presented to Joan by the Dauphin himself, made to fit her small form and decorated, apparently, with roses and floral motifs. She wore it constantly, even when sleeping, and it became the perfect emblem of the sealed virginal body, emblem of the inviolability of France. It has never been found. Like Grace Marks's secret, it remains unknowable but invites revisiting.

NOTES

1 Dexter (1985, 57–74).
2 Sissa (1990a, 78–83, 87, 91; 1990b, 340–3).
3 Hanson (1990) 309–38.
4 Douglas (1966).
5 Franchot (1994).
6 Monk (1836).

7 A parallel for this overriding of gendered differences by religious activity may be found in early bisexual gods of fertility and power, such as Aphroditos (transgendered Aphrodite) of Cyprus, whose worshippers cross-dressed while sacrificing (Macrobius, *Saturnalia* 3.8.1–3).
8 Salisbury (1991, 6–7).
9 Warner (1981, 140–8, 157–8).

1

The Invention of Virginity on Olympus

ELEANOR IRWIN

It goes without saying that the Greek gods and goddesses were social constructions. They arose from a social reality initially embedded in the Greek Bronze Age, and their characteristics were modified and adapted somewhat to suit the needs of later historical periods. They were, in other words, *invented*. To some degree their portraits mirrored the lives of Greek men and women, but in certain other ways their narratives sketch some dramatic departures from what we know of the everyday life of the Greeks. We can only conjecture why this was so, assuming that these divine constructs arose in order to accommodate some deeply held beliefs and concerns of the people: by exploring the dissonance between the patterns of Greek human and divine life we are rewarded with some important insights into the Greek conceptual framework.[1] One of these departures involves goddesses who remain eternally virgin, who refuse to make the transition from *parthenos* to *gynê*, from nubile young woman to the woman with sexual experience.

At the outset of the *Homeric Hymn to Aphrodite* 5 (7–33) we learn that three of the Olympian goddesses took no pleasure in the 'works of Aphrodite' and requested from Zeus the right to remain virginal: Athena preferred the pleasure to be found in warfare and craft; for Artemis it was the bow and hunting, and the dances and songs of her women followers; Hestia, despite the suits of Poseidon and Apollo, firmly resisted them and swore a great oath before Zeus that she would live forever virgin and become celibate guardian of the hearth fires of home and city. As virgins these immortals enjoyed a unique autonomy granted by their unmarried status, an independence that was denied to Greek women, who were perpetually under the guardianship of their *kyrios*. The specific strength of these immortal virgins in fact resided in their refusal to relinquish *partheneia*, the ephemeral state between childhood and motherhood experienced by all young women. This was a time of life that was filled with potency derived from a reservoir of as-yet-unreleased generative energy, a transitional phase in the life pattern of a mortal woman that was a time of crisis, when she exerted an attractive yet threatening wildness.[2] Mortal virgins therefore had to move beyond *partheneia* to transmute and shape its wild energy into the requirements of wifehood and motherhood.[3] But for goddesses virginity could be permanent or even (in the case of Hera, discussed below) renewable. Translated into a permanent state, *partheneia* became a source of eternal and unyielding power.

The Olympian family was no less patriarchal than Greek families of the historical period. Why did Greeks 'invent' a divine social construct that permitted certain females such a degree of independence from male would-be suitors? Why did their life stories differ markedly from others in the divine family – goddesses as well as gods – who were sexually active and reproductive? The answer lies in the fact that this family was headed by an immortal patriarch who did not wish to be replaced. Athena, Artemis, and Hestia did not pose the risk that would be presented by divine motherhood.

This particular configuration of the divine family of the Greeks included another powerful virgin, Hecate, sometimes conflated with Artemis. Hecate's unique relationship to Zeus is the result of her history: she was a goddess from the generation prior to the Olympians, the Titans, and retained honours that pre-dated Zeus. Hesiod honours her with the (so-called) 'Hymn to Hecate' in the *Theogony* (411–52), reflecting her unique power and autonomy within the patriarchal family. Hecate mediated between regimes – Olympian and Titan – but also between mortal and divine spheres.[4] She possessed the liminal qualities of the virgin – not those belonging to the transition from childhood to womanhood, but rather to two successive generations of gods. Zeus chose not to arrange a marriage for her, for by the logic of the succession myth she would give birth to a son who would overthrow him. Instead, she functioned as a daughter who could transmit the family legacy from one generation to another. Hesiod describes her as *mounogenês* ('only child,' 426), suggesting that she is to be thought of as an *epikleros*, one of those brotherless women who become the carrier of a family's wealth and estate.[5] But while it was required of the mortal *epikleros* that she marry and produce an heir, Hecate transmitted to Zeus the heritage of the Titans and in return received honours from Zeus 'beyond all others' (412). Precisely because she remained unmarried she continued to carry this balance of privileges.[6]

Greek virginity by definition excluded sexual submission to a male. The divine virgin remained *adamatos*, 'untamed' or 'unsubdued' in the fullest sense of the word. No husband controlled her, nor did she submit to the power of Aphrodite. The Greeks, who equated masculine sexuality with social dominance, also found it difficult to accept the inverse situation in which goddesses were active lovers.[7] If a goddess took a mortal lover she distorted the social order, for she would automatically become the dominant partner in the relationship. Virgin goddesses had no interest in exerting their powers in this way. Instead, the Greeks made them interact with mortal men in a kourotrophic capacity: rather than functioning as sexual partners, they became nurturing guardians of young men approaching adulthood or protectors of male heroes. Athena, for instance, functioned as just such a *kourotrophos*. Her tutelage benefited Athens, and she assumed responsibility for the nurturing of the autochthonous ancestor of the Athenians, Erichthonius.[8] Her relationship with Heracles and Odysseus contained no hint that they were sexually attracted to her nor she to them, and her micromanaging of their careers was not the result of maternal inclinations; the heroes survived and prospered because their tutelary deity had access to a storehouse of energy provided by her special status and nature, for which her virginity was essential. A Celtic tale provides some insight here: the Welsh Warrior King Math retained his martial powers by resting his feet in the lap of a virgin between battles. As long as his female footstool retained her virginity, Math was able to draw upon her special powers, to renew his strength, but should the woman become sexually active he was obliged to find another virgin or lose his kingdom.[9]

Virgin Artemis was a powerful kourotrophic divinity.[10] Her fierce attachment to Hippolytus is but one example, although his refusal to renounce virginity served as a reminder that only the immortals could remain celibate with impunity.[11] She was also a kourotrophic figure for Athenian ephebes: adolescent males were inducted into the rights of citizenship by swearing an oath in her sanctuary. She was the protecting deity in rituals involving *parthenoi*, at Brauron for instance. With *parthenoi* (historical and mythical) she was rigorous in demanding virginity in her followers. When Callisto became pregnant by Zeus, the goddess's anger was ferocious.[12] Pausanias (7.19.2–5) gives us an account of a priestess of Artemis *Triclaria* in Achaia named Comaetho, who loved one Melanippus. Unable to obtain permission from their parents to marry, the couple used the sanctuary of Artemis as a bridal chamber. Artemis sent disease and death upon the inhabitants of the region until Apollo commanded that the lovers be sacrificed to Artemis; an Achaean sacrifice was reenacted annually requiring for it the most beautiful young man and woman. In Cyrene, Greek women about to marry were obliged to engage in a prenuptial rite of appeasement to Artemis for the loss of their virginity.[13]

The ferocity of Artemis, virgin and patron of virgins, arose from her refusal to submit to the same mature sexual identity required of a human female. Resistance added value to human virgins before they married, however; this was the furthest apple on the highest branch of the apple tree, according to Sappho (105aV), a prize worth defending and fighting for. And patriarchal society would have it so, for girls before their marriage: a sexually reticent girl possessed the feminine virtues of *sophrosyne*, self-control, so important in a patrilineal inheritance system in which a man needed to know that he was the father of his heirs. The powerful virgin protected her valuable potential fecundity. The desirable and athletic young woman Atalanta, a denizen of the wild like Artemis, resisted her suitors by defeating them in foot races until one of them dropped a golden apple – symbolic of sexuality – in her path (Hesiod, fr. 72–6M-W). Io tried to resist the advances of Zeus by running through Europe, Asia, and Africa. Ovid gives us other – more successful – accounts of a virgin's refusal with Daphne, who (with the help of her father) protected her virginity by turning into the laurel tree, and Syrinx, who resisted the libidinous god Apollo by becoming water reeds.[14] Ovid exploits the fact that the virgins' resistance added to their erotic charm. The same qualities were found in another Greek invention, the Amazons, who figured prominently in Greek males' fantasies, to judge from their frequent representation in public and private art. The famous vase of Exekias depicts Achilles falling in love with the dying Amazon queen, Penthesileia, at the very moment he penetrated her with both his sword and his gaze. Amazons, archetypal figures who resisted sexual control by men, existed permanently in the liminal state of *partheneia*. Inverting the conventional role of married women, they lived outside, riding horses and carrying bows and arrows, and making war like men. By refusing to come inside and accept the traditional role of wives and mothers they created a separate society, a gynecocracy where patrilineal succession had no place or meaning. As warriors and hunters they combined the masculine traits of Artemis and Athena, who were likewise unconstrained by marriage. But unlike those immortals they were ultimately vanquished by men.

That there was an erotic charge to the nubile but sexually inactive *parthenos* is clear from stories of abduction of these young girls while they were performing rituals in honour of the virgin goddess overseeing their *partheneia*. Pausanias gives many such accounts, such as the occasion on which the Messenians abducted Spartan maidens dancing in honour of Artemis (4.16.9). Processions like that of *kanephoroi* honouring Athena were for the Greeks occasions that ill concealed the tension between the felt need to conceal the *parthenos* from male view and predation and the desire to display her potential fecundity.[15] There were mythical counterparts to this: Oreithyia, *kanephoros* at the Panathenaia, was abducted by Boreas (the North Wind) and taken from Athens to Thrace.[16] That the most erotically charged moments for *parthenoi* should occur during rituals for virgin goddesses betrays a belief in the heightened power of sexual energy when it is withheld.

The goddesses themselves manifested an erotic magnetism. Mythical narratives of both Artemis and Athena recount their being the object of a voyeuristic male gaze, which was repelled with brutal finality. It is important to remember that for the Greeks looking was a physical act in which rays of light emanated from the eyes of the beholder.[17] To look was to take a dominant, active role; to be looked at connotated passivity. Both virgin goddesses subverted the passive role of females as the conventional object of the gaze. One of the signs of their power to do this was the Gorgon, the apotropaic female head entwined with snakes that had the power to turn men to stone: vase paintings depicted Artemis with the Gorgon and Athena wearing the Gorgon on her aegis. But these two goddesses took other measures to repel the male gaze: when Actaeon looked upon Artemis as she bathed he was turned into a passive quarry by this *Potnia Thêrôn*, Mistress of the Animals. Becoming a stag, he was attacked by his own hounds.[18] In a similar fashion Athena did not tolerate the inadvertent gaze of Teiresias, who was struck with blindness for viewing her at her bath.[19]

Despite their erotic attractiveness to men, divine and mortal *parthenoi* displayed a kind of dynamic androgyny. A Greek *parthenos* did not assume her gendered identity until marriage: like the Amazons, she existed outside boundaries confining women and exhibited both male and female features. In the same way, the virgin goddesses – eternal *parthenoi* – partook of the gendered expectations of both males and females. Artemis *Potnia Theron* mediated between the masculine pursuit of hunting and the more feminine nurture of wild animals. The number of dedications of clothing at her cult site in Brauron attests to an association between the goddess and weaving, the definitive feminine occupation.[20] The warrior goddess Athena, born from her father's head in full armour, also presided over weaving, as Athena *Ergane*.[21] The androgyny of both goddesses was consistent with the idea of the virgin as pre-gendered, a belief not confined to the Greeks and one based upon the notion that the sexual identity of a young, unmarried woman was not yet fixed.[22] Greek and Roman medical writers described the flesh of the unpenetrated female body as dense and hard – that is, more like a man's – and not yet having the porous consistency of that of a sexually active woman. This physiological theory finds its ritual corollary in the athletic competitions in honour of Hera, the Heraia. Girls participating in the foot races wore a masculine *exomis*, which has been connected to the ritual transvestism associated with puberty rites.[23] Even more dramatic is evidence found of a cult of Artemis which, according to Hesychius, required girls to don the phallus.[24] The juxtaposition of innocent girlhood and such overt symbols of masculinity is not as odd as it first seems: the Greek imagination focused upon the *parthenos* as an incipient *gyne*, or woman, by recognizing in her an unformed being whose potential fecundity could take a variety of shapes until it was fixed in its final feminine form.

In preparation for her transition from *parthenos* to *gyne* the young Greek woman undertook a ritual bath. Water is routinely found in cultic contexts and combines the somewhat paradoxical features of purity and fertility – entirely appropriate for a girl who was nubile but sexually inexperienced. Statues of virgin goddesses were regularly bathed in the ritual known as the *Plynteria*.[25] This would have had a practical function, particularly for those statues placed outdoors. But the *Plynteria* was also connected with renewing the energy to be found in the *partheneia* of the goddesses, the energy of their fecundity withheld. In Athens the *Plynteria* involved bathing the ancient olive-wood statue of Athena *Polias*, along with her peplos, and this was done with a cache of vessels with 'breast-like protrusions,' betraying the connection between the ritual act and fertility.[26] After the *Plynteria* women anointed and dressed the statue in a manner reminiscent of activities of the Sumerian goddess Inanna or her Mesopotamian successors, whose bathing and elaborate dressing in robes of power was a prelude to a *hieros gamos*, the sacred marriage of goddess and consort that would ensure the fertility and prosperity of the city.[27] This may explain the curious phenomenon reported by Pausanias whereby Hera, Greek goddess of marriage and wife of Zeus, bathed annually, and in so doing – as the Argives believed – 'recovered her *partheneia*' (2.38.2).[28] Recovering their virginity would permit the goddesses to bring fresh sexual vitality to lovemaking but would also renew in them the power and independence of the *parthenos*.[29]

The association of water with fertility and virginity is ancient, rich, complex, and widespread, extending from the third millennium in Mesopotamia to sites of veneration of the Virgin Mary such as Lourdes, with the healing powers located in its holy waters. Mary is associated with springs and wells throughout Europe. Throughout Britain the custom of well-dressing persists in honour of such virgin saints as St Brigid. For the Greeks the Danaids, perpetual virgins, were also associated with Argive springs and wells.[30] The apparent paradox of water as both virginally pure and fecund is strikingly presented in Euripides' *Helen*, which begins with a description of the fertile Nile's 'beautiful virgin streams' (*kalliparthenoi rhoai*, 1).

The Greek virgin goddesses were, like their Mesopotamian forebears, connected with natural and human fertility. Although not a birth mother,

Athena was sometimes depicted as an adoring parent of Erichthonius. In pottery of the Classical period she adopts a maternal pose with the birth of Erichthonius, in contrast with her martial demeanour during this event in earlier representations.[31] Such portraits encapsulate the fertile potential of the virgin, even one as manly as Athena. Noel Robertson has suggested that she originally had strong connections to agriculture, with her festivals being organized around the grain cycle. That the Athenian women honoured her together with Demeter in the Skira, or Threshing Festival, lends support to Robertson's speculation that she had her origins as a fertility goddess.[32] The fertile potential of Athena's chastity can be seen in her gift to Athens, the olive tree: olive oil, bestowed upon victors in her Panathenaic games, was a major contribution to the prosperity of her city and hints at her virgin fecundity. In Aeschylus's *Eumenides* there is an alliance between Athena and the fertility deities, the Eumenides, who 'have no allegiance to another household and thus provide without reservation the fertility of Athens.'[33] The virginity of Athena, like that of the Eumenides, guarantees that she will never withdraw her generative powers from Athens. Athenian citizens exhibited an extreme anxiety about the potential disloyalty of young women who must exchange their natal household for another at marriage. Athena's loyalty to her city, however, would be assured by her virginity, validating her own decision to remain *adamatos*. Her inviolable body, clothed in armour since birth, repelled enemy attacks as fiercely as she guarded her chastity.[34]

Athena and Artemis as nurturing divinities were both connected with childbirth: Artemis is better known in this capacity; she is midwife at the birth of her brother Apollo and in cult was the recipient of votive gifts from women anticipating or experiencing childbirth, but there is also a tradition in which Athena brings Artemis into the world (Aelius Aristides 37.18). The principal birth goddess is Eileithuia (frequently associated with Artemis but also with Hera); it is no surprise that she was unmarried. The connection between virginity and midwifery is well attested in antiquity. The legend of the first Athenian midwife Agnodike, recorded by Hyginus, exerted an influence on the history of midwifery and the medical profession until the nineteenth century.[35] The power of a virgin midwife to ensure safe delivery was reflected in the early Christian period with the biography of his sister Macrina by Gregory of Nyssa, who recounts how the appearance of the virgin Thecla (devotee of the apostle Paul) mitigated his mother's labour pangs.[36] While tomb inscriptions attest to the fact that many midwives throughout history were wives and mothers themselves, the traditional concept of the chaste midwife testifies once again to the nurturing power of the virgin.

The centre of the Greek household and family life was the hearth. The third of the goddesses petitioning for and receiving virginity as a special honour in the *Homeric Hymn to Aphrodite* was Hestia, who stood for the sanctity of the household and was held in the highest regard by mortals:

Father Zeus gave her a high honour instead of marriage,
and she sits in the midst of the house and has the richest portion.
In all the temples of the deities she has a share of honour
and among all mortals she is first of deities. (29–32)

The hearth was appropriately embodied by a virgin goddess. Hesiod comments on the need to keep the hearth ritually pure by avoiding polluting it with sexual intercourse (*Op.* 733). Furthermore, the hearth was 'contained' within the walls of the house as a *parthenos* was contained within the house under the protection of her family. Marriage for a Greek girl meant a change from her father's hearth to her husband's, and this mobility was considered destabilizing for both bride and the groom's family. Hestia, like the Eumenides and Athena for Athens, acted as a counterweight to this threat, sexually inactive hence anchored and protective. The domestic cult had its parallels in the public cult celebrated where the hearth of the city was symbolically located. The hearth represented not only stability but security:[37] Hestia embodied this security by remaining virgin, her body having been neither penetrated by a male partner nor opened by giving birth.[38] As a goddess whose sacred space had not been invaded, she could be asked to protect the house and city where her hearth was established.[39] So powerful was the resistant and tutelary power of Hestia that even a foreign suppliant could seek refuge at the hearth rather than an altar.

Although Hestia was a colourless figure in Greek mythology – in essence little more than a personification – she nonetheless exemplified all the attributes of the divine virgin. As the focal point of the household she was connected with the prosperity of the family; she is another example of the 'virgin powerhouse' who could transmit fecundity to those within her sphere of influence. Athena's virginity was metonymic for her loyalty to the state, while Hestia's virginity symbolized loyalty to the household. The inherent semiotic value of an unmarried daughter in an aristocratic family was recognized in the late Roman period and was naturally absorbed by adherents of the early Christian church as an important choice for women when the primary loyalty shifted from family to cult.

Concerned to perpetuate a patriarchal system, the Greeks nonetheless invented female divinities who would be able to direct for human benefit the special energy available to them as *parthenoi*. But with this permanent virginal status came autonomy and agency that contrasted with the permanent infantilization of Greek girls and women. These Olympians were never inclined to submit to Eros, unlike human *parthenoi*, who were consistently presented as lustful and unrestrained. This immunity signifies a mastery of self,[40] a quality very much admired by the ancient Greeks, and one which reassuringly suggests that the virgin goddesses could not be swayed from their protective vigilance by any force.

NOTES

1 For discussions of this dissonance see Blundell (1995, 25–46) and Loraux (1992, 19–25).
2 On these features of the Greek *parthenos* see the article by Ann Hanson in this volume.
3 Those mortals who failed to make the transition were represented in myth as sacrificial virgins, achieving marriage in death. Iphigeneia is but one of many examples (Lyons 1997, 98–9, 137–9).
4 Hecate's influence was extensive: as Clay (1984, 33) observes, the beneficence she granted to mortal activities of various kinds was contingent upon her 'willingness' (conveyed elsewhere by the Greek word *heketi*).
5 Arthur (1982) 75.
6 Later writers reflect the fact that Hecate's autonomy and power led to the construction of her as a goddess of witchcraft, a baleful and unconstrained chthonic force who undermines male potency.
7 For a study of this see Stehle (1990). Goddesses who took mortal lovers also distorted the gender hierarchy. Aphrodite's congress with Anchises, for example, is a source of anxiety and embarrassment for both goddess and mortal (*Homeric Hymn to Aphrodite* 5.180–90, 247–55), as is that between Calypso and Odysseus (*Od.* 5.118–44).
8 The sexual misadventure with Hephaestus that led to the birth of Erichthonius was an isolated phenomenon; it did not involve sexual activity on Athena's part nor any continuing relationship with the god. On her 'maternal' relationship with Erichthonius see below.
9 For the story and an analysis of it see Dexter (1985, 66).
10 For a study of the cults of Artemis *Kourotrophos* and other nursing divinities see Price (1978).
11 The story of their problematic relationship is told in Euripides' *Hippolytus*.
12 Apollodorus (*Lib.* 3.8.2) gives us the traditional account in which Callisto, turned into a bear by Zeus in order to make love with her and escape the notice of Hera, was shot down because she did not preserve her *partheneia*.
13 The requirement is preserved in the Sacred Laws of Cyrene: 'a bride must go

down to the nymphaeum to Artemis, whenever she wishes at the Artemesia, but the sooner the better. Any woman who does not go down shall sacrifice in addition what is necessary for young women. If she has not gone down, she will purify the shrine and sacrifice in addition a full-grown animal as penalty.' (*SEG* 9.72.16).

14 Io, *Met.* 1.784–953; Daphne, *Met.* 1.628–783; Syrinx, *Met.* 1.954–97.
15 On this, see Scodel (1996, 113–14).
16 The details of the abduction, and the various sources that report this, are provided by Robertson (1996, 58–9).
17 Alcmaeon of Croton (late sixth century BCE) is the first Greek whose theory of vision has survived (fr. 14A5 DK = Theophrastus *de Sensu* 25), arguing that the eyes see through a fiery fluid surrounding them. Empedocles fr. 21B 84 DK = Arist. *De Sensu* 2.437b23 claimed that fire within the eye sent forth a ray that beamed upon its object.
18 The Ovidian account is found in *Metamorphoses* 3.163–317.
19 Callimachus, *Hymn to Athena* 51–136.
20 Dillon (2002) 19–23. Weaving, a principal activity of Greek wives from the Bronze Age to the Classical period, carried associations of both chastity (*sophrosyne*) and deception, cunning.
21 Athena, self-proclaimed exponent of wit and cunning (*Od.* 13. 296–9), was the appropriate patron of weaving. This craft was an important component of her Athenian cult: selected young girls, the *arrephoroi*, helped to set up the special loom for weaving the goddess's peplos for her Panathenaic festival. This was an important aspect of the training for their roles as adult women in a ritual that socialized them, and by proxy all Athenian girls.
22 Compare, for example, the German assignment of the neuter gender to 'das Mädchen.'
23 On this see Serwint (1993).
24 s.v. '*lomboi*.' Burkert (1985, 151, with n. 21).
25 The practice was widespread; a discussion is found in Dillon (2002, 132–6); for various locations in which the statue of Athena was ritually cleansed see Robertson (1996, 48–52).
26 Robertson (1996, 34).
27 Penglase (1994, 90). On the sacred marriage ritual, see Kramer (1969) and Avagianou (1991).
28 It is perhaps worth mentioning here that there is a convent today on the spot traditionally assigned to Hera's bath.
29 In the case of Hera, although Zeus was the supreme god on Olympus, she managed to sidestep his authority more than once (e.g., the famous episode in *Iliad* 14.152–360, but also 15.18–33; 19.98–110). On the annual washing of Hera's statue at her great sanctuary on Samos see Dillon (2002, 135).

30 Their fierce and murderous resistance to marriage posed a threat to the natural order, however, and for their crimes they were condemned in the Underworld to transport water in sieves, an appropriate symbol of fertility squandered.
31 Reeder (1995, 259–60), who discusses a kylix of the Kodros painter (440–430 BCE) on which Gaia emerges from the earth and presents the baby to Athena, gazing into his eyes 'like an affectionate young mother.'
32 Robertson (1996, 52–6).
33 Tyrrell (1984, 123) is commenting here on the relationship between Athena and the Erinyes in Aeschylus' *Eumenides*. Cf. Fletcher in this volume.
34 Her armour was the outward sign of her ability to control access to her body and an apt metaphor for her virginity. Cf. the introductory remarks in this volume on Joan of Arc.
35 Hyginus, *Fabula* 274, King (1998, 181–5).
36 Gregory of Nyssa, *Vita Macrinae* 2 (*PG* 46.961).
37 The stability represented by Hestia was assured by her remaining fixed at the hearth, by her immobility. Vernant (1983) studied this feature as the counterpoise of the mobility of Hermes, in an analysis of space and movement in ancient Greece reflected in Greek religion.
38 As a female who was never to know sexual experience with a man, Hestia resembles the *parthenos*, widely understood metaphorically as a container. See Lissarrague (1995, 91–100). For the *parthenos* like a jar with a closed mouth cf. Sissa (1990a, 138–44, 147–56).
39 Hestia's counterpart in the Roman world was Vesta, and the virginal body of her Vestals was essential for the welfare of the state. See Staples (1998, 129–30) and Parker's essay in this volume.
40 Compare with this Foucault's study of sexual activity in the Greek novel, where he examines in the protagonists the connection between self-mastery and virginity and writes: 'virginity is not simply abstention as a preliminary to sexual practice. It is a choice, a style of life, a lofty form of existence that the hero chooses out of the regard that he has for himself' (1986, 230).

2

The Virgin Choruses of Aeschylus

JUDITH FLETCHER

'Thundered voiced' Aeschylus, as his fellow citizen Aristophanes called him, produced dramas reverberating with clamorous, elemental violence. Often this sound and fury emanate from confrontations between male and female forces, battles of the sexes which characterize and symbolize not only the universal forces of the human psyche, but also the conventions and structures of Aeschylus's own society, democratic Athens. Although his tragedies (with the exception of *The Persians*) are set in the legendary past, they nevertheless address political and social concerns of the poet's own day: Aeschylus shaped his mythical female characters from a contemporary matrix. His portrait of the husband-killing Clytemnestra, for instance, supports the idea that women should not aspire to political power. Her daughter Electra behaves more appropriately by supporting the interests of her father and brother, and by staying out of public view.

Yet Aeschylus's most powerful and volatile females are not the famous, high-born women of ancient saga, but rather that often nameless and supposedly marginal group, the chorus. Five of his seven surviving tragedies feature female choruses; three of these represent virgins. Aeschylus's virgin choruses conform to societal expectations regarding the behaviour of young women, although they operate not in an intimate domestic space (like the female choruses of Sophocles and Euripides), but right in the centre of the public world of men. They negotiate with kings and princes, they move freely in the civic world, and they are, in all cases, a force to be reckoned with.

In the following discussion I examine three of Aeschylus's virgin choruses: the 'suppliant band of maidens' who form the chorus of *Seven against Thebes*; the Danaids, collective central character of *Suppliant Women*; and the Erinyes, chorus of *Eumenides*. This third virgin chorus is, unlike the Theban girls and Danaids, neither mortal nor adolescent; Apollo, however, refers to them as 'disgusting maidens *(kataptustoi korai)* old women who are eternally children, with whom neither god, nor man, nor beast has intercourse.'[1] In a sense they take the concept of virginity to its furthest limits.

Given that mortality is not a criterion for 'virginity,' the Oceanids, chorus of *Prometheus Bound*, might offer themselves for examination. Chaste as they might be, they differ from these other three choruses because they are not in a city, or *polis*, but occupy an uncivilized tract of land beyond Greece. This is, as we shall see, a significant distinction: the virgin or *parthenos* has an important role to play in the civic life of Greece; indeed her status is defined by state-authorized rituals including initiatory rites and marriage. I would like to examine how Aeschylean drama represents this unique relationship between the virgin and the state. What happens when the virgin is integrated into the political, public world of the city? The *Seven*, *Suppliant Women*, and *Eumenides* occur within a civic context; each virgin chorus is assimilated into the *polis* in a way that might recall some of the actual cultic and legal processes associated with the passage to womanhood in Athens, where the dramas were performed. I suggest that the transitional period in a young girl's life when she leaves the protective environment of childhood and assumes a new role as an adult is the paradigm which informs the behaviour of these three virgin choruses. They represent a temporary period of wildness in a young woman's coming of age, and they are possessed of a remarkable potency which must be incorporated within the state if the state is to survive.

Before we proceed we need to consider what the social construct 'virgin' or *parthenos* signified to the ancient Greeks. Childhood in general, both for males and females, was considered to be a state of wildness, although we hear much more about the bestial nature of young females. Greek poetry, myth, and ritual treat the *parthenos* as an untamed and hence unsocialized female. In general an unwed female is *adamatos*, 'untamed'; while to marry or even seduce a young girl is to *damazein*, 'tame,' her.[2] The lyric poet Anacreon teases a young woman by likening her to a 'Thracian filly' who has not yet tasted the bit (*PMG*, 335). Myths which feature women transformed into animals, for example Callisto, are usually specific to young women on the threshold of sexual maturity.[3] Girls' puberty rituals suggest a similar correlation between beast and maiden. In a puberty rite at Brauron selected Athenian girls emulated bears, and in Thessaly girls played the part of deer or fawns.

Life before man is idyllic for the virgin, if we are to believe our sources. Anacreon's Thracian girlfriend frolics in innocent pleasure beside her mother; Sophocles' Deianeira, wife of Heracles, envies the chorus of Trachinian maidens their peaceful existence (*Tr.* 144–5), but such a life is only temporary. When the *parthenos* becomes nubile she can turn nasty or even suicidal; the final stage of virginity, right before marriage and integration into society, is a dangerous period, it seems. The virgin is a powerful creature, full of a latent fecundity and incipient sexuality which cause problems unless properly channelled. The myth of the Danaids, who kill their husbands rather than consummate their marriages, illustrates the dangerous potential of the virgin; both Plutarch (*Mor.* 249) and the Hippocratic corpus record stories of virgins hanging themselves.[4]

But these are exceptional cases which suggest how turbulent the transition from childhood to womanhood can be. Greek religion institutionalized the passage into adulthood with rituals such as the Arkteia, which acknowledged the feral nature of young females who 'danced the Bear' and incorporated at least a token group of them into the state by means of public processions featuring maiden choruses, or various cultic functions such as carrying the basket of first fruits at the Panathenaia (as *Kanephoroi*), or weaving Athena's new *peplos* (as *Arrephoroi*).[5] There was even a temple to Artemis Brauronia, who presided over the virgins' transition, on the Athenian Acropolis. Because she would bear citizen children, the virgin was an essential component of the city-state; she was a valuable commodity, an *agalma*, a treasure displayed by her family in assorted public venues.[6] But even after marriage she retained her status as a minor with no voice in the legislature or judiciary and constantly under the economic guardianship of an adult male, her *kyrios*.[7] The most salient exception to the list of disabilities suffered by the Athenian woman, and one pertinent to this discussion, was her participation in the religion of the state, especially her role as cultic functionary or celebrant. Even so, women's involvement in civic cult had to be authorized at some level by men such as a priest or archon.

Simply put, the *parthenos* required someone to help her fit into civilized life; she would be too powerful and disruptive a force if left to her own devices. The necessity of male intervention in the life of the virgin, or at least the virgin about to pass into womanhood, is an idea which runs through Greek thought. Plutarch tells how a group of suicidally inclined Milesian virgins were prevented from hanging themselves by a quick-witted man. Various medical texts represent different forms of hysteria in virgins, where the prescribed solution is cohabitation with a man or pregnancy. In mythology, the raging daughters of Proeteus, the Proetides, are cured of their madness by Melampos, who subsequently marries one of them (Hesiod fr. 37.10). Io, afflicted by a version of 'mad cow disease,' runs in a frenzy across three continents (*Supp.* 541–85) until she is finally restored to her human form and calmed by the touch of Zeus, who impregnates her.

In Greek myth and medicine sexual intercourse was supposed to be an effective remedy against virginal bedlam, but it was not simply sexual inexperience which defined virginity for the Greeks.[8] Virginity was a social status: a *parthenos* was an unwed girl; marriage and childbirth were definitive events in her gradual transition to womanhood. In other words a young girl became a member of society through marriage or cohabitation, and thus by assuming her position in society, insignificant as it may seem to us, she exchanged nature for culture, or childhood for adulthood. The acceptance of masculine control signified the maiden's entry into adult life. The legal and economic reality of the *kyrios*, or 'guardian,' is replicated in the cultic practice of the male *choregos*: a chorus leader would preside over public choral performances[9] where nubile girls would be displayed, perhaps to prospective husbands.

It is this pattern, I suggest, which informs Aeschylus's articulation of the virgin persona in his choruses. All three virgin choruses are situated in the *polis* or at its borders. All are represented as chaotic and threatening to the *polis* but eventually are accepted into the city-state to become an organized and coherent unit capable of bestowing great benefits on the state. Thus Aeschylus characterizes his maiden choruses in a manner consonant with the social construction of virginity in fifth-century Greece.

In particular it is the language of these three Aeschylean choruses which is initially troublesome. The undisciplined language of the virgin choruses is consistent with the representation of women's communication in Greek drama generally. Women like Clytemnestra, who speak in public and without the authorization of men, are represented as a public menace. In the following discussion I examine how the chaotic and potentially dangerous discourse of Aeschylus's virgin choruses conforms to this stereotype. From there I explore the politics of communication, specifically how the disorderly voice of the chorus is modified in order for it to become part of the civic voice. This taming of the chorus's speech is performed by civic entities – Eteocles, king of Thebes, Pelasgos, king of Argos, and Athena, the *polis* incarnate. The newly domesticated chorus receives specific instructions on how to communicate within a civic context. As a result, the chorus's language is no longer threatening but becomes beneficent; the women offer prayers, an appropriate genre for women's public discourse, on behalf of the city in all three plays.[10] In the case of Aeschylus's choruses this approved discourse takes the form of a prayer; the puissant energy of the virgin is thus directed into an appropriate and useful form of communication within a civic space.

Seven against Thebes

Seven against Thebes is the final, and only surviving, play of a trilogy which follows the afflictions of Oedipus, his father, and sons. It dramatizes the course of an ancient familial curse about to close in on Eteocles, king of Thebes. After the exile of Oedipus, his sons, Eteocles and Polyneices, had agreed to rule Thebes in alternating years. When Eteocles refused to give up the throne at the end of his first year Polyneices mustered an army of Argive supporters to enforce his claim. The seven chieftains are at the gates of Thebes when the tragedy opens. The *Seven* would be a static play – a messenger reports the invasion; Eteocles arms himself and departs for battle; the messenger relates the mutual fratricides at the gates of Thebes – were it not for the chorus of Theban virgins. They impart a sense of the turmoil and cacophony of war; they fill the play with motion, tension, and noise; and they mirror the discord outside the gates within the city. They are an unruly group whose behaviour contributes in a very large way to the themes and symbolism of the play. When Eteocles scolds them it is as if he were attempting to suppress his own fears. On the other hand, their virginity is a perfect symbol for the sanctity of the innermost part of the city where the drama takes place, while their fear of rape corresponds on a personal level to the public violation of the citadel.[11]

The chorus sings a terrified prayer as they enter and appeal to the gods for protection. As the young women clutch at the statues of the gods, their prayers are chaotic and punctuated with fearful interjections and phatic utterances: '*Oa, Ioh, Ee, ee, ee, ee.*' This undisciplined form of supplication is of no benefit to Thebes and in fact may intensify the panic of its citizens – such are the sentiments of Eteocles. He sternly rebukes the maidens for 'howling' (186). *Lakazein* is the word he uses, a term often employed for animals barking or yowling. This is a wild, chaotic, even animalistic pack of women who are unable to communicate in a rational and civilized manner. Eteocles' desperate attempts to quell them testify to their enormous power.

This first episode focuses on his repeated attempts to silence the chorus; there are no other characters present, and the exchange between king and chorus is the only real *agon* or 'contest' enacted in the play itself. The king worries about how the young women might influence the rest of his city, so he berates and threatens them with harsh punishment unless they obey him immediately.[12] Although Eteocles tries to remove the women from the public space and insists that they retreat indoors, which is where the Athenians felt all women belonged, the chorus maidens ignore the command; they remain where they stand in the public venue and continue to voice their anxiety. Of course the young women will have to remain outside and in view of the audience to fulfill their function as a tragic chorus, but their debate with Eteocles exploits this technical necessity to draw attention to their continued presence in the civic space. The first episode is devoted to this negotiation between the chorus, who continue their fearful outbursts and terrified prayers, and Eteocles, who perseveres in his attempt to impose silence and submission. He is especially concerned about how the virgins are praying. The tension increases as the agitated maidens disregard Eteocles' threats and commands, and Eteocles continues to demand silence. Eventually, however, the 'chorus' leader gives in to the king's control: 'I am silent' (263), she finally says on behalf of the chorus. This protracted contest has focused on the issue of speech, particularly prayer, as Eteocles attempts to restrain the young women's speech. When the chorus does finally agree to be silent, Eteocles instructs them in their supplication. He recommends that they 'make a better prayer, that the gods be our allies' and that they 'sing with good heart the sacred victory chant, the customary Greek song of sacrifice' (266–70). Eteocles is not trying to silence the women permanently but rather to channel the energy of their supplication into a more favourable form of appeal. His efforts to control the discourse of the women actually reflect his attempts to gain some control over the escalating crisis of his city, and his own doomed life.

It would seem, then, that the relationship between Eteocles and the chorus is analogous to a genuine cultural institution: Eteocles functions as the *choregos*, who organizes and instructs maiden choruses in Greek ritual. We know this kind of relationship existed in ancient Greek society partly because fragments of maiden songs composed by the lyric poets Alcman and Pindar survive. In his important study of this institution Claude Calame discusses the roles of the *choregos* or the director of the chorus. Calame is not discussing tragic choruses, but the role of the *choregos* as the director of young women who sang and danced in civic ceremonies throughout Greece. The ancient lexicographer Hesychius gives several definitions of the term *choregos*, including the person, either male or female, who sets the chorus going, who gives the signal for the dances or the songs to begin. Apollo, for instance, is often depicted as the leader of the chorus of the Graces. The semantic range of the term covers three components: organizing, beginning, and conducting.[13]

Considered in this context, Eteocles acts as a marshalling force, a *choregos*, for the maidens: specifically he tells them how to sing, how to arrange their prayers. And the chorus does need organizing. To judge from the excited metre of their lyrics, they probably would have poured into the theatre in scattered disarray. At some point in their showdown with Eteocles they must fall into the rank-and-file position of the typical tragic chorus; thus the organizing force of Eteocles is expressed spatially. When the king leaves the acting space the maidens continue to be afraid, but they are now in the prescribed formation of the tragic chorus.

It could be argued that the chorus has hardly settled down after Eteocles leaves, since their next song, the first *stasimon*, is a fantasy of a raped and pillaged city. The chorus is certainly still very much afraid, but the young women no longer blurt out their disjointed prayers. While their first song had a very disturbed structure, once they accept Eteocles' advice their ode is far more harmonious and coherent in terms of metre and content.[14] At any rate, they do not seem to disturb Eteocles, who returns to give the messenger his orders for the forthcoming battle. The chorus is now a much more composed group and more disciplined in its language as Eteocles' instructions take effect. The central section of the play consists of six paired speeches in which the messenger describes the shields of the attacking Argive captains and Eteocles assigns a corresponding Theban warrior to each of the seven gates. The seventh warrior is his brother Polyneices, whom Eteocles will fight (and eventually kill and be killed by) at the seventh gate. The chorus is present throughout this important strategy session, and after each set of speeches they sing a short choral verse which complies with Eteocles' earlier request for auspicious prayer. The first verse, for example, is a prayer that the gods give victory (417–21). In the remaining lyrics they wish for their enemy's destruction (e.g., 452–6) and pray for success (481–5). This is precisely the manner of speech which Eteocles prescribed for them, although his own speech becomes increasingly dangerous and out of bounds.

For the remainder of the play the chorus is sober and self-controlled – so much so that some scholars have suggested that they actually change character (and masks) from innocent maidens to wise counsellors, an unprecedented occurrence in Greek tragedy.[15] Yet this is not a different chorus, but a civilized chorus which has evolved from the chaos of the early part of the play to the structured and coherent odes and prayers in the remainder of the play until the death of Eteocles. The choral ode after Eteocles leaves to meet his brother at the seventh gate of Thebes is an authoritative and precise narrative of the house of the Labdacids, a far cry from earlier inchoate utterances. Now the women demonstrate a detailed knowledge of the family's history and a prophetic understanding of how Oedipus's curse will manifest itself in the mutual fratricide that is indeed occurring even as the chorus women describe it. The chorus has developed from a group of distressed maidens whose words were inappropriate for a public venue to a controlled group which offers prayers for the city's safety and is able to place the action of the drama in the pattern of Theban history. Interestingly, as their linguistic competence grows it seems to parallel the actualization of Oedipus's curse against his sons. As William Scott points out, 'Eteocles' action of calming the women and seeking to organize the war effort is in fact fulfilling [his father's curse] by trapping himself in his own war plans.'[16] Needless to say, the evolution of the chorus is not the central concern of this drama, although, as I argue, it does help to delineate the activity of the curse by providing us with an authoritative and focused narrator.[17]

The Suppliant Women

The chorus of *Seven against Thebes* is but one example of what are arguably the most invasive and threatening choral groups in Greek tragedy. Virgins are powerful young women with a great potential for disruption, but when they do agree to operate within cultural boundaries they can offer great benefits for the state. The chorus of Danaids in *The Suppliant Women*, like the Theban women, display a tendency towards irrational behaviour. This play was probably first in a trilogy dealing with the myth of the Danaids, fifty descendants of Io and Zeus who were forced to marry their cousins, the sons of Aegyptos. When the action begins, they are arriving at the city of Argos, having fled with their father, Danaos, from Egypt. They enter the drama in an orderly manner because they are under his supervision; Danaos instructs them how to speak correctly and tells them exactly when and what to sing. In the eyes of the Athenian audience he is their legal guardian or *kyrios*, but in a performance context he is their *choregos*. With a few notable exceptions he authorizes practically every song that they sing, usually by telling them to sing or pray, or comments on the nature of their language in some way. In the first episode Danaos coaches his daughters on verbal decorum in preparation for their meeting with the Argives: he advises them to speak with self-restraint and modesty, for, as he says, 'it is not seemly for inferiors to be bold in speech' (203). The correct use of language is the strongest theme in this scene and is a major preoccupation of Danaos, whose concern for the propriety of his daughters' speech is, we soon discover, entirely justified.

The Danaids have come to petition the city for refuge by exploiting an ancestral link with the Argives through Io, but the business of supplication is stressful and complex. The Danaids need to negotiate with King Pelasgos, who has serious misgivings about including the young women within the protective scope of the *polis*. The threat posed by the Danaids' potency arises from their nascent sexuality: to accept responsibility for this group of fertile young women is to risk war with their impassioned pursuers. In their meeting with the Argives the women display the contradictory features of their virgin personality; commentators for the play aptly describe the chorus as 'pathetic, sinister, docile, pertinacious, hysterical, euphoric,' but above all independent in thought and action.[18] It is important to recognize that the young women negotiate on their own behalf in a highly charged political situation. They are effective agents in securing a position for themselves within the city, although their methods of persuasion are anything but conciliatory. Several times Pelasgos chides them for their unruly and impolite speech. In their attempt to coerce the king into granting them sanctuary the maidens even threaten to hang themselves on Argive altars – typical virgin behaviour. It is the threat of moral pollution, *miasma*, which finally persuades Pelasgos to argue their case before the assembly; he dispatches Danaos to the city and then sends the daughters to a nearby public grove, where he bids them pray to the local gods for what they desire (520–1). He thus takes over the role of *choregos*, instructing the chorus of virgins in their hymns, in a public venue. The symmetrically structured first *stasimon*, one of three choral prayers in this play, ensues. In it the chorus sing the story of Io and beseech Zeus to protect them. The beautiful ring composition of this coherent narrative reflects the regulating force of Pelasgos on the maidens.

What happens to the language of the Danaids when they are not under the protective control of Pelasgos or Danaos? As the chorus await the return of the king and their father, the Aegyptids' herald arrives, intent on leading the maidens away. Unfortunately, this passage is deeply corrupt, and there is great uncertainty over the number of characters involved or even the distribution of lines.[19] Nonetheless, it is obvious that once the enemy herald approaches, the Danaids are no longer capable of coherent song. They blurt out inarticulate expressions of terror – phatic utterances such as '*aiai, aiai, oioi, oioi, otototoi, ma Ga ma Ga*' and so forth. Without the tutelage of their protectors, and in the presence of an uncivilized and threatening male, the maidens are unable to speak lucidly. The herald remonstrates with them for crying and howling (*lakaze*, the same word Eteocles used for the yelps of the Theban virgins), but unlike Eteocles he is incapable of controlling the young women's outbursts. Not just any man can rein in such a powerful group of women. The herald is a specimen of utter barbarity who rejects Greek gods (891), attempts to abduct virgins in spite of their father's prohibitions, and, as Pelasgos will point out, does not know how to be a guest (917), a serious transgression in the eyes of the Greeks. Such an uncultured, barbarian lout could not possibly act as a *choregos*. When Pelasgos comes to the rescue, the Danaids regain their composure and, at the bidding of their father, make a prayer of benediction for Argos which Danaos approves: 'I praise these seemly prayers, dear girls' (710). Since they have been admitted to the state as new citizens, their prayers for the prosperity of Argos are reminiscent of the contributions of the young woman who replenishes the citizenry by parenting new citizens. The transfer of custody over the maidens resembles marriage negotiations, while it simultaneously seems to refer to the bestowal of new citizenship rights.[20]

Of course, in the subsequent lost dramas the Danaids are somehow compelled to marry the Aegyptids, and all but one will murder their new husbands. That exceptional Danaid, Hypermnestra, will make the transition to adulthood successfully and eventually found an Argive dynasty which will include Heracles. Since all but a few fragments of the remainder of the trilogy are lost, very little can be said about how Aeschylus presented this story, but as we have seen, the first tragedy has the virgins securely installed in the civic space of Argos.

As I have attempted to demonstrate, the characterization of both these Aeschylean choruses accords with popular conceptions of virgins as powerful but wild creatures. In both cases the young women's speech is at some point out of control when not governed by a civic authority figure. And in both dramas the most significant form of discourse is prayer. The civic figures tell the chorus how to pray, petitioning for benedictions for the city. The virgins then become part of the civic structure in a process which recognizes the great potential of their public voice while seeking to regulate it in a way that uses it to maximum advantage.

The *Eumenides*

The final play of Aeschylus's great trilogy the *Oresteia* shows how the young son of Agamemnon, Orestes, flees from Delphi to Athens to seek purification and exoneration for killing his mother, whom he killed to avenge his father. He is pursued by the avenging spirits, the Furies or Erinyes of his mother, Clytemnestra, whose ghost urges them to hunt her son like a wild animal. The Erinyes comprise the chorus and, like the Danaids and the chorus of the *The Suppliant Women*, this group is a major player in the tragedy. The Erinyes are far more dangerous than the two human virgin choruses. While the Danaids and Theban virgins feared the violent potential of male sexuality, the Erinyes fear another type of masculine power, namely assimilation and domination by the patriarchal order of the Olympian gods ('the younger gods,' 162, 778–9). The Erinyes are devoted to the interests of blood-kin (and hence oppose the matricide) and do not recognize the bonds of marriage; in their opinion Orestes committed a far greater crime in killing his mother than she did in killing his father.[21] They belong to the old pre-Olympian order of gods, chthonic powers (connected with the earth), and there is something strikingly primitive about their behaviour. The first noises that they make are not music at all but inarticulate groans and grunts: '*mu, mu ... oh, oh*' etc.; Clytemnestra's ghost declares 'you bark (*klangaineis*) like a dog' (131).[22] And while the howls of the human virgin choruses in the other two plays obliquely suggest their feral nature, the Erinyes are obviously like a pack of animals, like dogs pursuing a deer, as they themselves put it (246). Furthermore, they do not appear initially in the rank and file of the regular tragic chorus, but probably arrive in the theatre at random, like the Theban virgin chorus.[23]

Here is a female chorus that functions without the control of men, and it is a very menacing group of women indeed. Aeschylus underscores their great power by having them enter, unconventionally, through the *skene* building, which represented the temple of Apollo at Delphi. There are apparently no limits on their mobility, and in their pursuit of Orestes to Athens they actually leave the orchestra, another bold violation of convention. They have no *choregos*, no tutelary figure to instruct them in their singing. They themselves decide to become a chorus: 'Come let us form a chorus,' they say at the beginning of the first *stasimon* (308). In this ode the Erinyes sing their binding song, a verbal enchantment meant to imprison Orestes, as they encircle their victim. Such magical incantation is a form of speech traditionally associated with women and one that they can use to exercise control over men.[24]

In this case the Erinyes fail to detain Orestes with their spell. The virgin monsters are still an extreme exponent of the dangers of unsupervised female speech, however. They follow their quarry right to the civic heart of Athens, where they participate in a forensic debate; indeed, they come very close to arguing successfully for their claim on Orestes (since the trial results in a tie vote). Considering that this is *the chorus* (whom we expect to be somewhat subsidiary to the action), they are remarkably voluble, mobile, and active. They actually identify themselves as *Arai*, 'Curses,' and after the acquittal of Orestes they threaten to curse Athens.[25] Their language is at least as problematic as that of the terrified Theban women, or the truculent Danaids whose threat of suicide bespeaks pollution.

The ultimate taming of the Furies occurs in the very public milieu of the Areopagus. Another virgin, Athena, in voting for and representing the male principle, channels the Erinyes' power, and through the agency of her persuasion the daughters of Night take their place within the Athenian patriarchy. We might expect Athena to try persuading the Erinyes to leave Athens after Orestes returns to Argos, but instead she convinces them to assume the role of protectors of Athens, which will incorporate their force.[26] The debate between Athena and the chorus corresponds to similar contests between Eteocles and Pelasgos and their respective choruses. In all three plays the language of the chorus threatens the stability of the *polis*. In the *Eumenides*, despite Athena's insistence that they will not be dishonoured, the Erinyes repeatedly threaten to curse Attica with venom, disease, and death, which they can apparently accomplish with a word.[27] Athena continues to offer them the power to grant wealth and fecundity to the land and households of her city; the chorus leader is at last persuaded and asks, 'What do you bid me to invoke upon this land?' (902). In essence the chorus has put its voice under the control of a more rational force, a *choregos*. A masculine virgin, Athena, asks that they grant the city fecundity and protection, and in accordance with her wishes the chorus sings a hymn of benediction for Athens. Although it has taken most of the play for this to happen, the debate between Athena and the chorus follows the same principle that we have already seen in *Seven against Thebes* and *The Suppliant Women*: a civic figure directs the volatile potential of the virgin voice into a format that is beneficial to the *polis*.

The trilogy ends with the chorus being escorted to their new homes in a torchlight parade, a ritual that looks very much like a marriage procession. But the newly installed *Semnai Theai*, or 'Venerable Goddesses,' as they are now called, will retain their virginity, for this is where their power resides. In her examination of the roles of these spirits, Sarah Iles Johnston describes Aeschylus's version of the Erinyes as 'eternal virgins, divine paradigms of the girls whose transitions they could thwart if they wished.'[28] In addition to their many functions they are 'transitional' goddesses who preside over young women in their safe passage to womanhood. Thus the land of Attica subsumes the power of these virgins who will never marry and who will forever be childless (*paides apaides*, 1034). With some degree of irony, however, a type of marriage has occurred between these fatherless children of the goddess Night, who champion the cause of maternity and blood kinship, and the motherless child of Zeus, who 'approves the male in all things, except in marriage' (737).

As these three tragic dramas illustrate, Aeschylus used the passage from wildness to civilization, an idea inherent in coming-of-age rituals, as a model for the behaviour of his virgin choruses. He depicts the remarkable power of the virginal voice as a chaotic, untamed clamour which threatens the equilibrium of the state. This power is diverted by a civic figure who virtually 'tames' the chorus and guides it toward a propitious function. Laura McClure has argued that Greek tragedy represents women's 'vital role in perpetuating the values and ideals of the community by reaffirming the social and religious roles of men and women.' She has also pointed out that 'choruses of girls and women ... suggest the existence of women's public and authoritative speech in ancient Greece.'[29] As she so rightfully acknowledges, ancient Athens did recognize the power of the female voice.

It is interesting that Aeschylus sets his virgin choruses in a civic drama, especially when we consider the female choruses of Sophocles or Euripides. These women seldom have such stressful relationships with male characters.

There is a definite civic flavour to all three of these Aeschylean tragedies; some scholars have gone so far as to suggest that the plays could be an allegory for the installation of new citizens in the *polis*.[30] The prenuptial wildness of virgins as perceived by the Greeks was a stage in their movement towards marriage, and marriage was their 'civic duty.' Ancient Greek society recognized the enormous power of the virgin and needed to enclose and tap into her budding fertility. The alternatives would be societies like the mythical Amazons, who lived on the edges of civilization, perpetual virgins who even stormed the Athenian citadel, according to legend. In the Greek imagination powerful and threatening young women could live outside the confines of the city. Although we encounter the occasional man in Greek literature who wishes he could live in a world without women, the mythopoeic mind prefers to harness female power, most potent in the virgin.

NOTES

1 *Eu.* 68. As Alan Sommerstein (1989) 95 comments, 'nothing qualifies the Erinyes to be called *korai* except their virginity.'
2 The fourth-century BC philosopher and historian Xenophon (*Oec.*7.5) makes his character Ischomachos use the term to explain how he instructed his young wife in the niceties of civilized life. Cf. Calame (1997) 239, n. 123: 'In a female context, the metaphor of domestication refers both to a girl's education and to her marriage.'
3 If we accept J.E. Robson's suggestion in (1997) 80–2, even mythical victims of bestial rape, such as Europa, who was abducted by Zeus disguised as a bull, testify to the feral nature of young women, who can turn their admirers into beasts as well; Robson argues that gods turn themselves into beasts to match young girls' feral nature.
4 The Hippocratic corpus represents various forms of hysteria in young women and reports that 'virgins who do not take a husband at the appropriate time for marriage experience visions and suicidal impulses' (Hippocrates, *On Virgins* 8.466–70). Seaford (1988, 119) remarks: 'The ritually expressed reluctance of the girl to pass from the parental to the marital home is widely attested as a traditional feature of Greek marriage.' See especially Ann Hanson's essay in this volume.
5 See Sourvinou-Inwood (1988) and Dowden (1989).
6 Ruth Scodel (1996, 111–12) remarks on how the tragedians represent virgins as luxury goods, similar to a fine *peplos* or statue. Most representative of this concept is Agamemnon's description of Iphigenia as 'the ornament of my house' (*Ag.* 208).

7 On the role of the *kyrios* ('guardian' or 'master') see Just (1989, 26–30). Although much has been written about the restrictions imposed on ancient Greek women in public life, the fact remains that Athenian women of citizen parentage enjoyed certain rights and privileges which set them apart from *metics* (resident aliens) and slaves. See Schaps (1998, 161–88). Citizen women were an almost indefinable, yet crucial, part of the state. They were legal entities who could testify in court, make public prayers, and bestow citizenship. The paradox of course is that women were not full-fledged members of the state and were always seen as being somehow incompetent. Roger Just sums up this incongruity: 'By their very nature women belonged *as a whole* to the disordered and irrational side of life. Their integration into society was, as it were, artificial – the result of their subjugation and domestication by men. Left to themselves, women would be both ignorant of and incapable of conforming to society's demands.' Just (1989, 26–30).

8 The state of *partheneia* does not simply end with intercourse or even childbirth, as Sissa (1990a, 76–7) argues, since numerous children in Greek mythology are described as *parthenios*, 'born of a virgin.'

9 A 'well attested model' which was a 'microcosm of the social hierarchy' according to Jennifer Larson (1995, 33). As Larson reminds us, there are no instances of male choruses guided by a female *choregos*. I am not suggesting that only men are leaders of women's choruses, of course. There is evidence that older women (perhaps like Sappho) taught young girls to sing and dance.

10 The pattern which I identify is compatible with the observations of Laura McClure (1999), who notices that classical Greek drama represents women's speech as subversive or pernicious unless it is directed into socially prescribed formats. Also Josine H. Blok (2001).

11 Thalmann (1978, 102) observes that 'they embody much that is fragile and precious in the city's life.' See Holt Parker's similar remarks on Vestal Virgins in this volume.

12 Eteocles' invective against the chorus has provoked various scholarly responses. Solmsen (1937) finds Eteocles' policing of the chorus to be a necessary corrective to their dangerous outbursts. Caldwell (1973) suggests that Eteocles, son of Oedipus, hates all women because of his dysfunctional family background. Stehle (2005) focuses on the performative effects of his language, through which the curse is manifested.

13 Calame (1997, 43–9).

14 Scott (1984, 160–1).

15 Solmsen (1937, 201) argues that since the chorus give advice to Eteocles and call him *teknon*, 'child,' at 686, they must now be wearing different masks, a rather improbable suggestion which Brown (1977, 316) counters by pointing out this is merely a term of affection.

16 Scott (1984, 162). Cf. Eva Stehle (2005), who analyses how the curse of Oedipus is manifested in Eteocles' language. As the chorus gain control of themselves, and eventually accomplish a proper prayer, Eteocles loses control of language.
17 Let us remember too that Thebes is one of the most crisis-ridden cities in Greek myth and that this is the final installment in a trilogy detailing its history. And finally, there are doubts about the authenticity of the extant ending, an extensive lamentation which introduces Antigone and her sister. Assuming that the ending is genuine, I would suggest that the chorus has now taken on a stereotypical adult feminine role as mourners. That their lamentation is perhaps excessive and somewhat disordered may be attributed to the fact that their *choregos* no longer lives.
18 Friis-Johansen and Whittle (1980, 39).
19 The text does not designate any change of singers in the lyric portions, but as Friis-Johansen and Whittle (1980, 172) point out, the Danaids could not sing verses 836–42, 847–53, and 859–65. The scene might have more force with a secondary chorus of Egyptian henchmen here, but their presence or absence does not substantially affect my arguments.
20 See Zeitlin (1992, 203–52) for parallels between virgins and suppliants.
21 They are '[d]aughters who will not leave the self-contained family unit in its simplest form.' Johnston (1999, 255).
22 117–29 are rare examples of stage directions or *parepigraphai* in the manuscript. On the sounds made by the Erinyes see McClure (1999, 107–8).
23 Texts of Greek tragedy do not usually print stage directions (although see n. 22 above), so it is difficult to know exactly how or when the Erinyes make their entrance. Sommerstein (1989) 93 suggests that they are presented sleeping around Orestes on the *ekkyklema*, which is wheeled out of the building representing the temple of Apollo at Delphi. Unfortunately we have no conclusive evidence that the *ekkyklema* was in use at this time. The most conservative reconstruction would have the chorus entering through the side entrance of the theatre (the *parodos*) after the ghost of Clytemnestra has awakened them. In any staging, however, the chorus members' entrances must be sporadic, since it appears that they are waking up in fits and starts. So Clytemnestra's ghost says to them, 'get up, and you and you' (140).
24 McClure (1999, 65–7, 80–92, 108).
25 Prins (1991) suggests that they are the incarnations of speech acts.
26 Sommerstein (1989, 239–40).
27 '[T]he Erinyes' blighting poison is here, it would seem, conceived as being contained in the bitter words they are uttering.' Sommerstein (1989, 247).
28 Johnston (1999, 253).
29 McClure (1999, 55).

30 Podlecki (1972, 201) notes similarities between the Erinyes and Danaids in that both groups are received into the *polis* as *neopolitai* ('new citizens'). Bakewell (1997, 208–28) suggests that the Argive reception of the Danaids reflects contemporary Athenian policy towards *metics*, or resident aliens.

3

The Hippocratic *Parthenos* in Sickness and Health

ANN ELLIS HANSON

Medical writers of the Hippocratic Corpus, composing their anonymous treatises in the fifth and early fourth centuries BC, situated the *parthenos* at the brink of a perilous transition from child to adult.[1] No English word overlaps well with Greek *parthenos*, although we approximate it with the translations 'young girl,' 'virgin,' 'maiden.' The body of the *parthenos* was no longer that of the genderless child, such as she had inhabited it from birth, nor was her body yet able to function like that of a fully mature woman (*gyne*). As wife, mother, and mistress of her husband's household, the *gyne* birthed the offspring that perpetuated family and community into a new generation, and the legitimacy and gender of her children were of intense interest to the family and to the citizen body of her community.[2] While modern Western society emphasizes the menopausal changes that take place in the woman's body at the close of her decades of fertility, Greek society of the Classical period problematized menarche and the beginning of a female's fertile life, marking the transition with elaborate rituals.[3] Most Hippocratics shared their society's preoccupations, including these first changes in the female body, endowing them with medical seriousness. The embryological treatises expected the female fetus to develop more slowly than the male in the space of the womb, but the author of *Eight Months' Child* claimed in addition that daughters reached puberty and a prudent maturity more quickly than sons and grew old more rapidly due to the weakness of their female bodies and their manner of living (7.450L).[4]

Genderless Child, Fertile Wife, and *Parthenos* in Between

Although gender difference was marked in some Hippocratic descriptions of fetal development and birthing, once the baby was born medical writers of the *Corpus* spoke of 'children' (*paides, paidia*), paying scant attention to whether the child was a boy or a girl. The Hippocratic author of the embryological treatise *Nature of the Child* described the child's body as compact and firm because the inner passageways which led from diverse parts to the organs of generation were narrow, constricted, and blocked up. This was, for him, the reason why boys did not secrete sperm and girls did not menstruate:

Children's interior passageways[5] are narrow and filled up, and this prevents generating seed[6] from passing through them, so that a stimulating irritation does not occur in the same way [as in adults]. As a result, fluids in the body are never sufficiently agitated for generating seed to separate out. Nor do menses flow for *parthenoi* while they are young for this same reason. (*NC* 2.2–3, 7.472L)

Because the bodies of children appeared similar, Hippocratics expected them to suffer the same sicknesses in similar fashion. The children growing up in a town with northward exposure and waters hard, cold, and indigestible were likely to suffer from dropsy and pass through puberty later than those in a more beneficent climate (*AWP* 4, 1.78LCL). The author of *Epidemics* I described the fevers prevalent during an unusually damp year on the island of Thasos and noted that children were the ones who died – 'those recently weaned, older ones eight and ten years old, and however many were still prepubescent' (I 10, 1.162LCL). Children were also alike in that important bodily changes hovered on the horizon for them as they grew older.[7] The most famous Hippocratic collection of short, pithy utterances of medical wisdom, *Aphorisms*, claimed that maladies either ceased with puberty, or, if they did not, they then became chronic (III 28, 4.132LCL), and that children who suffered from seizures could also anticipate alterations in their disease at this time (V 7, 4.158LCL). While the Hippocratic gaze sometimes fastened upon children, noting how their bodies responded to specific diseases or environmental conditions, Hippocratics never approached the more elaborate pediatrics that survive from Roman times,[8] and their attention was more often focused on adults.

Throughout antiquity medical writers tended to give fourteen years as the age of puberty, no doubt fastening upon 'twice seven years' as particularly plausible because of their culture's long-lived preference for multiples of seven when applying periodicity to human life.[9] As the boy and girl grew in stature and their bodies increased in size, their inner passageways expanded, making a path for generating seed to reach the organs of generation. Now there was space in which the potent fluid was agitated, heated, and set in motion; once delivered to the uterus, the seed of generation from both partners combined, solidified because of the warmth, and a new life began within the body of the now mature female. Secondary sexual characteristics were outwardly visible, while the expansion of the inner passageways was hidden from view, and the medical writer of *Nature of the Child* emphasized swelling of breasts, growth of pubic hair, in addition to the production of menses and seed. Growth of hair on the young man's chin signalled that his generating seed, drawn from all parts of the body and flowing down from head to penis, was now sufficient to nourish this outcropping of hair, much as rain nourished plants in earth.[10] Hormonal explanations for the appearance of secondary sexual characteristics lay several millennia in the future, yet this Hippocratic's invoking of connected interior passageways provided him with mechanical explanations for the phenomena of puberty that occur simultaneously in widely separated parts of the body.

Once childhood was left behind, the social lives of girls and boys within the family and the city-state of the Classical period in Greece differed as markedly as the medical construction Hippocratics gave their bodies. Body growth alone accounted for maturation in boys, but girls required further opening and widening for them to process the additional fluids that exited the mature female as menses, milk, and postpartum flows. Only intercourse and pregnancy completed the transformation of the girl-child's body to that of a mature woman. The gynecological treatises of the *Corpus* occasionally referred to old virgins, grouping them with young widows, both of whom were expected to be unhealthy.[11] While the youngest *parthenos* was the young girl for whom the menses did not yet flow, the age of the oldest *parthenos* in the case histories of *Epidemics* was twenty years (*Epid.* V 50, 7.190LCL). This pretty daughter of Nerius, as the medical writer described her, died nine days after she was struck on the forehead by a friend while playing. In all likelihood she had begun to menstruate, since nothing is mentioned to the contrary, and the medical writer would surely have considered amenorrhea medically significant to her case history if she had not. She was, of course, unmarried.

The Hippocratic author of *Nature of the Child* placed his discussion of the second widening brought about by pregnancy and childbirth at the beginning of the gynecological treatise *Diseases of Women* I, to which he contributed many sections.[12] Once again mechanical paradigms played a conspicuous role in his discussion. Mature female flesh must become porous and the mature female body equipped with empty spaces in order for the woman to manage successfully the menses and other fluids that accumulated within her prior to their evacuation, and her uterus required room for expansion so as to accommodate a fetus:

I say that a woman who is childless suffers more intensely and more readily from menstruation than one who has given birth: for when she gives birth, her interior passageways become more receptive to menstrual blood. The lochial flow makes them receptive, even if only some of her body is broken down.[13] In particular, the passageways near the belly and the breasts are broken down; in addition, the rest of the body is usually broken down. I have explained how this happens in my *Nature of the Child in Childbirth*: when the body is broken down, it is inevitable that the passageways are more open and more receptive to menstrual blood. The uterus is also more open – as, for example, when the child has moved through it and has caused pressure and pain. (*DW* I 1.1–4, 8.10L)

The *parthenos* was poised between child and woman, her body moving ever closer to that of the sexually mature *gyne*. *Diseases of Women* I explained the anatomical and physiological changes occasioned by birthing and by the menses, postpartum flows, and the milk that exited the body of the mother. These fluids persuaded Hippocratics and later medical writers that inner female nature was moister than male nature, and in order to manage these flows successfully in full maturity, the body of a *parthenos* had to be broken down and opened up. Menarche showed that the interior changes had commenced, but further widening and straightening came only with the penetration of intercourse, pregnancy, and childbirth when the infant struggled to free itself from the confining membranes of the womb and thrashed its way outward, accomplishing its own birth.[14] The rambunctious baby spread the bones of the pelvic region apart and widened the path to the outside, while the subsequent movement of fluids within the mother's body – lochial flows and milk – completed the breaking down of her compact and genderless flesh. Thus opened up and broken down, the now feminized body better managed the surplus fluids that for Hippocratics characterized a wife and mother. While Hippocratics admitted that the birth of a first infant might be difficult, they assured the uniparous that subsequent births would proceed more easily.[15] She who had birthed many children, the multiparous, was in their view the one who had transformed from young girl to productive wife and mother, the healthiest of women.

Hippocratics considered reproductive activities essential to female health once the transformations of puberty had begun, and their exhortations to intercourse and childbearing as salubrious continued throughout the woman's fertile life. Male seed, the liquid of choice, moistened the womb and kept it from drying out, contracting overmuch, and turning toward moist organs, such as the liver or lungs; without this moisture, maladies such as womb displacement and chronic amenorrhea caused her considerable distress. Intercourse heated her blood, rendering it more fluid and better able to find its proper path of downward descent in monthly purgings. Vigorous menstruation was healthful, but amenorrhea fatal after six months (*DW* I 2.12–18, 8.16–18L). In short, as the author of *Nature of the Child* put it, 'If they have intercourse with men their health is better than if they do not' (*NC* 4.3, 7.476L). The therapeutic treatises of gynecology noted that uterine suffocation, caused by the movement of the uterus to moist areas elsewhere in the body and resulting in blocked passageways, 'happened especially to old *parthenoi* and widows too young in their widowhood, and it often happened to barren women and to those who were sterile after menopause' (*DW* II 127, 8.274L). The close join between woman's reproductive activities and female health was everywhere apparent, and refrains such as 'if she becomes pregnant she will be healthy' and 'persuade the *parthenos* to sleep with a husband' resonated through Hippocratic gynecology.[16]

Hippocratic Therapy and Theory of the *Parthenos*: *Superfetation* 34 and *Diseases of Young Girls*

Healers inhabited the Greek world for centuries prior to the Hippocratic development, and Machaon and Podalirius, sons of Asclepius, had according to Homer accompanied the Greek forces to Troy, medicating battlefield wounds of the heroes. The poet of the *Odyssey*, with his far greater interest in the social mores of the home and family, portrayed Nausicaa, the young daughter of King Alcinous, as preoccupied with finding a proper suitor for eventual marriage as she set out with her maids and young friends to wash the family's laundry in *Odyssey* VI. Her preoccupation coloured the entirety of the interaction between her and Odysseus, and the delicacy with which Odysseus responded to the nubile princess underscored the fact that she was not only of royal blood but also at that liminal state between childhood and female maturity. Even before Nausicaa encountered the shipwrecked Odysseus on the shore, his clothing lost and only branches to cover his nakedness, Athena, disguised as Nausicaa's young friend, the daughter of Dymas, observed to her, 'You will soon be a *parthenos* no longer' (VI 33). The Homeric line may have influenced the thoughts about *partheneia* expressed by the archaic Greek poetess Sappho (fl. ca. 600 BC), for surviving fragments of her poems contain a number of references to *parthenoi* and *partheneia*, the abstract quality of being a *parthenos*. In some instances the context seemed to be a wedding and the *parthenos*, a bride accompanied by an attendant chorus of singing *parthenoi*.[17] Sappho's emphasis in such instances was on the sexual innocence of the *parthenos* and her chorus, for at a certain point in the joining of bride and groom the accompanying maidens were sent away (Frag. 27.10V). One fragment, cited by a certain Chrysippus[18] for its use of negatives, emphasized more general qualities of the *parthenos* – her youth and lack of worldly experiences:

I do not imagine that any *parthenos*
who has looked on the light of the sun will have
such [poetic?] skill at any time in the future (Frag. 56V).[19]

Demetrius of Phaleron, Peripatetic philosopher, rhetorician, and politician (b. ca. 350 BC), also quoted Sappho in his *On Style* because of the elegant repetition of the abstract in the first line, adding that the two lines represented a dialogue between bride (*nymphe*) and *partheneia* personified:

'*Partheneia, partheneia,* where have you gone, deserting me?'
'Never again shall I come to you: never again shall I come' (Frag. 114V).

Despite textual uncertainties in the second line, it seems to me that Sappho was here lamenting both the specific loss of sexual innocence as well as youth more generally, with all its attendant carefree pleasures.[20] Two relatively recent English translations divide in their response to Sappho's abstract *partheneia*, with one choosing 'virginity,' the other 'childhood.'[21] The *parthenos* must become a *gyne*, speeding along in a transition that writers of the *Hippocratic Corpus* later facilitated through their medical interventions. For poetess and medical writers alike, *partheneia* was a temporary state: it could not and never did return once the *parthenos* became a *gyne*, properly married off to a husband as wife and mother.

The Hippocratics of the fifth and fourth centuries BC were fashioning a more sophisticated medical discourse – one that explained how ailments disrupted inner mechanical processes and how the cures they recommended rectified, or at least ameliorated, malfunctions. They were also expanding Greek medical horizons to embrace the anatomy and physiology of the female body, and the same author in the gynecological collection *Diseases of Women* I quoted above thought it necessary to stress how his own punctiliousness in the treatment of female patients saved women's lives: 'the healing of the diseases of women differs greatly from the healing of men's diseases' (62.6, 8.126L). At several points in the text this same Hippocratic writer noted mistakes of other healers who endangered their female patients because they attempted to heal them in ways appropriate for the male body, but not for the female.[22] The writer's careful concern in such matters counted for something in the struggle to save women's lives.

Hippocratic anatomy and physiology gave medical meaning to the social role of the Greek woman in the Classical period as wife and mother of children. The precise chronology of Hippocratic treatises remains problematic, and definitive criteria for assigning specific dates to individual works are lacking, despite the general consensus that most works in the *Corpus* were composed in the latter decades of the fifth century and the early decades of the fourth. Nonetheless, special attention to the *parthenos* in sickness and health gives every indication of being one of the later developments within Hippocratic gynecology, an appendage to their concern for the *gyne*. Puberty was a time to expect changes, physical as well as social, and the medical implications for Hippocratics lay in facilitating these transformations for the *parthenos*, underscoring the notion that the metamorphosis from genderless child to fertile woman was simple only when the transition was effected speedily. The healthy young girl soon became pregnant and birthed babies, hopefully male, while delays in her transition brought physical illness and mental aberrations. One of the demonstrably later treatises in the Hippocratic gynecologies, *Superfetation*, described the maladies that afflicted young girls as the time for menarche approached, together with the therapies for medicating these:

Whenever menarche[23] does not take place for a *parthenos*, she is dominated by bile and feverish; she suffers pain; she is thirsty and hungry, she vomits; she is mad and then again becomes sane. (*Superfet.* 34.1, 8.504L)[24]

Some of the therapies prescribed specifically aimed at diminishing the menstrual blood trapped within her body: 'Put warmed sheepskins on her belly and ... have her fast as much as possible.' The warmed sheepskins caused sweating, a recognized Hippocratic means for evacuating fluid residues through the skin; fasting prevented her from producing additional blood out of the food she was ingesting. The physician also advised vaginal fumigations, a common therapeutic procedure endorsed by most medical writers throughout antiquity.[25] While neither the fumigation itself, nor its ingredients, appear unusual, the means to deliver the fumes into the womb of the *parthenos* are unparalleled elsewhere, for he ordered her to sit over a long-necked jar such that the neck extended into her uterus. This Hippocratic apparently intended that the jar's neck simulate the first penetration of intercourse and simultaneously bring on the menarche that would alleviate her suffering. In common with his Hippocratic fellows, he identified the bleeding that accompanied defloration with menstrual blood.[26]

The anatomy and physiology of the *parthenos* were elaborated in a single Hippocratic work, *Diseases of Young Girls*, which, as we have it in the earliest Greek manuscripts, is less than fifty lines long. The Hippocratic author of the embryological *Nature of the Child*, portions of the gynecological *Diseases of Women* I, and a treatise of general medicine known as *Diseases* IV, identified works from his own hand through cross-references from one treatise to the next.[27] At *Diseases of Women* I 2.31 (8.22L) he made reference to his discussion in *Diseases of Young Girls* claiming to have discussed there how retained menstrual blood at times exited the body of the *parthenos* more readily through her anus than her vagina. Nothing in the short treatise we have, however, made any mention of this phenomenon.[28] Thus, either this short Hippocratic treatise on the *parthenos* is but a fragment of a once longer work by the author of *Nature of the Child*, *Diseases* IV, and portions of *Diseases of Women* I, or a second, early medical writer also composed a work dealing with diseases of young girls.

The treatise we have did describe a malady that afflicted the *parthenos* at the time menses were to appear for the first time. The young girl's senses were deranged because the blood that accumulated in her uterus flowed out and moved upward in her body, 'for,' as the author observed, 'the blood has yet to find its proper path of exit.' It journeyed upward in her body, not down and out, wreaking havoc, particularly at the centre section of her body and the diaphragm, the area in which this Hippocratic and many others located the organs of sensation and cognition. The misdirected blood clogged passageways for breath; it putrefied and numbed her intelligence in the same way as sitting still for too long and having all the blood in one's thighs and legs run down to one's feet made the feet numb. In the author's analogy, the young girl's mind was as useless for thinking as were one's feet for walking, once they had gone to sleep:

[The blood that gathered in the feet], however, goes back up very swiftly ... whenever one stands in cold water and soaks the area above the ankles. This latter numbness is easy to manage, for the blood flows back again speedily because of the straightness of the vessels [in the legs], and the place in the body is not a crucial one. But blood flows back slowly from the heart and the diaphragm, because the veins here proceed crosswise and the place is critical for both mental aberration and madness. When these parts themselves are filled, a chill with fever rises up. (8.466–8L)

The *parthenos* thus afflicted saw visions, and these persuaded her that death was a good thing. The author knew of many young girls who had hanged themselves, or others who had thrown themselves down wells, 'more women than men, for female nature is weaker and more troublesome.' Not only did this Hippocratic writer deny the medical efficacy of religious rituals performed in the young girl's behalf, but he closed by urging marriage and pregnancy upon her as soon as possible:

When the female is recovering her senses, the women dedicate to Artemis many things, especially expensive female clothing, at the orders of the goddess's priests. But the women are being deceived. Release from this comes whenever there is no impediment for the flowing out of the blood. I urge, then, that whenever young girls suffer this kind of malady they should marry as quickly as possible. If they become pregnant, they become healthy. If not, either at the same moment as puberty, or a little later, she will be caught by this sickness, if not by another one. Among those women who have regular intercourse with a man, the barren suffer these things. (8.468–70L)

The medical writer did not explain the 'impediment' that was preventing the onset of menstruation, but it was clearly not the hymen of modern anatomy. Hippocratics did not practise systematic dissection, and many of their notions about the anatomy, physiology, and nosology of the uterus were little more than elaborations on popular traditions about the body. Even the sophisticated Greek anatomists of later centuries failed to isolate the hymen as a specific bodily part in young girls.[29] I have argued elsewhere that this Hippocratic's 'impediment' was a fantasy membrane, thought to lie at the mouth of the uterus – deep within, unseen and unseeable. Positing such a membrane not only explained why menstrual blood, accumulating prior to menarche, did not flow out, but also why first coitus was prophylactic for the *parthenos*, especially in cases in which the menses had not yet appeared spontaneously.[30] Hippocratics saw the uterus as an up-turned jar, its bottom on top and its mouth at the bottom, turned in a downward direction.[31] The uterine mouth in the mature woman learned to purse its lips and close when its contents were to be retained but to open the lips again at the proper time in order to release what was within. Thus, in conception the mouth of the uterus closed to retain male seed and in gestation to hold in the menses, for the latter were nourishment for the developing fetus; in childbirth the mouth was forced open by the strenuous movements of the child. It also opened monthly for the release of the menses, but closed thereafter. Tales contemporary with Hippocratics and also from later times suggested that even as the lower neck of the *parthenos* widened after first penetration, so too did her upper neck and her voice deepened.[32]

Hippocratic therapy and theory viewed the transition from genderless child to wife and mother as particularly dangerous when the process did not progress as anticipated. Delays, whether real or imagined, made space for medical interventions that aimed to bring about release of the menstrual blood unable to find its proper path of exit. If the blood should remain trapped within, Hippocratics expected both physical symptoms and mental derangement to ensue. While the consequences of amenorrhea were dire for all fertile women, said to be fatal after the sixth month in the *gyne*, the situation was particularly acute for the *parthenos* because her flesh was still firm and her inner passageways not fully opened. There was little or no empty space in which blood might lodge harmlessly, even for a short time, and any accumulation was likely to cause crowding and result in overheating. Genderlessness characterized the body of the Hippocratic *parthenos* until growth initiated the series of changes that irreversibly transformed her masculine body into one with wide interior passageways and porous flesh. Virginity was physical in the sense that the body of the *parthenos* was different from other bodies, and it awaited the onset of the menses, intercourse, pregnancy, and childbirth to complete the transformation. Given the salubriousness Hippocratic theory and practice attached to intercourse, prepubescent defloration seemed more healthful for the *parthenos* than a delayed onset of menstruation. The status of *parthenos* was temporary, and the sooner she became a mother, the better.

Hippocratic Data on *Parthenoi*: Case Histories

A case history in *Epidemics* V was cited above for information it gave about the medical writer's attendance on the pretty daughter of Nerius, who died on the ninth day after being struck on the forehead. Although this patient was individualized in the sense that 'daughter of Nerius' was her name and 'twenty years' her age, the medical writer's description of her fatal illness seems laced with current theory about the virginal body. Case histories recorded the progress of an illness, but commonalities among the symptoms recorded for the young girls the doctors were attending suggest that this cadre of writers in the *Epidemics* tradition shared unenunciated assumptions about the *parthenos* that shaped what they were observing and determined the symptoms they recorded as worthy of note.[33] They did not interpret what they observed, but in what follows I borrow Hippocratic theory on the *parthenos*, explicit in *Diseases of Young Girls* and echoed in *Superfetation* 34, to flesh out these case histories.

In addition to noting that the daughter of Nerius was a *parthenos*, the author of *Epidemics* V mentioned that she was immediately blind and breathless after receiving the blow to her forehead and that high fever seized her as soon as she got home. Early on there was redness about her face; on the seventh day of her illness the foul-smelling, reddish pus that exited through her ear brought some relief, and she seemed better. But afterward the high fever returned, and she became depressed and speechless, with spasmodic trembling, paralysis of the tongue, and a fixed eye close to the time of her death. The medical writer was apparently assuming that men-

commonplace but a mythical and historical reality. There is a running theme[4] wherein two specific charges of sexual impurity in women – violation of virginity in the Vestals and adultery in wives – were made responsible for danger to the state. This series of strange incidents, spanning a thousand years of Roman history, reveals a world-view deeply rooted in sympathetic magic, where women in their strictly limited societal roles embodied the state, and where the inviolability and control of women were objectified as the inviolability and control of the community.[5]

Previous Work

Most previous work on the Vestal Virgins has focused not on the function of the cult but on its form. Apart from George Dumézil and a few others, little effort has been directed at explaining the cult's social functions and ideological purposes.[6] Instead, scholars have been absorbed in etymological speculation about its putative origin in the domestic structures of the early kings of Rome. Thus the question most often posed about the Vestals is whether they reflected the daughters or the wives of a supposed original royal household.[7]

Three brief points should be made about what we may call the 'paleontological' approach to the study of religion. First, the preoccupation with origins conceals a methodological bias. This search, though interesting in itself, is firmly rooted in the notion that ontogeny recapitulates phylogeny. In the sphere of ritual, that is, a rite is taken as primarily an amalgam of earlier rites, while features that seem archaic are explained as 'survivals' of an original structure. The nineteenth-century concern with evolution is evident. Second, the search for origins or etymologies does not in itself constitute an explanation of the god, myth, or ritual. The very fact of the 'survival' and the reasons for it must be explained. Projecting synchronic facts back onto a diachronic axis simply shoves the explanation a step back. Further, there is considerable range for error in the act of creating a historical event or supposed circumstance out of each individual aspect of a ritual or myth. In particular, this form of historicizing ignores the fact that a myth or rite may not in fact reflect the 'survival' of anything but rather may be the narrative or ritual recreation of what the culture assumes or wishes had occurred.[8] Third, the assumption that the origins of the cult must lie in either the daughters of the kings or else their wives shows a desire for a monolithic explanation for the features of the Vestals and obscures the fact that the rituals and persons of the cult of Vesta, as in others, are overdetermined and multivalent.

The emphasis on the putative origins of the cult has led to an obscuring of the role of cult. Oddly enough, little emphasis had been placed on the fact that

strual blood was present in her body, perhaps dislodged from her uterus by the blow. Some displaced blood headed upward immediately, causing her to gasp for breath and hampering her sight; her flushed face and high fever were symptomatic of the blood's continued presence in her head. Blood exited from her ear in the pus that was reddish and putrefied by the seventh day of her illness. What did not depart then remained within, impeding the functioning of her tongue and eye as her end drew near. The pretty daughter of Nerius died without completing the transition to wife and mother.

The author of *Diseases of Women* I related high fevers directly to the accumulation of blood in the *gyne* – 'her body becomes full of blood unless some flows off, [and] she experiences pain when her flesh is full and heated' (I 1.15, 8.12L). The fevers said to afflict the *parthenos* in both *Diseases of Young Girls* and *Superfetation* 34 were also caused by accumulation of blood, although rather than localized in spongy flesh, as was the case in the mature woman, blood moved wherever it could discover any space at all. Even a small amount speedily resulted in fever, because of the cramped conditions within. The breathlessness the daughter of Nerius exhibited marked the presence of displaced menses in passageways at the centre of her body; her depression was caused by the blood's putrefaction; and her subsequent flushed face and malfunctions of sight and speech indicated that blood eventually reached her head.[34]

The medical writer of *Epidemics* III 17 recorded his observations in case histories about three young girls, all suffering from the high fever brought on by accumulation of menstrual blood. One *parthenos* lived in Abdera, and during the course of her illness she menstruated for the first time (case 7, 1.268LCL). Among the symptoms he thought worth recording about her case were: persistent redness, nausea, insomnia, deafness, delirium, and a loss of reason. A copious nosebleed brought some relief on the seventeenth day of her illness, as did a slight one on the twentieth; she recovered completely on the twenty-seventh day after copious sweating, although the pains in her feet that commenced on the twentieth day persisted afterward. Her purging through nosebleeds and the achievement of menarche were sufficient to bring recovery, but it was not a complete purging, as the pain in her feet continued, occasioned by blood left behind and trapped where the pain was.[35] The second *parthenos* lived in Larisa and recovered on the sixth day the doctor was observing her (case 12, 1.276–8LCL). In addition to charting the insomnia, copious watery stools, and thin, scant urine that plagued her on the second to fourth days, she was also delirious during the fourth night. On the sixth day her fever broke in the midst of a chill, followed by sweating and the appearance of her menses for the first time. Her face was flushed throughout her illness, her eyes ached, and her head felt heavy – again suggesting that he thought menstrual blood was at first clogging her central trunk in its journey upward but was subsequently lodged in her head prior to finding the proper path for evacuation. The third *parthenos* attended by this author, the daughter of Euryanax, had a sore near her anus that burst on the sixth day, and on the day following she experienced a chill and sweating (case 6, 1.228–30LCL). Her stools were small, her urine thin and scant. On the tenth day, she again sweated copiously; but instead of recovery, delirium followed, and some people said the trouble was due to the fact she had eaten grapes. From then until her death some seven days later, she was plagued by nausea, loss of appetite, and bouts of delirium. The medical writer noted that a rash was present throughout her illness and her throat red and painful; she was depressed and despaired of herself. Again, the anal suppuration, the redness and rash, and mental aberrations were symptoms expected in a *parthenos*, struggling to reach maturity.

All female patients caught in an epidemic of high fever on Thasos who were attended by the author of *Epidemics* I survived in greater numbers than did the males who became ill, provided the women experienced copious bleeding, either as menses, nosebleed, or bloody stools (I 16 and 19, 1.170 and 174LCL). A *parthenos* among those who took sick, the daughter of Daitharses, experienced both nosebleed and menarche at the same moment and speedily recovered. These Hippocratics imagined that menstrual blood, when trapped within the female, searched for and sometimes found alternate paths of exit from her body. The gnomic *Aphorisms* put the matter into concise form: 'When menstruation is suppressed, a flow of blood from the nose is good' (V 33, 4.166LCL).[36]

Helen King has drawn attention to the case history of the daughter of Leonidas in *Epidemics* VII, for at first glance it seemed to belie Hippocratic confidence in the salubriousness of a nosebleed whenever menses were suppressed:

In the case of the daughter of Leonidas her menses[37] rushed forward, but they were repulsed, and, repulsed, she bled from her nose. Having bled from the nose, a change occurred. But the doctor did not understand, and the girl-child (*pais*) died. (*Epid.* VII 123, 7.414LCL)

King was surely right to argue that what the attending doctor did not understand was the bodily state of this girl-child, for at any given point in the transition to womanhood her passageways were not necessarily widened sufficiently to convey menstrual blood through the central trunk, on to the head, and out the nose in quantity adequate to save her life. Exterior signs of growth perhaps deceived the doctor into thinking that full pubertal development was more advanced for the daughter of Leonidas than it actually was. After all, the capacity of her interior to manage surplus blood and dissipate noxious accumulations into fleshy areas for benign and temporary storage determined survival, while the fact that her breasts were beginning to develop only guaranteed that maturation was beginning and a first spongy locus was starting to form. The changes within were unseen and unseeable, and while the doctor misinterpreted the nosebleed as a positive sign for recovery, he who reported the case did understand the additional complications the body of the *parthenos* presented. For a doctor dealing with a young girl, confidence in the efficacy of a nosebleed was at times unjustified, and the exit of insufficient quantities of blood signalled death, not recovery.

The medical writer of *Epidemics* II also reported on a *parthenos* not further identified:

[Her] right arm and left leg were paralyzed after a brief cough, not worthy of mention. She experienced no other change, neither in her face, nor her intelligence – at least nothing conspicuously so. She began to improve about the twentieth day. It happened that her menses burst forth[38] for her then, and perhaps it was the first time, for she was a *parthenos*. (2.8, 7.32LCL)

In common with the writers of *Superfetation* 34 and *Diseases of Young Girls*, this medical writer anticipated that complications of difficult menarche would appear for this young girl. He inspected her face for visible signs of menses striving to discover alternative paths of exit – redness, a rash, impairment of tongue or eye – but none materialized. He anticipated mental aberrations, should blood clog breathing spaces at the centre of her body and putrefy. But again he waited in vain, and the young girl recovered when menstruation came on spontaneously. Despite the fact that her cough was brief and not worthy of mention, he nonetheless felt compelled to mention it in conjunction with the paralysis in her right arm and left leg. My guess here is that for this Hippocratic a cough operated in much the same way as a sneeze, functioning as a means to shake the uterus.[39] In this young girl even a mild cough was sufficient to disperse accumulated blood from the sensitive centre of her body to her extremities, a right arm and a left leg, causing a relatively harmless and temporary paralysis only there. The displacement prevented the menses within from disrupting the sensitive areas of perception and cognition. This *parthenos* exhibited no symptoms in her face because the blood did not rise to her head, nor did she become delirious, mentally deranged, or depressed, as he feared. Rather, around the twentieth day her menses burst forth, initiating for her the process of breaking down her body.

Nearly six hundred years later Galen wrote commentaries to the Hippocratic *Epidemics* I, II, III, and VI, and to *Aphorisms*, and, in common with many other ancients and moderns, he interpreted Hippocratic case histories according to the medicine he was currently practising. His was still a medical system based on constitutive bodily humours, but many views he attributed to 'Hippocrates'[40] were the result of his own reinterpretations. Galen did not write a commentary to *Epidemics* VII and apparently did not comment on the case of the daughter of Leonidas, but his comments on this latter young girl in *Epidemics* II, now preserved only in Arabic translation, reveal the extent to which he silently reworked outmoded Hippocratic views, such as that which accorded the *parthenos* special bodily status.[41] This young girl had, in Galen's view, clearly reached the age for marriage but had not yet achieved menarche. As could be expected, he went on, she developed a cough, as all women did, 'both *parthenos* and wife,' whenever menses were suppressed, for excess fluids were prone to gather in the chest. He praised Hippocrates' correct choice of the word *katarrhexis* for the 'breaking forth' of the menses because it conveyed the sudden force with which blocked menses usually appeared – 'for both young girls of an age for marriage and women already married.' Galen thought the bodies of both the *parthenos* and the mature woman functioned in approximately the same fashion as regards suppressed menses. This is not to say that Galen was repeating the errors of judgment committed by the doctor who attended the daughter of Leonidas. Rather, Galen coupled 'young girls' and 'married women' twice in his discussion of this case history because the anatomy and physiology of the female body he endorsed was based on systematic dissection, and more accurate knowledge about female insides had important consequences for the women and young girls Greek doctors of the Roman period were treating.

The medical community of the fifth and fourth centuries BC in Greece bound female health closely to the frequency and vigorousness of her reproductive activities, and the Hippocratics' efforts as doctors aimed at speeding the transition of the *parthenos* from child to mother. By contrast, the Greek doctors of the Roman period, building upon the anatomical advances of Herophilus and others in Hellenistic Alexandria, decisively separated female health from reproduction, a separation that had already taken place for males in the dietetic treatises of the *Hippocratic Corpus*.[42] This is not to say that societal pressures for early socialization of young girls for marriage and motherhood had altered significantly in the nearly six centuries since Hippocratics wrote. In both the Greek city-states and in Rome of the Imperial period the patriarchal regime impelled all women who were able to take up the wifely burdens of childbearing, and these were considerable, given the high rate of infant mortality.[43] Still, medical priorities had also expanded, and the Greek doctors at Rome paid considerably more attention to the general health and well-being of female patients, medicating the person in addition to the illness or conditions that came to them because of their gender. Soranus's *Gynecology*, in particular, discussed menarche and defloration in ways that looked to the comfort of the *parthenos* as she became an adult.

Soranus, Galen, and the *Parthenos* at Rome

Hippocratics characterized females by their medical Otherness, but medicine was retreating from so stark a view of gender asymmetry already by the middle of the third century BC in the face of Herophilus's assimilative interpretations of the female bodies he was dissecting in Alexandria during the reign of Ptolemy II Philadelphus (285–246 BC). His decision to employ the same nomenclature for male and female generative parts underscored similarity, not difference, as did his judgment that the uterus was made of the same stuff as other parts of the body.[44] Dissection demonstrated that human bodies were demonstrably more alike on the inside than Hippocratics supposed. Doctors even began to argue whether or not female ailments and conditions required a separate medicine, although Soranus, living and practising at Rome in the reigns of Trajan and Hadrian (AD 98–138), in the course of writing his own gynecology, agreed with those who argued that they did.[45] At the same time, Soranus also claimed that women contracted men's diseases, such as satyriasis (unceasing desire for intercourse, and in the male characterized by continous erection, but in the female by a clitoris engorged with blood) and gonorrhea (in the ancient sense, a continual flow of seed), and he introduced such discussions with 'as in men, so also in women.' Hippocratics had vacillated on the question of woman's innate heat, but after Aristotle's pronouncement at the end of the fourth century BC that females were by nature colder than males, the woman's coldness became canonical.[46] Galen, court doctor to the emperors from Marcus Aurelius to Septimius Severus (ca. AD 161–213), constructed a gendered thought experiment that likewise underscored similarity between male and female bodies on the inside. He compared pulses, which were, in his view, determined by innate bodily heat and, perhaps surprisingly, decided that a specific woman under certain conditions might have more innate heat and a stronger pulse than a particular man:

[H]ave the woman dwell in Egypt, eat hot food, exercise strenuously; have the man dwell in Pontus, eat cold food, pass the day indoors and idle. This woman's pulse is greater than that man's! (*Caus. puls.* III 2, 9.109K).

For Galen, environment, age, diet, and lifestyle were more important determiners of sickness and health than gender difference.[47] As a vigorous dissector of animal bodies (pigs, oxen, pregnant goats, apes), Galen was attracted to the similarities he saw on the inside and he provided considerable impetus to the notion that female organs of generation were analogous to the male ones, albeit on the inside of the woman's body.

Hippocratic confidence in the salubriousness of pregnancy for the *parthenos* was countered by Soranus, who declared perpetual virginity healthful for both males and females and repeated childbirth exhausting for the mother (*Gyn.* I 30–3). He viewed menstruation as harmful, albeit the necessary antecedent to pregnancy (*Gyn.* I 27–9). Amenorrhea was natural in young girls and menopausal women and was likely to occur without consequence in women of mannish appearance, in female athletes, and competitors in choral singing, since these latter expended their surplus fluids on strenuous activities and had nothing left over for monthly purgings (*Gyn.* III 6–7). Should they wish to conceive a child, however, Soranus advised those who were not menstruating to convert to a more feminine way of life, as necessary precursor to conception. He accepted the Roman view that 'men married for the sake of children and succession, and not for mere enjoyment' but went on to criticize the Roman habit of inquiring about the excellence of a prospective bride's lineage and fortune while, at the same time, neglecting to learn whether she could conceive and bear a child (*Gyn.* I 34). He too relied on the criteria of age and breast development to predict the approach of menarche but urged that proper care of the young girl begin in the thirteenth year, so as to encourage a spontaneous flow prior to defloration. This included walks, passive exercises (such as riding in a chariot, swinging, and rocking), massage with rich oils, a daily bath, and diversions for her mind that would promote relaxation in her body.[48] When the menses were flowing for the first time, he prescribed adequate rest, gentle but wholesome foods, and vaginal suppositories soaked in warm oil (*Gyn.* I 26).

Soranus was firm in his belief that defloration should take place after spontaneous menarche, repeating it several times, yet he still anticipated that both events would take place about the fourteenth year, 'for menses are a definite sign that the uterus is able to fulfill its proper functions, one of which ... is conception' (*Gyn.* I 33). Precocious pregnancy in a womb too small to carry its burden endangered the lives of both gravida and child. Particularly at risk for premature conception, in his view, were *parthenoi* not prudently brought up. Because they had not been taught proper control over their appetites, novel pleasures and new experiences were enticing to them, and they senselessly aroused premature desires in themselves with disastrous consequences. Soranus did not approve of abortion as means to hide an adulterous affair or preserve youthful beauty, but it was more than warranted if the gravida's uterus was too small and unable to accommodate a growing fetus (*Gyn.* I 60). Although he seems not to have practised dissection, Soranus not only knew well the discoveries of earlier anatomists, but was also a keen observer. Nonetheless, he too seemed not to know the hymen of modern anatomy, declaring, 'It is a mistake to suppose that a thin membrane grows across the vagina and causes pain in defloration, or during a violent outflow of blood at the menarche' (*Gyn.* I 17).[49] Such a membrane was not found in dissection, nor, when Soranus himself inserted a probe into the vagina of a *parthenos*, did he find that it met with resistance, but penetrated deep within. He attributed the bleeding that accompanied defloration to the bursting of vessels in the vaginal wall that were holding the vagina taut and narrow.

Galen wrote a treatise entitled *Remedies Easily Prepared*, but according to Oribasius, court physician to the emperor Julian (AD 361–3), it was already lost by his own day.[50] At some point, probably subsequent to Oribasius, three separate collections of recipes became attached to the Galenic corpus, and although they circulated in Greek under the title *Euporista*, printed editions of the sixteenth to eighteenth centuries affixed Latin titles, such as *De remediis parabilibus libri* III, on the mistaken assumption that this actually was Galen's *Remedies Easily Prepared*. The second book of the treatise circulating under Galen's name offered three recipes for vaginal pessaries, all of which promised to make a *gyne* at least seem like a *parthenos*.[51] The three recipes occurred in chapter 26 under the general heading 'For women's diseases'; thirty-eight subheadings followed that ran the gamut from aids to conception to recipes for dysmenorrhea and suppressing milk when the infant was to be weaned. Subsection 12 bore the heading 'So that a woman who has been violated may appear a *parthenos*,' and a prescription followed containing plant substances (wood-cassia, dried roses, white pepper, etc.) and oak galls, soaked for eight days in water, with ground rumex seeds inserted as an afterthought. The other two recipes appeared in subsection 38 with the heading 'So that the vagina does not become overly moist during coitus,' although this title was appropriate only for the first recipe that extended the promise to prevent accumulation of moisture in the uterus for the user's entire lifetime. Six recipes in all are grouped under this last heading, and the second and third boast that 'she will be like a *parthenos* in coitus'; the one that makes use of perfumed wool for the pessary suggested it could be reused, if the woman so desired. The list of ingredients is short in the latter pair, but oak galls are the principal ingredient in one, rumex seeds in the other.[52] These two ingredients contain tannins, particularly concentrated in the oak galls. Modern herbal medicine prescribes oak galls externally as a powerful astringent and styptic, while rumex also possesses astringent and cleansing properties and is employed for chronic skin diseases, as well as internal uses. Herbalists, for example, prescribe both for the treatment of hemorrhoids.[53]

The families of Greek and Roman antiquity prized the *parthenos*-daughter, about to go forth as bride and representative of her family in another man's household.[54] As Soranus suggested, it was her considerable youth and careful upbringing that guarded her reputation and guaranteed her sexual innocence. The prescriptions in the pseudo-Galenic *Remedies Easily Prepared* would have temporarily dried and tightened up the vaginal wall through their astringent properties, but their efficacy is perhaps of less interest than the milieux in which they originated and the contexts in which temporary simulation of virginity through medicaments seemed attractive and perhaps even necessary. Recipes immediately following in chapter 27 made explicit claims to enhance or diminish sexual prowess, and these perhaps suggest the prostitute community, the sex manual, and the like, as sources of and consumers for virginity-simulating prescriptions. Still, there is no way to know whether or not a Greek or Roman father from the respectable classes, or the doctors he introduced into his household, subjected a young daughter to such medicaments prior to her wedding night, if there were doubts to forestall, gossip to quell.

What can be said is that recipes to simulate virginity had not previously found a place among the written prescriptions of Greek medical writers that have come down to us. Recipes promising to counterfeit a virginity lost did appear in collections of recipes from late antiquity onward, perhaps reaching their greatest number in the seventh book of the *Compendium medicine* of Gilbertus Angelicus (d. ca. 1240). The fact that these same recipes were excised from the translation of Gilbertus into the vernacular underscored the fact that their content was yet controversial.[55] In the three pseudo-Galenic recipes from *Remedies Easily Prepared*, however, we are at, or near, the beginning of the paper trail the recipes left behind them; the trail stretched forward in time from pseudo-Galen and the fully Christianized late Empire through the next millennium and beyond – but not backward to the Rome of Galen's day. At the least, it seems to me unlikely that Galen would have been pleased to have such recipes circulating under his name.[56]

The medical writers of Greek and Roman antiquity afford us a glimpse of the social world they serviced as medical professionals. The fact that they lavished as much attention as they did on the *parthenos* and her transition from genderless child and sexual innocent to wife and mother underscores how important she was to family and society, valued for the fact that she produced the next generation of legitimate offspring. Menarche was probed and problematized, not menopause, and, in striking contrast to contemporary Western society, it was the beginning of the young girl's fertile life that drew medical attentions, not its passing. Young girls were early socialized to the burdens of childbearing throughout the ancient Mediterranean world: virtually all women married and the fertile bore babies year after year, since nearly half of those born were likely to die before a fifth birthday. Nonetheless, the insistence of Hippocratic physicians in the fifth and early fourth centuries BC that reproductive activities were essential for health in the sexually mature woman was modified in succeeding centuries, as dissection of human and animal bodies revealed how similar on the inside were males and females. If intercourse and the ejection of seed were not thought salubrious for the male, perhaps this was also true for the female, especially because her body not only provided the locus in which the fetus developed, but her body was also the nourisher of the fetus *in utero* and of the baby once born. However much virginity, *partheneia*, was valued in the pagan family's nubile daughters, it was but a passing prelude to the adult responsibilities thrust upon young girls with marriage. Men married for the sake of children and succession.

Primary Sources

– *Supplementum Epigraphicum Graecum* IX.72.16
Angelicus, Gilbertus. *Compendium medicine.* Lyon: Jacobus Sacconus 1510.
Galen. *Claudii Galeni Opera omnia.* C.G. Kühn, ed. (= K), Leipzig: Andernach 1821; 2nd reprint, Hildesheim, Zürich, and New York: Olms 1997. Greek with Latin tr.

Individual Treatises Cited from the Galenic Corpus

Caus. puls. III = *Causes of pulses* III (*De causis pulsuum*). 9.105–155K.
Comm. to Hipp. Epid. II = *Commentary to Hippocrates' Epidemics* II. Galeni In Hippocratis Epidemiarum Libros I et II (CMG V 10.1). E. Wenkebach and F. Pfaff, eds, Leipzig and Berlin: Corpus medicorum graecorum 1934. Greek, with German tr. of Arabic.
Remed. II = *Remedies Easily Prepared* (*De remediis parabilibus* II). 14.390–491K.
Gregory of Nyssa, *Vita Macrinae* (*Patrologia Graeca* 46.961)
Hippocrates. *Hippocrates. Opera omnia.* Émile Littré, ed. (= L), Paris: Baillière 1839–61; reprint, Amsterdam: Hakkert 1961–2. Greek with French tr.
– *Hippocrate.* Robert Joly and Jacques Jouanna, eds, vols. I, II (in two parts);

IV (3rd part); V (1st part); X (2nd part); XI, XIII. Paris: Les Belles Lettres 1967- . Greek with French tr.
– *Hippocrates* 1–8. W.H.S. Jones, Paul Potter, and Wesley D. Smith, eds. (= LCL), Cambridge MA (and London, 1–4 only): Harvard University Press (and William Heinemann, 1–4 only) 1923– . Greek with English tr.

Individual Treatises Cited from the Hippocratic Corpus

Anc. Med. = Ancient medicine (*De prisca medicina*). 1.12–62LCL.
Aph. = *Aphorisms* I-VII (*Aphorismi*). 4.98–220LCL.
AWP = *Airs, Waters, Places* (*De aere, aquis, locis*). 1.70–136LCL.
Coan = *Coan prognoses* (*Coa praesagia*). 5.588–732L.
D IV = *Diseases* IV (*De morbis* IV). 7.542–614L.
   Joly (1970) 84–124. Greek with French tr.
   Lonie (1981) 22–42. English tr. and commentary.
DW I–III = *Diseases of Women* I–III (*De morbis mulierum* I–III). 8.10–462L.
   Countouris, *Hippokratische Gynäkologie*. Hamburg: Med. diss. 1985. Greek with German tr. (selection, *DW* I–II).
   Grensemann (1982) 88–140. Greek with German tr. (selection, mostly *DW* I).
   Hanson (1975) 567–84. English tr. (selection, mostly *DW* I).
DYG = *Diseases of Young Girls* (*De virginum morbis*). 8.466–470L.
   Flemming and Hanson (1998) 248–52. Greek with English tr.
8mos. = *Eight-months child* (*De octimestri puero*) 7.436–60L.
   Hippokrates. Über Achtmonatskinder (CMG I 2.1). Hermann Grensemann, ed., Berlin: Corpus medicorum graecorum 1968. Greek with German tr.
Epid. I–VII = *Epidemics* I–VII (*De morbis popularibus*). *Epid.* I and III, 1.146–286LCL; *Epid* II, IV, V–VII, 7LCL.
   Jouanna (2000) 2–118 (*Epid.* V and VII). Greek with French tr.
NC = *Nature of the Child* (*De natura pueri*). 7.470–540L.
   Modern editors, following Hippocratic manuscripts, divide the treatise into two parts with separate titles, but consecutive numbering of the chapters (*Generation*, chapters 1–12; *Nature of the Child*, chapters 13–31). *NC* is used here to refer to both parts of the treatise.
   Joly (1970) 44–83. Greek with French tr.
   Lonie (1981) 1–21. English tr. and commentary.
NW = *Nature of Women* (*De natura muliebri*). 7.312–430L.
   Ippocrate. Natura della donna. Valeria Andò, ed. Milan: Rizzoli 2000. Greek with Italian tr.
Reg. I = *Regimen* I (*De diaeta*). 4.224–294LCL.

Superfet. = *Superfetation* (*De superfetatione*). 8.476–508L.
  Hippokrates. Über Nachempfängnis, Geburtshilfe und Schwangerschaftsleiden (CMG I 2.2). Cay Lienau, ed. Berlin: Corpus medicorum graecorum 1973. Greek with German tr.
Nestorius, *First Sermons* (Loofs 1905).
Sappho. *Sappho et Alcaeus*. Eva-Marie Voigt, ed. (= V). Amsterdam: Atenaeum-Polak & Van Gennep 1971.
  David A. Campbell, ed. *Sappho and Alcaeus*. Cambridge MA and London: Harvard University Press 1982. *Greek Lyric* I, 2–204LCL.
Soranus. *Gynaeciorum libri IV*, etc. (CMG IV). Johannes Ilberg, ed., Berlin: Corpus medicorum graecorum 1927. Greek.
  Soranos d'Éphèse. Maladies des Femmes I–IV. Paul Burguiére, Danielle Gourevitch, and Yves Malinas, eds, Paris: Les Belles Lettres 1988–2000. Greek text with French tr.
  Soranus' Gynecology. Owsei Temkin et al., eds. Baltimore: Johns Hopkins Press 1956. English tr. (based on Ilberg).

NOTES

1 Abbreviated terms are explained in the list of primary sources at the end of this chapter. In the body and notes of this paper references are to volume and page number in the Loeb Classical Library (= 'LCL'), when available, and, when not, to earlier editions from the nineteenth century: for the Hippocratic Corpus, volume and page in the edition by Émile Littré (= 'L'); for the Galenic Corpus, volume and page in that by C.G. Kühn (= 'K').
2 Helen King has written extensively on the *parthenos*, beginning with King's unpublished 1985 PhD thesis at University College, London, and culminating in her monograph *Hippocrates' Woman* (1998), especially chapters 3, 4, and 10. King (2004) carries her discussions of the diseases afflicting young girls into the early modern period.
3 The bibliography on Greek rituals for young girls around the time of puberty is large; for a reasonable summary, see, e.g., King (1998, 75–98); for medical emphasis on menarche, not menopause, see Dean-Jones (1994, 105–7).
4 For Hippocratic views on the instability of female nature, not only as a fetus in the womb, but also in full maturity, see Hanson (1992, 52–6). Hippocratics considered a mature woman's body more wet than that of a man, due to the gender-specific fluids it produced, and this wetness (and weakness) is here projected back to the female fetus in the womb.
5 Hippocratic physiology thought in terms of a system of conduits, or channels, that conducted blood and other fluids about the body and into the major organs,

which were viewed as receptacles. Important passageways were called 'roads' (*hodoi*), and while the *hodos* between mouth and anus was common to all, the *hodos* between nose and womb/vagina was fully operative only in the mature woman. Smaller conduits were called *phlebes*, or *phlebia*, as here; although *phlebes* and *phlebia* denoted 'veins' in later anatomical terminology, Hippocratics did not distinguish arteries from veins, nor were they always careful to separate nerves and tendons from blood vessels.

6 Hippocratics endorsed the notion that both parents produced 'generating seed' (*gone*), although the mother's contribution to her offspring remained controversial in the society at large; for the opinion that male seed was the sole source of generation, see, for example, Apollo's speech for the defence of Orestes in Aeschylus, *Eumenides* 658–66 and Aristotle, *Generation of Animals* I 20, 727b 31–728a 21.
7 For similar statements by other Hippocratics, see also *Epid*. VI 1.4 (7.218LCL) and *D* IV 54.3 (7.596L).
8 For Greek medical writers of pediatrics in the Roman period, see Hummel (1999, 13–93).
9 For the age groups 'prior to puberty' and 'from 14 to 42 years,' or 'from puberty to 63 years,' see *Coan Prognoses* 502 (5.700L).
10 *NC* 20.1–4 (7.506–8L).
11 E.g., *DW* II 127 (8.274L) and *NW* 3 (7.314L).
12 For *DW* I–III as the work of several authors, see Grensemann (1982, 1–10).
13 The Greek verb for 'break down' (*katarrhegnunai*) is also used by Greek agricultural writers for the action of the plough as it broke up clods of earth and readied soil for the sowing of seed; agricultural metaphors punctuated the gynecological treatises of the *Corpus* – see Hanson (1992, 36–41). See also below, n. 38.
14 That Hippocratic doctors, like the rest of their society, were unaware of uterine contractions and the active role played by the uterus in bringing about a birth; see Hanson (1999, 235–54) and (2004, 265–80).
15 The birthing of a male was considered the more salubrious for the mother; see Hanson (1989, 48–9) and King (1998, 180).
16 For this advice to the *gyne*, *DW* I 37 (8.92L), 63, (8.130L); *DW* II 119 (8.260L), 121 (8.264L), 131 (8.280L), 134 (8.304L), 135 (8.308L), 162 (8.342L); and *NW* 2 (7.314L), 35 (7.378L). For this advice to the *parthenos*, *DW* II 127 (8.274L), *NW* 3 (7.316L), and *DYG* (8.468–70L, quoted below in the next section). Cf. also Hanson (2000, 149–65).
17 E.g., Frags. 27V, 30V, 44V (marriage of Hector and Andromache).
18 Either a little-known first-century BC scholar and grammarian who commented on Pindar, or the better-known third-century BC Stoic philosopher.
19 Translation by Campbell, *Greek Lyric I*, 1.99LCL.

20 Cf. also Frag. 107V: 'Do I still long for *partheneia*?'
21 For 'virginity,' see Campbell, *Greek Lyric I*, S Frag. 114 (1.139LCL), but 'childhood' in Groden (1966, 62).
22 E.g., *DW* I 2.26–9 (8.20L): 'In some women, when accumulated menses are two or three months old ... and they have fallen toward her side, they form into a sort of tumor above the pubic area which is headless, large, and red ... Many doctors have not recognized what kind of a thing this is and they cut it open; they have accordingly brought their patients into danger ... The flesh has soaked up blood because the mouth of the woman's womb lies near her side ... and it forms a projection because it is now full of blood. If the mouth of the womb changes its position and extends down the vagina and if the menstrual blood exits through the vagina, the protrusion which formed along the side sometimes recedes.'
23 There is no single Greek term for 'menarche' – see King (1998, 60). Here, the Greek word is *ta horaia*, 'the things that occur at their due season,' perhaps the 'timelies.' Cf. also below, n. 37.
24 Before prescribing medicaments, the author of *Superfet.* 34 also wrote: 'Her uterus is moving, and whenever it turns toward her innards, she vomits and is feverish and out of her mind. When the uterus moves away, she is hungry, thirsty, and very feverish.' Although some scholars (including C. Lienau, an editor of *Superfet.*) have assumed that the author was speaking about 'uterine suffocation,' his language does not compel this interpretation, since nothing is said about choking (*pnix*). Rather, the uterus moved toward inner organs (of digestion) and the crowding its presence brought forced the young girl to vomit; heat spread because the uterus's movement released menstrual blood into her body. Once the uterus moved away, her belly returned to normal, for she became hungry and thirsty; her fever, however, increased, because the blood was trapped, crowded in wherever there was a bit of space. The malady described in the Hippocratic *DYG* (see below, this section) has also been interpreted as one of 'uterine suffocation,' but again this is by no means required by the text – see King (1998, 79, 240–1), although she is tempted to see *Superfet.* 34 as involving suffocation, but not the *DYG*.
25 For uterine fumigations, see Hanson (1998a, 84–7).
26 For Hippocratic identification of the blood of defloration with menstrual blood, see Dean-Jones (1994, 52).
27 At *NC* 4.3 and 15.6 (7.476L and 496L), the author appeals to his discussion of the prophylactic benefits of menses and the dangers of amenorrhea and scanty periods in *DW* I 2–4; at *D* IV 57.6 (7.612L), to his discussion of dropsy in women in *DW* I 61; at *DW* I 1.3 (8.10L), to his discussion of childbirth in *NC* 30; at *DW* I 44 (8.102L) and *DW* I 73 (8.152-154 L), to his discussion of how milk comes to the breasts in *NC* 21. In other words, his cross-references elsewhere are accurate; see also Lonie (1981, 51–3).

28 Also unmentioned in *DYG* is this author's reference to the *parthenos* at *DW* I 41.2 (8.98L), where he noted that she lived for a shorter time than did the mature woman, should her menses, appearing for the first time, rise upward in her body.
29 Evidence that Greeks and Romans were unaware that the hymen of modern anatomy was the natural physical attribute of a *parthenos* is assembled by Sissa (1990b, 339–61). As Sissa also pointed out, the unmarried young girl might bear a child and still be labelled a *parthenos* and her child a *parthenios*.
30 The point is argued for more extensively in Hanson (1990, 324–30).
31 See, for example, *Epid*. VI 5.11 (7.258LCL) and King (1998, 34–7); for these same notions in uterine amulets popular during the Roman period, see also Hanson (1995, 281–99).
32 Ancient references in Armstrong and Hanson (1986, 97–100); see also Sappho, Frag. 153V, where the *parthenos* was called 'sweet-voiced.'
33 In his commentaries on the Hippocratic texts, Galen said that *Epid*. I and III were prepared for publication by the great Hippocrates, but *Epid*. II, VI, and perhaps IV, were notes the old man left behind at his death that were subsequently reworked by a son; V and VII were perhaps from the hand of a grandson – see Hanson (1998b, 28–35). There is little agreement as to the number of authors involved in the *Epidemics*, although some books were much read in the Roman period; see Smith (1979, 237–40), and, for a descriptive view of the authors of *Epidemics*, see Smith's Introduction to LCL 7. The case histories in the present discussion derive from *Epid*. II, III, and VII, each from a different one of Galen's three groups, and it seems likely that different medical writers produced them.
34 For the Hippocratic view which saw the head as an organ that, like the uterus, attracted blood and other fluids because of its shape and similarity to cupping instruments, see *Anc. Med.* 22 (1.58LCL).
35 Despite the straightness of the conduits for fluids in the legs, noted by the author of the *DYG*, whatever was trapped in a toe, 'not sufficient to receive the sickness,' could cause death, as was the case for Timenes' niece in *Epid*. II 1.7 (7.24LCL). Cf. also the case history of Philistis, wife of Heraclides, in whom trapped menses also resulted in fever and a flushed face (*Epid*. VII 120, 7.410LCL).
36 Cf. also *Aph*. V 32 (4.166LCL): 'A menstrual flow cures a woman vomiting blood.'
37 The Greek word for 'menses' in this instance of menarche was *physis*; see also above, n. 23.
38 The Greek used the abstract noun *katarrhexis*, derived from the verb *katarrhegnunai*, for which see above, n. 13.
39 For the gnomic statement, see *Aph*. V 35: 'When a woman suffers from womby diseases or difficult childbirth, sneezing is beneficial' (4.166LCL). For sneezes in

Hippocratic therapy for dystocia, intended to dislodge an infant experiencing difficulties in effecting its own birthing, see *DW* I 68: 'Offer [the parturient] a sternutative: take hold of her nostrils, make her sneeze, and press her mouth closed so that the sneeze will have maximum effect. One should also employ shakings' (8.142L).

40 For the most part, Galen referred to treatises in his copy of the *Hippocratic Corpus* as by 'Hippocrates' and showed little interest in the 'Hippocratic Question' (worrying about which treatises in the *Corpus* were by the great Hippocrates), a question that occupied students of the *Corpus* until quite recently: see Smith (1979, 31–44) and King (1998, 61–7).

41 For German translation of the Arabic, see *Comm. to Hipp. Epid. II*, 204 Wenkebach and Pfaff. Galen's text of Hippocrates apparently also noted that a paralysis in the extremities lacked the force of paralysis on the side of the central trunk, and he also commented on this. Galen did not view the paralyzed limbs as the site of misplaced menstrual blood dispersed by the cough, for his sophisticated anatomy would have regarded such transfer impossible.

42 The Hippocratic conviction that a man's regimen must be based on an aesthetic balancing of intake of food and drink and the expenditure of the same in urine, feces, sweat, etc., was well emphasized by Foucault (1985, 97–139).

43 For the mortality functions likely to have prevailed in the Roman Empire of Galen's time, see Bagnall and Frier (1994, 75–110) and Saller (1994, 12–42).

44 See von Staden (1989, 183–6 [Frag. 61] and 167–9, and also 365 [Frag. 193]), who underscores the degree to which Herophilean anatomy demystified the uterus.

45 Soranus recounted the debate at *Gyn*. III 1–5, and the list of doctors' opinions he quoted suggest that the debate was in full flower by the days of the Alexandrian anatomists Herophilus and Erasistratus.

46 See *Gyn*. III 25, for satyriasis, and *Gyn*. III 45, for gonnorhea. For the Hippocratic disagreement as to whether women were hotter or colder than men, compare *DW* I 1.16, 'a woman has hotter blood, and because of this she is hotter than a man; yet if only the present surplus flows out, there is neither pain nor heating of this blood' (8.12L), with *Reg*. I 27, 'females, inclining rather to water, grow from the cold, wet, and soft among foods, drinks, and habits' (4.264LCL). For Aristotle's pronouncement, see *Generation of Animals* I 19–20, 726b 31–727a 4 and 728a 17–21.

47 For the 'one-sex' theory of the body, visible at times in Hippocratic gynecology, but far more prominent from the Alexandrian anatomists onward into the early modern period, see the summary in King (1998, 7–11).

48 As a doctor of the 'Method,' Soranus did not structure his medical thinking in terms of inner bodily humours, but rather the bodily states (constricted,

49 relaxed, or mixed) common to all bodies; see Hanson and Green (1994, 988–1006).
49 Soranus was aware of the morbid condition *atresia*, in which a membrane lacking perforation occluded the vagina and had to be excised (*Gyn.* III 9); Hippocratics also seem to have recognized *atresia* (*DW* I 20, 8.58L, and *DW* III 223, 8.132L), on which passages, see Sissa (1990b, 354–7).
50 Oribasius, *Ad Eunapium*, preface 5, *CMG* VI 3, 317–18 Raeder. For the possibility that Galen's own treatise has now been found in a Syriac version, see Nutton (1995, 60).
51 *Remed.* II 26.12 (14.478K) and II 26.38 (14.485–6K).
52 In the first recipe: *omphakitis*, gall of the Quercus infectoria, and *oxylapathon*, Rumex crispus; in the second, *kekis*, a general term for 'oak gall,' and, in the third, again *oxylapathon*. See also Dioscorides, *Materia medica* II 114, for *lapathon*, 'also called *oxylapathon* ... [which] the Romans call rumex'; this plant is illustrated on fol. 244 in the early sixth-century codex MS Vindob.Med.Gr. 1.
53 See Chevalier (1996, 126, 258, 302); Bown (1995, 338, 344). On oak galls, see also Riddle (1992, 94–5).
54 Marriage contracts from the Roman province of Egypt occasionally mentioned that the bride was a virgin (*P.Stras.* VIII 764.19, 109 AD; *CPR* I 30.15, 184 AD, and *Stud.Pal.* XX 15.6, 190 AD), and so did a marriage contract from a Jewish family in the newly constituted Roman province of Arabia (*P.Bab.* 18.4, 34, 128 AD). For abbreviations of papyrus editions, see Bagnall et al. (2001).
55 For the recipes to simulate virginity in the printed edition (11510), see *Compendium medicine* fol. 300recto-a to fol. 302verso-a. I am indebted to Monica Green for information about Gilbertus Anglicus.
56 For Galen's complaints about treatises falsely circulating under his name, see references in Hanson (1998b, 22–30).

4

Why Were the Vestals Virgins? Or the Chastity of Women and the Safety of the Roman State

HOLT N. PARKER

[The Pontifex Maximus] was also the overseer of the holy virgins who are called Vestals. For they ascribe to Numa also the dedication of the Vestal Virgins and generally the care and worship of the inextinguishable fire which they guard, either because he considered the nature of fire to be pure and uncorrupted and so entrusted it to uncontaminated and undefiled bodies or else because he compared its fruitlessness and sterility to virginity. In fact, in all of Greece wherever there is an inextinguishable fire, as at Delphi and Athens, virgins do not have the care of it but women who are beyond the age of marriage. (Plutarch, *Numa* 9.5)[1]

Plutarch seems puzzled. Why did the Vestals have to be virgins? The explanations offered up until recently have tended to be, like Plutarch's own, unsatisfactory. The work of Mary Beard and Ariadne Staples's recent *From Good Goddess to Vestal Virgins*[2] represent major advances in our understanding of the cult of the Vestals. I believe we can go even further. By looking to analyses of similar symbolic structures in a variety of cultures, especially in the area of witchcraft, and by drawing on the work of Maureen J. Giovannini, René Girard, and Mary Douglas, we can offer not only an explanation of the specific function of virginity in the cult but also at least a partial solution to three other puzzles about the priestesses of Vesta. First, what accounts for their unique legal status? Second, how can these women, vital to the religious and magical functioning of the Roman state, be murdered so routinely at moments of political crisis? Third, what accounts for the odd details of those murders?

I also want to go beyond virginity to look at a wider symbolic role played by women's chastity. Feminine virtue was used in antiquity as a sign of the moral health of the commonwealth as commonly as it is in some places today.[3] However, for Rome the connection was not merely a rhetorical

the Vestals had to be intact virgins. The usual explanations were that their pure state represented that of the original royal daughters who tended the household fire before their marriage, or, among those who held that the Vestal Virgins came from the king's wife or wives, some kind of more generalized sexual purity.[9] The first is clearly inadequate. The emphasis of the sources and the symbolism of the cult are not those of youth or girlish innocence but of absolute physical virginity. Virginity as merely a characteristic of youth is clearly inapplicable to Vestals, whose term of service, though beginning at ages six to ten (Gell. 1.12.1), was thirty years and frequently lifelong (Dion. Hal. 1.76.3, 2.67.2). Beard rightly criticized the second explanation:

It is unacceptable special pleading to suggest that the virginity of the Vestal was merely representative of a very generalized form of chastity, comparable to the *pudicitia* of the Roman matron. Throughout all the ancient sources which deal with the priesthood great stress is laid on the physical virginity of the women and their total abstinence from sexual intercourse during their thirty years or more in the college.[10]

It is true one needed to be sexually pure to perform many rites in both Greek and Roman religion,[11] but sexual purity and virginity are not identical, and Plutarch (*Numa* 9.5, quoted above) pointed out that virginity was not everywhere required or indeed even the norm. So we may ask with Plutarch, why virgins? If the Vestals represented the wives of the early kings, why was not the pure flame in charge of virtuous matrons, *univirae*, or widows? If the Vestals represented the original young (and hence virginal) daughters of the early kings of Rome tending the royal fire, why was not the cult of Vesta confined to young girls?[12] For an answer we must look to the symbolic functions of the Vestal Virgins and of virginity itself.

The Virginity of the Vestals

Our understanding of the symbolic role of the Vestals was greatly advanced by Mary Beard's 1980 paper 'The Sexual Status of Vestal Virgins,' in which she carefully elucidated the fusion of aspects of the two categories of 'virgin' and 'matron' in the Vestals.[13] More recently, Ariadne Staples's *From Good Goddess to Vestal Virgins* presented an insight fundamental to a correct interpretation of their role and cult. In brief: the primary role of the Vestal Virgin was to be an embodiment of the city and citizenry of Rome.[14] I have reached similar conclusions by a different route, that of cultural anthropology. Staples's work rightly returns our focus from putative origin to actual function. This symbolic role of the absolute virginity of the Vestal Virgins was the aspect to which the ancient texts gave the greatest prominence and which they explicitly labelled the most important. Their embodiment of the city of Rome is clear throughout the sources.

Whether or not the cult of Vesta originated in the household of the Roman kings, one fact must be emphasized: from the beginning of the historical record it was not a private but a public cult.[15] The role of Vesta herself in symbolizing Rome is abundantly clear. She was the hearth and heart of Rome.[16] She stood literally at the centre of the city and served to bind the city together. The common hearth and the common wall together signified the unity of Rome.[17] The goddess's official title was *Vesta publica populi Romani Quiritium*.[18] The historians appealed to Vesta to demonstrate the impossibility of abandoning Rome.[19] For the poets Vesta was the metonym for Rome.[20]

Equally clear is the role of Vesta's priestesses. The Vestals were 'taken' in a complex ceremony, whose formula stressed their service to the Roman people.[21] The Vestals prayed for the people of Rome.[22] Cicero ordained that the Vestal Virgins guard the public hearth of the city.[23] Their temple was explicitly open to all by day, though shut to men at night.[24] Their *penus* was the storehouse of the state, holding not merely state documents, but also the Palladium, the 'guarantee of Roman power.'[25] The Vestals tended the eternal fire, whose extinction was not just unlucky, but a grave prodigy, specifically said to presage the destruction of the city.[26] Rome, said Horace, would stand 'as long as the pontifex climbs the Capitoline beside the silent Virgin.'[27]

It is here that we can seek the symbolic function of the Vestal's virginity. Just as she embodied the city of Rome, so her unpenetrated body was a metaphor for the unpenetrated walls of Rome. This is manifest from the ancient sources. The powers of a Vestal were conterminous with the city walls.[28] Pliny the Elder (*NH* 28.13) stated: 'We still believe that our Vestals root to the spot fugitive slaves, if they have not yet left the city' (cf. Dio 48.19.4). Their lives and deaths were bound by the limits of the city. Vestal Virgins were given the honour of burial within the *pomerium* (Serv. *Aen.* 11.206), most strikingly even when they are buried alive after being convicted of unchastity (see below). However, the Vestals' virginity was more than merely the symbol of the inviolability of Rome. It was also the guarantee. The whole state depended on the state of being whole. The Vestals did not just hold the repositories of the state; they were the repositories of the state.

Rome and Mediterranean Anthropology

The roles of women as symbolic counters in men's codes of honour and the special function of virginity within those codes have been a major concern in what has come to be called 'Mediterranean anthropology.'[29] Maureen J. Giovannini's observations[30] on the function of Woman as Sign in symbolizing and mediating various aspects of the family can help us in understanding this complex of contradictory ideas. Giovannini identified six archetypal categories into which women were placed by the citizens of the Sicilian town that she calls 'Garre.' At the centre is the pair of *la Vergine* (the Virgin) and *la Mamma* (the Mother) representing woman in her two societally sanctioned roles, unpenetrated and penetrated. Each has an anti-type: *la Puttana* (the Whore) and *la Madrigna* (the Step- or Anti-mother). On the supernatural level, just as *la Madonna* unites the beneficent aspects of woman, so *la Strega* (the Witch) unites the figures of *la Puttana* and *la Madrigna*. The honour of the family is synonymous with the chastity of its women, who, because of their inherent vice of feminine sexual weakness, are in constant danger of becoming whores and adulteresses.[31] For *la Vergine*, Giovannini notes:

Her physical intactness is also viewed as a sign that her family possesses the unity and strength necessary to protect its patrimony ... As family member, *la Vergine* can synecdochically (part for whole) convey the message that her family is a viable entity with its boundaries intact ... *la Vergine's* (and, as we shall later discover, *la Puttana's*) corporal being constitutes a kind of cognitive map for the family unit by concretely representing the boundaries of this social group along with its internal unity.[32]

For ancient Rome, the cult of Vesta was the symbol for the unity of all families. Hence Giovannini's analysis applies not merely to the individual units but to the Roman state as a collective. Mary Douglas's remarks on the use of the human body as a microcosm of the social order in various societies, especially those with strong witchcraft beliefs, relate directly to the symbolic value of the Vestal Virgin:

The group is likened to the human body; the orifices are to be carefully guarded to prevent unlawful intrusions ... The most fundamental assumptions about the cosmos and man's place in nature are coloured by the socially appropriate image of the human body ... The idea of a cherished bodily form vulnerable to attack from without tends to be transferred from one context to another. It can serve as a theory of misfortune by pinning blame on hidden enemies of society; it can serve as a guide to action, requiring the enemies to be unmasked and disabled ... Injustice can be rectified merely by purging the system of internal traitors allied with outside enemies ... Bodily symbolism in the witch fearing cosmology is endlessly rich and varied, but always the emphasis is on valuing the boundaries, guarding the orifices, avoiding improper mixtures.[33]

This same bodily symbolism, where the safety of the group is bound to the bodily integrity of a chosen figure, is found in a number of cultures. Turner, in a famous analysis, remarks on the Lunda-Ndembu of modern Zambia:

> The position of senior or paramount chief among the Ndembu, as in many other African societies, is a paradoxical one, for he represents both the apex of the structured politico-legal hierarchy and the total community as an unstructured unit. He is, symbolically, also the tribal territory itself and all its resources. Its fertility and freedom from drought, famine, disease, and insect plagues are bound up with his office, and with both his physical and moral condition.[34]

Magical Virginity

The Vestal was not merely a mode of representation. She was also a symbol that could be manipulated. Archaic Roman religion was based on and steeped in magical practice.[35] By 'magical practice' I mean that technology of analogy as defined by Tambiah: 'Magical acts ... constitute "performative" acts by which a property is imperatively transferred to a recipient object or person on an analogical basis.'[36] Magic, since Frazer, has traditionally been divided between the imitative and the contagious. In imitative magic the law of similarity applies: 'like produces like'; in contagious magic, the law of contiguity applies: 'objects which have been in contact, but since ceased to be so, continue to act on each other at a distance.'[37] The Vestal, who preserved the inviolability of Rome by preserving the inviolability of her body, exemplifies both forms of magic and indeed shows their overlap and a certain arbitrariness in the distinction. Imitative magic is perhaps better characterized as metaphoric (*similia similibus*): as she remained *integra*, so did the city. The Vestal's body served as the microcosm of the city.

Again, this is abundantly clear from the ancient sources. The Vestal must be not merely a virgin but physically perfect in every respect. The potential candidate was examined by the Pontifex Maximus to guarantee this. Both parents must be living, and neither she nor her father emancipated, since this would make her technically an orphan and hence imperfect.[38] Her parents' marriage must have been perfect. Neither of them could be divorced or ex-slaves or found to have engaged in *negotia sordida*. Should she even fall sick, she must be removed from the *aedes Vestae* and cared for outside the holy area by a married woman, but not a family member (Pliny 7.19.1). Most important, as we have noted, her life and powers were circumscribed by the walls of the city.

Contagious magic, on the other hand, is metonymic or synecdochic: 'The part is to the whole as the image is to the represented object.'[39] The Vestal represents not only the idealized role of Woman – a fusion of the archetypal roles of *la Vergine* and *la Mamma* into the figure of *la Madonna*[40] – but also the citizen body as a whole.[41] Many cities are symbolized by women. Athens, symbolized and guarded by the virgin goddess Athena, is an obvious parallel but does not supply an explanation for the choice of a virgin female to represent a citizen body composed of men and their dependents. Pomeroy points towards an answer: 'Since a virgin belongs to no man, she can incarnate the collective, the city: she can belong to everyone.'[42] This insight, however, is incorrect in one important respect: an ordinary virgin in Roman law does belong to a man – she belongs to her father. Accordingly, for a virgin to incarnate the collective, she must be extraordinary. She must be freed not only from her father but from all possible and catalogued forms of familial tie.

Legal Status

In the past the legal status of the Vestal Virgin was not correctly conceptualized, since it was approached almost entirely from a purely descriptive point of view.[43] Her unique legal status should be viewed less as a mark of respect than as a magical function that made it possible for her to incarnate the collective. Once the ritual and symbolic purpose of the laws is considered, the legal status and consequences of that status become clear. Gardner summarizes:

The oddities of her position seem rather to arise from her position as one in charge of a worship central to the state and not belonging to any one family in the state. She was taken out of her family, with certain legal consequences, but she did not cease to be a woman.[44]

It is necessary to go further. She was taken out of her family and not added to any other. Moreover, she was not just in charge of a worship central to the state; she was also the embodiment of that state. She did not cease to be a woman, but she ceased to be like any other woman.

Roman society was governed by a strict series of exogamic rules, and the principle of Woman as Sign is more visible there than in many other cultures.[45] The exchange of women to seal interfamilial bonds and political ties was a marked feature of Roman society.[46] Thus if the Vestal Virgin were to represent the society as a whole, she must be exterior to all families. Because a basic principle of Roman law was that a woman always belonged to someone, the procedure to free the Vestals from ownership was both complex and comprehensive. The first step in the process was to exempt the Vestal initiate from the power of her father (*patria potestas*). Since this was normally accomplished by *coemptio*, a form of sale that merely placed her in someone else's power, she was specifically said not to have undergone emancipation, which normally simply passed a woman into the *tutela* of her nearest male relative. She was then freed from any form of *tutela*, but uniquely without loss of status (*capitis minutio*) – that is, without falling into the *manus* of any other man.[47] Though she was under the formal discipline of the Pontifex Maximus, who could scourge her for minor offences, he exercised neither *patria potestas* nor *tutela* over her.[48] Thus the complex legal procedure prevented her from being an orphan while still guaranteeing that legally and religiously she had no family. She was completely removed from her agnatic family and yet did not pass to the ownership of any other family.

A Roman woman existed legally only in relation to a man.[49] A woman's legal status was based entirely on this fact. The act of freeing a Vestal from any man, so that she was free to incarnate all men, removed her from all conventional classifications. Thus she was unmarried and so not a wife; a virgin and so not a mother; she was outside *patria potestas* and so not a daughter; she underwent no *emancipatio*, no *coemptio*, and so was not a ward.[50]

This unique status entailed a number of consequences. Since she had no family, she no longer inherited property; nor did she leave property to her family if she died intestate. Rather than her property reverting to the *gens*, as would be the case for an intestate woman freed by ordinary emancipation, it reverted to the state, of which she was the embodiment.[51] As a free agent, she necessarily acquired the right to dispose of her property by will and the right to be a witness.[52] It is to this unique status that I would assign the 'male aspect' that Beard and Dumézil have identified.[53] Her 'masculine' rights and privileges were side effects of the act of freeing her from all masculine ownership and not necessarily constructs designed to increase the ambiguity of her classification and thus further mark her out as sacred.[54]

The Vestal was thus the *totem* of Rome, and her sacred character derives from her status as the embodiment of the clan.[55] Her virginity is a type of binding spell familiar from ritual observances in many cultures. A single totemic item is invested with the safety of an individual or state. As long as it remains unharmed, so does that which it signifies.[56] For Rome there was significantly the Palladium, which the Vestal Virgins guarded and with which they were associated and identified as the 'guarantee of Roman power.'[57]

Thus, as long as the Vestal remained intact, so did Rome. This symbolic function is explicitly stated. For example, a Vestal's epitaph reads: 'The republic saw with good fortune day after day her exceptional discipline in morals and most exact observance of the rituals.'[58] Thus the Vestal Aemilia, when the sacred fire went out, prayed to Vesta (Dion. Hal. 2.68.4): 'If anything unholy has been done by me, let the pollution of the city be expiated by my punishment.' Most tellingly, the Vestal Cornelia, on her way to be buried alive by the order of Domitian, ties the safety of Rome explicitly to her virginity and reveals the underlying magical logic: 'Does Caesar think that I have been unchaste, when he has conquered and triumphed while I have been performing the rites!'[59]

The Sacrifice of the Vestal Virgin: A Theoretical Outline

The question now arises: how can a people sacrifice its symbol? How can the incarnation of the state be ritually murdered? Burkert's explanation for the sacrifice of a virgin in his reconstruction of prehistoric ritual (and perhaps in Greek myth) will not do. He proposes: 'Man declines love in order to kill: this is most graphically demonstrated in the slaughter of "the virgin" ... In the period of preparation, maiden-sacrifice is the strongest expression of the attempt to renounce sexuality.'[60] However, there is no necessity for 'virginity' in a renunciation of sexuality. Further, there is nothing in the Roman ritual of the sacrifice of the Vestal Virgin to show the connection that Burkert proposed between maiden-sacrifice and hunting or preparation for warfare (as distinct from the threat of external warfare). Rather, to summarize what the Roman sources cited below make clear, the sacrifice of a Vestal Virgin was the sacrifice of a scapegoat, in both the popular and the ritual sense. For it is important to note that the sacrifice of a Vestal Virgin is a ritual, a precisely delineated social construction.

René Girard's careful exploration of the roles and patterns of sacrifice[61] can aid in isolating elements and functions of the ritual sacrifice of the Vestal Virgin.[62] In turn, by using the society of ancient Rome as a source of anthropological data, we can cast light on and make some corrections to Girard's theory. Certain features of his analysis illuminate the sacrifice of the Vestal Virgins. A summary of his complex ideas may be presented under the two headings of the nature of the sacrifice and the nature of the victim.

For all societies, says Girard, the greatest danger is that of unchecked reciprocal violence.[63] As the cycle of violence increases, the society reaches a 'sacrificial crisis,'[64] which can be, almost miraculously, resolved by further violence, but of a specifically controlled type, namely sacrifice. In sacrifice, 'society is seeking to deflect upon a relatively indifferent victim, a "sacrificeable" victim, the violence that would otherwise be vented on its own members.'[65] Through sacrifice and the sacrificial victim, improper vio-

Why Were the Vestals Virgins? 75

lence is channelled into proper violence. All are united in this single act, which Girard defines as 'the sacred.'[66]

For sacrifice to work in this way, it is essential that the violence be unanimous.[67] Anyone left outside is a potential avenger, a source of new violence. As Girard says, 'Such an attitude requires absolute faith in the guilt of the surrogate victim.'[68] To restate Girard's thesis, no victim is ever sacrificed and then found not to have been guilty.[69]

For Rome, we may note in the historical record the total lack of any protest against the sacrifice of a Vestal Virgin, even from the Vestal's family.[70] Pliny's eyewitness account of the murder of Cornelia is revealing. Though Pliny hated Domitian, was deeply suspicious of his motives for attacking the Vestal, and denounced the illegality of her trial and execution, he could not bring himself to believe that the charge was utterly without foundation. He was able only to go as far as writing 'I don't know whether she was innocent, but she certainly acted as if she were innocent.'[71]

Further, to eliminate the possibility of a new cycle of revenge, the sacrificial act must be sharply marked off from any non-sacred act of violence. The nature of the sacrifice must be in some form, as Girard says, 'disguised': 'A properly conducted ritual killing is never openly linked to another bloodletting of irregular character.'[72] The murder of the Vestal was a precise form of sanctioned human sacrifice: violence broke out in a predictable pattern and the sequence of events that led to the accusation of a Vestal was as formalized as the details of her trial and execution.[73]

It is clear that the victims in Girard's analysis must possess a stringent set of qualities if their deaths are to unite the society in a unanimous act of sacrifice. First, since 'sacrifice is primarily an act of violence without risk of vengeance,' all sacrificial victims 'are invariably distinguished from the nonsacrificeable beings by one essential characteristic: between these victims and the community a crucial social link is missing, so they can be exposed to violence without fear of reprisal. Their death does not automatically entail an act of vengeance.'[74] However, the exact opposite must also be simultaneously true. Since the victim 'is a substitute for all the members of the community, offered up by the members themselves,' the victim must also be similar to and part of the community it represents. Therefore, says Girard, 'the proper functioning of the sacrificial process requires not only the complete separation of the sacrificial victim from those beings for whom the victim is a substitute but also a similarity. This dual requirement can be fulfilled only through a delicately balanced mechanism of associations.'[75] Anthropological data reveal that the human victims share a common status:

[They] are either outside or on the fringes of society: prisoners, slaves, pharmakos ... What we are dealing with, therefore, are exterior or marginal individuals, incapable of establishing or sharing the social bonds that link the rest of the inhabitants. Their status ... prevents these future victims from fully integrating themselves into the community.[76]

Following this pattern, the Vestal Virgin is both interior and exterior. She is the child of citizens, originally confined to the upper classes, perfect to represent the whole citizenry.[77] Yet at the same time she is carefully segregated, legally removed from all familial ties, as outlined above.

Likewise, the victim must be innocent – for vengeance on a guilty party may lead to another act of vengeance – and at the same time guilty, since only a collective belief in guilt can guarantee the necessary unanimity.[78] Ritual measures are taken in order to increase the future victim's guilt. The victim is frequently charged with the most hideous crimes, violating the society's most basic taboos, notably incest.[79] I use the words 'charged with' in two senses: both charged with sin and charged with power. One form of charging the victims with magical power (the familiar Polynesian *mana*) is to force the members of the group of potential victims to violate taboos (as done by the kings in various African cultures). The other is its opposite: a strict and compulsive guard on the victims, but with the purpose of holding the victims all the more guilty for violating these taboos. Thus the Vestals were bound by a complex series of duties and prohibitions. The lesser violations were punishable by a scourging from the Pontifex Maximus, but the most awesome violation, accusation of the loss of virginity, by burial alive.

The Vestal Virgin as Victim

The Vestal Virgin thus provides a perfect example of the *pharmakos*, as known from Greece, as described by Frazer, and as analysed by Girard.[80] Even as she was a physically perfect priestess, so she can become a sacrificially perfect victim. However, Girard notes a striking exception in his description of the marginality of the victim:

It is clearly legitimate to define the difference between sacrificeable and nonsacrificeable individuals in terms of their degree of integration, but such a definition is not yet sufficient. In many cultures women are not considered full-fledged members of their society; yet women are never, or rarely, selected as sacrificial victims.[81]

This statement is contradicted not only by the analogous worlds of myth and Greek tragedy to which Girard applies his theory, but also by a wide range of cross-cultural data.[82] He has neglected, in particular, evidence from

Why Were the Vestals Virgins? 77

anthropological discussions of witchcraft (see below).[83] Girard, however, offers an argument for his exclusion of women:

> There may be a simple explanation for this fact. The married woman retains her ties with her parent's clan even after she has become in some respects the property of her husband and his family.[84] To kill her would be to run the risk of one of the two groups interpreting her sacrifice as an act of murder committing it to a reciprocal act of revenge.[85]

Girard need not have confined himself to married women. The deaths of women in their role as daughters are equally subject to revenge.[86] To restate, though Girard does not use these terms, the role of Woman as Sign makes the use of Woman as Sacrifice dangerous. Women, however, are the most obviously sacrificeable class of victims; indeed they are the perfect victims. Better than any other group, they have been endowed with the marginality crucial to sacrifice. Yet it appears they cannot easily be sacrificed. Girard's own remarks point the way to the solution that culture after culture has found. If Woman as Sign prevents her use as victim, she must be made to be a sign for something else; she must be exempted from vengeance and removed completely from all social bonds.

Thus, the special status of the Vestal Virgin made it possible for her to be this perfect victim. The sacrifice of the Vestal Virgin reveals a deeply rooted cultural technology of the *pharmakos*. The magical ways of thinking are evident from the sources. A single example may suffice. Livy (2.42.9–11) described the sacrifice of the Vestal Oppia in 483 BC:

> War with Veii then broke out and the Volsci resumed hostilities. Roman resources were almost more than sufficient for war against an external enemy, but they were squandered by the Romans fighting among themselves. Adding to everyone's mental anxiety were heavenly prodigies, occurring in Rome and the countryside, which showed the anger of the gods almost daily. The prophets, after consulting first the entrails and then the birds about both the public and the private omens, announced that there was no other reason for the gods being so moved, except that the sacred rites were not being performed correctly. These terrors finally resulted in the Vestal Virgin Oppia being condemned for *incestum* and executed.[87]

Note the flat narrative tone, the logical sequence of events. Girard writes: 'Whenever violence threatens, ritual impurity is present.'[88] As Livy and the other sources make clear, this magical law is both resultative and causal. The logic runs: We are in trouble; therefore, the rites designed to protect us are not being performed properly; therefore, those entrusted with those rites have betrayed us; therefore, the way to restore safety is to sacrifice those who have betrayed us.[89]

Vestal Virgin as Witch

Throughout his work, in my opinion, Girard overemphasizes the role of internal violence at the expense of external threats. Here the Roman data can qualify his broad formulations. As various historians ancient and modern have noted, the sacrifice of the Vestal Virgin occurs primarily in times of 'extreme religious hysteria and political crisis.'[90] The crisis, however, is not exclusively one of internal dissension but also external military threat (see Appendix). As an example, note the emphasis that Livy places on both elements in his account of the sacrifice of Oppia. Girard, however, rightly links internal and external threats by identifying an element of 'betrayal.' Girard writes on African magicians:

As soon as the community becomes aware of a backlash of violence, it will shift the responsibility to those who led it into temptation, the manipulators of sacred violence. They will be accused of having betrayed a community to which they only half belonged, of having used against this community a power that had always been mistrusted.[91]

Those who work with and are in contact with the sacred are especially likely to become its victims. The primary notion is that of contagion. This fear of the contaminated insider abetting an external enemy is crucial to the thinking of many societies, and anthropological analyses of witchcraft can help illuminate how this fear manifested itself in Rome as well. Thus Philip Mayer in a famous article describes the witch as 'The Traitor within the Gates':

The figure of the witch, clearly enough, embodies those characteristics that society specially disapproves. The values of the witch directly negate the values of society ... However, I think that another or a more particular kind of opposition is also vitally involved. I mean the opposition between 'us' and 'them' ... The witch is the figure who has turned traitor to his own group. He has secretly taken the wrong side in the basic societal opposition between 'us' and 'them.' This is what makes him a criminal and not only a sinner.[92]

These remarks cast an important light on the Vestal Virgin.[93] For the Vestal accused of *incestum* was held not only as a sinner but as a criminal as well, and the worst criminal of all: a trait*oress*. The specifically feminine form is significant. In undoing herself, she has undone Rome.

I say 'undoing herself' in the same sense as 'got herself pregnant.' The entirely optional presence of a man is a feature usually unnoticed or unremarked by both ancients and moderns. The sequence of events is inconsistent: misfortune results in suspicion of unchastity; unchastity implies a seducer; one is occasionally sought and found. While we know the names of several men executed or exiled for having had intercourse with Vestal Virgins,[94] and while such a charge clearly might be used for political purposes,[95] Vestals were most often tried for unchastity quite by themselves, with no male co-defendants, or (just as revealing) the existence of male co-respondents was not considered worthy of record.[96] There is no case recorded of a Vestal Virgin suspected or convicted because she was pregnant or any case where a Vestal was charged with unchastity because she had been raped.[97] Vestals always sinned willingly. It was necessary for them to do so.

In Giovannini's analysis, just as *la Vergine* serves to mark the family's boundaries, so her anti-type, *la Puttana*, 'can act as a synecdoche (part for whole) for her family's weakness in the face of external threats ... Also, because she was willingly penetrated, this female figure connotes individual disloyalty to the family. In fact, people commonly referred to such a woman as *una traditura* (a traitor).' Likewise, the supernatural Witch (*la Strega*), who unites Whore and Stepmother, 'while actualizing the penetration of Woman,' is called upon 'to represent the uncontrollable forces that undermine family unity.'[98]

Thus the penetrated Vestal Virgin becomes a witch – that is, when a witch was needed, a Vestal was deemed to have been penetrated. Here we see one of the most frequent uses of witchcraft: to protect other value systems. The failure of sacred ritual can be attributed to witchcraft, specifically to betrayal by those very technicians of the sacred whose duty it was to perform the rituals that protect society.[99]

This linking of betrayal and unchastity in the figure of the traitoress (*traditura*) ran deep in the Roman mind. It is an intimate part of the cultural encyclopedia. It features prominently in myth and mythical history (Horatia and Tarpeia) as well as rhetoric and rhetorical history (Sempronia).[100] It is also enshrined in law, which allows the torture of slaves to provide evidence against their masters only for cases of *incestum* and for treason.[101]

The Trial: Legal Status

The ambiguous legal status of the trial for *incestum* of the Vestal Virgin has excited the curiosity of many commentators. Two divergent views are held: one, that the trial of the Vestal was a purely secular procedure; the other, that it was a purely religious matter. Koch and others have claimed that Roman law had no procedures for dealing with offences against the gods.[102] This is not precisely correct[103] but leads them, nevertheless, to view the trial of the Vestal Virgin as a strictly criminal matter, with the Pontifex Maximus exercising a purely judicial and paternal authority in a trial for *incestum*.[104] Koch believed that the Vestal was held guilty of incest (in the English sense, German *Blutschande*) since all Romans were somehow the brothers of the Vestal.[105] He then likened it to a trial by a father for a daughter's adultery. Koch, however, misunderstood the very nature of the term *incestum*. *Incestum* was not just 'incest,' nor was it the same as *stuprum* (sexual defilement, which covers adultery and rape).[106] Both familial incest and the Vestal's *incestum* were types of a specific genus of un-chastity, united by the fact that each involved, unlike *stuprum*, not just legal but religious consequences, and so danger to the state as a whole.[107] Likewise, the trial of a wife accused of adultery before the family tribunal and the trial of a Vestal accused of *incestum* before the entire pontifical college differed in numerous aspects, most importantly in the unique specification of the Vestal's death by being buried alive.[108]

Wissowa and others, noting the obvious ritual significance of the trial and punishment of a Vestal, argued that they were not criminal procedures at all but the purely religious matter of the discovery and purification of a *prodigium* (*procuratio prodigiorum*).[109] Cornell objects that the unchastity of a Vestal was not in itself a *prodigium*, but a crime that a series of *prodigia* served to disclose.[110] This is not quite correct. Rather, it is the case that prodigies give rise to prodigies.[111] The accused Vestal shared with other *prodigia* the essential feature of pollution.[112] She was a contradiction in terms, a penetrated virgin, the impure pure, and so a *miasma*. Like a hermaphrodite, she crossed boundaries that must not be crossed, and so she must be removed and destroyed.[113] The details of her execution were those of the expiation of a prodigy.

Again, each single explanation is inadequate. The crime of the Vestal was neither against the gods alone nor against the Pontifex Maximus alone. The trial and execution of the Vestal Virgin was unique because it was simultaneously both a religious rite to drive out the pollution of *incestum* and a judicial rite for the punishment of treason.[114] The penetrated virgin was a monster and so must be expiated as a *prodigium*. Yet she sinned willingly and so was a traitor.[115] The trial therefore had two corresponding functions. First, the trial guaranteed the unanimity of the sacrifice, the 'absolute faith in the guilt of the surrogate victim.'[116] It separated the Vestal Virgin from the community and increased the sacrificially necessary guilt. She was made responsible for all the evils that occurred in the time of crisis, especially sterility of women and diseases of cattle – common witchcraft charges.[117] Second, the trial served as the disguise necessary to the proper functioning of the sacred. The Greek and Latin sources themselves carefully distinguished between the execution of the Vestals in 215 and 113 B.C. and the sacrifice of the two Greeks and two Gauls along with them (see Appendix). The disguise has worked extraordinarily well. Pliny is not the only one to be unable to convince himself of the possibility of wrongful conviction. Modern authors commenting on the historical texts hold to an oddly naive and credulous style of reporting. The trials and executions of the Vestals are never referred to as – what they so palpably are – human sacrifice.[118]

Execution and Burial: The Vestal as *Prodigium*, *Pharmakos*, and *Devotio*

As *Prodigium*

The execution of the Vestal followed the same magical and religious logic as the expiation of a *prodigium*. In each case the first principle was to remove all traces of the *prodigium*.[119] Thus two oxen that had climbed up the stairs to the roof of a block of flats were burned alive and their ashes scattered in the Tiber (Livy 36.37.2). A person who had changed sex is said by Pliny the Elder to have been left on a desert island (*Hist. Nat.* 7.36). A hermaphrodite was sealed alive in a chest and set adrift at sea.[120] Cornell rightly compares the hermaphrodite with the case of M. Atilius, who was convicted of revealing parts of the Sibylline books on the testimony of a slave, sealed in a sack, and thrown alive into the sea: 'The ritual purpose of [this] *culleus* is clearly to remove all trace of an unholy and polluting object.'[121] The goal, however, of such rituals is not only to remove the polluting presence of a *prodigium*, but to do so without incurring that pollution. Thus the *prodigium* is burned or abandoned alive. Death is left up to a natural force and no one is personally responsible for the death and so tainted. No one, therefore, is the object of a further act of vengeance for that death. Girard explains the mechanism in these terms:

It is best, therefore, to arrange matters so that nobody, except perhaps the culprit himself, is responsible for his death, so that nobody is obliged to raise a finger against him. He may be abandoned without provisions in mid-ocean, or stranded on top of a mountain, or forced to hurl himself from a cliff ... the object is to achieve a radically new type of violence, truly decisive and self-contained.[122]

Thus the details of the Vestal's execution. She was uniquely buried alive, yet provided with a small amount of food, which Plutarch explicitly said was done to prevent the death of a sacred person from being attributable to anyone but herself (*Quaest. Rom.* 96, *Numa* 10). The execution of a Vestal was in itself her trial by ordeal. If she were pure, Vesta would no doubt rescue her. Since the goddess never did, the Vestal's guilt was proved.[123]

As *Pharmakos*

The Vestal Virgin was the symbol of the city, specially set apart in order to incarnate the impregnable boundaries of Rome. When Rome was subject to violence, it was because the Vestal had been violated. Yet it was this very status that made it possible for her to be used as a witch figure whose sacrifice averted the anger of the gods. She could become a *pharmakos*.[124]

Like the *pharmakos*, she was a ritually pure victim. Seneca (*Cont.* 4.2) explicitly compared the physical perfection of the sacrificing priest to the physical perfection of the sacrificial victim. Yet we hear of no examination to determine a loss of virginity, apart from the trial by ordeal of burial alive. To have definite medical evidence one way or the other would destroy that precarious balance that Girard points out, since the victim must be simultaneously pure and yet guilty. Like the *pharmakos*, she was paraded through the town in order 'to absorb all the noxious influences that may be abroad.'[125] She partook therefore of the dual nature of the *pharmakos*, even as *pharmakon* has a dual sense. The ritual victim is both disease and cure. Dion. Hal. 9.40.1 (on the murder of Urbina in 472) makes the mechanism clear: once the Vestal was buried alive, the plague that had afflicted the women with sterility and miscarriages ceased (again, note the standard association of witchcraft with plague).

As *Devotio*

The Vestal Virgin's status as *pharmakos* means that after her execution, she was paradoxically a protection to the city. She was a prodigy: sacred before as Virgin and Mother, she was still sacred (that is crossing category boundaries) when defiled, as both penetrated and unpenetrated. Like Oedipus, the presence of her body helped guard the very city that she was held to have betrayed. This explains the fact that not only were the bodies of Vestals ordinarily given the honour of burial inside the city walls, but even Vestals found guilty of *incestum* were buried alive within the *pomerium*. Most important, this explains the fact that yearly sacrifices were made on the now holy site of the burial, the *campus sceleratus*.[126] Plutarch expressed astonishment that the site of the burial of a traitoress should receive yearly sacrifices. Only the Vestal's status as *pharmakos* can explain this.

The Vestal Virgin was thus the most magically effective form of *devotio*.[127]

Just as the Roman general could devote any soldier from the army as a substitute for himself, and as a representative of the army and the Roman people as a whole, so the Vestal Virgin was devoted as sacrifice for the Roman people to expiate the anger of the gods.[128] Indeed, only comparison with the *devotio* explains the fact that the Vestal was *buried* alive. The standard punishment for both treason and incest was to be thrown off the Tarpeian rock.[129] However, if someone survived after being made an involuntary *devotio*, an image had to be buried seven or more feet deep and the spot was declared sacred (Livy 8.10.2). The Vestal was thus an image of the Roman people and a *devotio* for them.

Death and the Matrons

The Vestal Virgin functioned as Sign, Stranger, and Sacrifice. She was *the* Sign for the Roman people, incarnating the collective. Yet in order to serve as the totem of Rome, she was made a Stranger, removed from all familial ties. This combination made her the ideal Sacrifice: both interior and exterior, she could serve as *prodigium*, *pharmakos*, and *devotio* to expiate and protect the city.

These uses of women were not confined to the Vestal Virgins. Rather, Roman society reveals a deep misogyny, erupting at times of crisis into murderous fear directed against its own matrons, against women in their roles as wives and as mothers.

Again, the logic of sympathetic magic is evident. The emphasis is on the element of control. Even for the Vestal Virgins, the sources are emphatic that although the Vestals no longer belonged to any man, they were still under the discipline of the Pontifex Maximus, whose punishments extended to beatings for minor infractions and to execution for *incestum*. To control women and their sexuality was to control the state. As the state escaped control, among the omens was the escape of women from proper male control. The danger to the *Urbs* could only be warded off by the punishment of women and the subsequent foundation of public cults of chastity with admonitory and apotropaic functions.[130] Again this was a common ploy of rhetoric and is reflected in a number of historical or quasi-historical events (see Appendix for the sources).

As in the case of the murder of the Vestals, these outbreaks of witch-hunts against the matrons of Rome cluster around times of external threat and internal danger. Thus in 491 BCE, the cult of Fortuna Muliebris was founded, open only to *univirae*, celebrating the salvation of Rome by the mother and wife of Coriolanus. In 331, a year of plague, twenty patrician wives were charged with a city-wide poisoning conspiracy.[131] The women were forced to drink the drugs that they claimed were beneficial and of course died – an obvious trial by ordeal.[132] A further 170 matrons were executed as a result of the subsequent investigation.[133] In 296, the cult of Plebeian Chastity was founded.[134] In the following year an unknown number of matrons were found guilty of adultery, fined, and the money used to build the temple of Venus Obsequens as a warning to adulteresses.[135] In 215, following the disaster at Cannae, the Oppian law was passed, the temple of Venus Verticordia dedicated, and the Vestal Virgins Floronia and Opimia executed, together with more explicit human sacrifice.[136] In 213, there was a suppression of foreign cults and an unspecified number of wives exiled for adultery.[137] In 204, there was the trial by ordeal of Claudia Quinta, charged with adultery.[138] In 186, the Bacchanalia crisis erupted, when unknown numbers (in the thousands) of women were executed by family tribunal or the state.[139] In 184, there was a further series of poisoning trials, including both men and women.[140] In 180, Hostilia Quarta was condemned for poisoning her husband in order to advance her son by an earlier marriage, while in Rome and environs three thousand people were found guilty of poisoning.[141] In 154, Publilia and Licinia were accused of poisoning their husbands, tried by family tribunals, and strangled.[142] In 113, following the condemnation and execution of the Vestal Virgins, the temple of Venus Verticordia was rededicated.[143]

Two questions arise: Why was this fear directed against matrons, women at the centre of society, rather than solely against the old, the widowed, the unprotected, or other societally marginal women, as in the European witch craze?[144] And why was the charge of adultery the expression of that fear? These eruptions of rage against women reveal a profound fear at the core of Roman society. In brief, the role of Woman as Sign has led to the role of Woman as Stranger: the very interchangeability and exchangeability on which Rome was based necessitated that a woman still be attached to, and a member of, her father's family for her to have value as an exchange.[145] As a result, she was still a stranger in her marriage family and feared as a stranger, that is, as a potential traitoress to her new family, as a potential witch to her husband, and as poisoner of his children.[146]

This fear, though best known to folklore as centring on the figure of the step-mother, was not confined to her. Rather, since for Rome the children were the husband's, both legally and biologically, all mothers were step-mothers, fostering another's children.[147] Anthropological data from a variety of cultures demonstrate the way in which accusations of witchcraft are frequent against brides brought into virilocal or patrilineal villages.[148] For Rome a single example may serve to illustrate this nexus of adultery, poisoning, and betrayal. According to Plutarch (*Rom.* 22.3), the laws of

Romulus specified that a husband may divorce his wife only for poisoning his children, counterfeiting his keys, or adultery.[149]

This very marginality of women, as we have seen, makes them the perfect victims. In times of panic, the society can easily be restored to health by the sacrifice, exile, or punishment of wives, who are central to the family, yet not fully members of it; who are necessary to produce children, yet expendable; who are, in short, human but less than human.[150] Yet why do Girard's objections to women as the ideal sacrificial victim not apply? The execution of a wife would appear to be fraught with the dangers of reciprocal violence from either her birth family or her marriage family that Girard noted. Here we can see the role that the charge of adultery played. Adultery of a wife was the betrayal of all her male relatives, both by birth and by marriage. Only for adultery did both husband and father have the right, indeed the duty, to kill a matron. Only the charge of adultery could sever a woman from both her agnatic and her marriage families.[151]

The list in the Appendix makes clear the prevalence of the theme of *conspiracy*. We hear not of individual women put on trial, but masses. We are told of monstrous women acting not alone, but in concert, and not merely with adulterers, but more terrifyingly with the other outsiders, with slaves and foreigners, and most terrifyingly with each other. They formed an anti-society, an underground where women were adulterous and poisoned their husbands, even their children. They created a witch-world whose values were distorted parodies of the values of patriarchal society: women as active, rather than passive; as sexual subjects, rather than sexual objects; as murderers, rather than victims.

Thus the magical and liminal functions of women were not confined to the Vestal Virgins. Female sexuality under male control was the basis of and the paradigm for keeping society under control. Yet in times of crisis, the society turned on those elements which it feared would threaten social stability, the very categories it created in order to have stability at all. The unpenetrated virgin and the well-regulated wife both embodied the city, in the symbolic universes of sympathetic magic and ideological praxis.

Appendix: Chronology

c. 750 BCE (traditional): Vestal Tarpeia. Only three sources call her a Vestal: Varro *LL* 5.41, Prop. 4.4, Plut. *Numa* 10.1. The rest merely label her *virgo* or *parthenos*: Livy 1.11.5–9; Ovid *F.* 1.261–2; Dion. Hal. 2.38 (citing Piso, Fabius, Cincius); Val. Max. 9.6.1; Plut. *Rom.* 17–18.1 (citing Juba, Sulpicius Galba, Simylus, Antigonus of Carystus); Festus 496L (464L, frg.).

c. 616–579 (traditional): Vestal Pinaria (under Tarquin Priscus). Dion. Hal. 3.67.3, Zonar. 7.8 (no name).

491: Foundation of Fortuna Muliebris, open only to *univirae* (widows and others excluded since they were unlucky: Dion. Hal. 8.56.4; Tert. *Monog.* 17). Livy 2.40.12; Festus 282L; *De Vir. Ill.* 19; Val. Max. 1.8.4, 5.2.1, 4.1; App. 2.5; Plut. *Cor.* 1.2, 4.3–4, 34–6.

483: Vestal Oppia (during the Volscian War, with signs of 'divine anger'). Livy 2.42.11; Dion. Hal. 8.89.4 (Opimia); Oros. 2.8.13 (Popilia); Euseb. 2.101 (Pompilia).

472: Vestal Orbinia (during a year of plague which caused miscarriages). Dion. Hal. 9.40.3.

420: Vestal Postumia (spoke and dressed too freely; acquitted). Livy 4.44.11; Plut. *Mor.* 89ff. (Pont. Max.: Sp. Minucius).

337: Vestal Minucia (same charge as Postumia; condemned). Livy 8.15.7–8 (*RE* Minucius 68), *Per.* 8; Hieron. *Adv. Iovinian.* 1.41; Oros. 3.9.5. Cf. *Hell. Oxy. (P. Oxy.* 12. col. iii, 33–7 = *FGrH* 255, 1155.6–8) under Olympiad 111, Year 1 (= 336 BCE), which mentions plural Vestals.

331 (a year of plague): 20 patrician wives executed for a poisoning conspiracy. Further 170 matrons subsequently executed. Livy 8.18 (170), Val. Max. 2.5.3 (170), Oros. 3.10 (370).

296: The cult of Plebeian Chastity founded. Livy 10.23; Prop. 2.6.25.

295: Matrons found guilt of adultery, fined and the money used to build the temple of Venus Obsequens. Livy 10.31.9.

275: Vestal Sextilia. Livy *Per.* 14; Oros. 4.2.8.

266: Vestal Caparronia (plague). Oros. 4.5.6–9.

c. 230: Vestal Tuccia. Livy *Per.* 20: *Tuccia, virgo vestalis, incesti damnata est*; all others know her as proven innocent by the trial of the sieve: Dion. Hal. 2.69; Val. Max. 8.1 abs. 5; Pliny *HN* 28.12; also Aug. *Civ. Dei* 10.16.

228: Sacrifice of two Gauls and two Greeks for the first time; in the Forum Boarium.

215: (following Cannae) Vestals Floronia and Opimia.
  a) One Vestal executed, the other commits suicide, together with more explicit human sacrifices. Livy 22.57.2, *Per.* 22; Plut. *Fab.* 18.3 (no names).
  b) The Oppian law is passed. Livy 26.36, Tac. *Ann.* 3.34, Val. Max. 9.1.3, Oros. 4.20.14, Zonar. 9.17.1.
  c) The temple of Venus Verticordia dedicated. Val. Max. 8.15.12, Pliny *NH* 7.180.

213: Wives exiled for adultery. Livy 25.2.9–10.

207: Lightning strikes Temple of Juno (among other prodigies). Matrons summoned and fined. The occasion of Livius Andronicus's hymn. Livy

27.37.8–10.
206: Sacred fire goes out; Vestal scourged by Pont. Max. P. Licinius. Livy 28.11.6.
204: Trial of Claudia Quinta. Livy 29.14.12; Ov. *F.* 4.305f.; Lactant. *Inst. Div.* 2.7, App. *Hann.* 56.
186: Bacchanalia suppressed; women are executed by family tribunal or the state. Livy 39.8–18.
184: Poisoning trials involving both men and women. Livy 39.41.5–6.
180: a) Trial and execution of Hostilia Quarta for poisoning husband C. Calpurnia Piso (cos. 180) in favour of her son from a previous marriage, A. Fulvius Flaccus. Livy 40.37.1–7 (184: *Hell. Oxy.* 39).
b) 3000 people found guilty of poisoning. Livy 40.43.2–3.
178: Vestal Aemilia: fire went out, and eventual miracle proving her (or her disciple's) innocence. Dion Hal. 2.68.3–5; Val. Max. 1.1.7. Cf. Livy *Per.* 41, Obseq. 8.
154: Publilia and Licinia accused of poisoning their husbands, tried by family tribunals, and executed by strangling. Livy *Per.* 48, Val. Max. 6.3.8; see Licinius 178, *RE* XIII.196.
114 (Dec.): (a) Helvia, a girl, blown up by lightning.
(b) Vestal Aemilia condemned (16 Dec.), but apparently not executed immediately; Saturnalia intervened (17 Dec.); Licinia tried (18 Dec.) but found innocent.
113: (a) The other two Vestals, Licinia and Marcia, condemned, again with more explicit human sacrifice.
(b) The temple of Venus Verticordia rededicated.
Macr. *Sat.* 1.10.5 (citing Fenestella, our source for the dates); Dio 26 (frg. 87); Ascon. *Milo* 45–6 (§32) Clark; Oros. 5.15.20–2; Plut. *QR* 83; Obseq. 37; Livy *Per.* 63; cf. Cic. *Nat. Deor.* 3.74. For Venus Verticordia: Val. Max. 8.15.12; Ov. *F.* 4.157–60. (Val. Max. 3.7.9, 6.8.1, cited by *MRR* I.536 and others, concern a vague charge of *incestum* against the orator M. Antonius.)
73: (a) Accusations against Licinia (Licinius 185, *RE* XIII 498) for intercourse with Crassus (charge brought by Plotius: see *MRR* II.114). Plut. *Crass.*1.2, *Mor.* 89e.
(b) Accusations against Fabia for intercourse with Catiline. Cic. *Cat.* 3.9, *Brut.* 236: Sal. *Cat.* 15.1; Plut. *Cat. Min.* 19.3; Oros. 6.3.1.
83 CE: Trials of the Vestals by Domitian: Oculata, Varronilla, Cornelia. According to Suetonius, Oculata and Varronilla were allowed to choose the methods of their deaths; their lovers banished. Chief Vestal, Cornelia, buried alive; her lovers beaten to death, with the exception of one ex-praetor who was exiled. According to Pliny, Cornelia buried alive; her

(possible) lover, Licinianus, exiled; other accused lover, Celer, scourged. According to Dio, many Vestals (no names) put to death, but not by being buried alive. Suet. *Dom.* 8.3-5; Plin. *Ep.* 4.11; Dio 67.3.

213: Caracalla said to have raped Clodia Laeta; she was buried alive, protesting her innocence; Aurelia Severa and Pomponia Rufina buried alive; Cannutia Crescentia committed suicide. Dio 77.16, Herod. 4.6.

219: Elagabulus 'lives with' the Vestal (Iulia) Aquilia Severa (Dio 77 [78].16); *incestum* (SHA *Ant. Elag.* 6.6-8). His marriage to her is known only from coins: see *PW* Iulius (Severa) 557. Dio 77 [78].16, SHA *Ant. Elag.* 6.6–8, Herod. 5.6.2, Zonar. 12.14.

Late 4th cent. (c. 390): *Incestum* of Primigenia, Vestal at Alba, with a certain Maximus. Punished 'in the custom and institution of our ancestors.' Symm. *Ep.* 9.147–8.

NOTES

This paper is a slightly revised version of 'Why Were the Vestals Virgins? Or The Chastity of Women and the Safety of the Roman State,' *American Journal of Philology* 125 (2004) 563–601, and is reprinted with the permission of Johns Hopkins University Press. Versions of this paper have been previously delivered at APA 1988 (Baltimore); University of Arizona, March 1989; Miami University, April 1992; Vassar College, March 1993; and at the conference 'Virginity Revisited,' University of Western Ontario, October 1998.

1 Cf. Dion. Hal. 2.66.1.
2 Staples (1998).
3 For example, Aristotle points to the luxury of Spartan women as revealing an essential weakness in their constitution: *Pol.* 2.6.5–11 (1269b–70a). Cf. Ath. 12.517. For Roman examples: Juv. 6, Livy 1.57.6 (Roman vs. Etruscan), Tac. *Germ.* 19. See Pomeroy (1975, 211–12). Modern parallels are discussed later in this article.
4 In the anthropological sense as defined by Turner (1985, 57): 'a postulate or position ... usually controlling behavior or stimulating activity, which is tacitly approved or openly promoted.'
5 An Appendix lists the chronology and sources.
6 For criticism of previous work, see Dumézil (1970, 311–26); Beard (1980, esp. 15–16) and Beard (1995) (a self-criticism); Staples (1998, 135–8, and 182 n. 13 for some of Beard's previous positions).
7 Beard (1995, 167).
8 This idea of a 'creative era,' familiar from the Australian Aborigines' 'dream

time,' has found its principal proponent in Eliade (1954) and (1961). For a brief outline and criticism see Kirk (1974, 63–6). For its application to the status of women in various societies and myths, see Bamberger (1974).

9 For the first idea, see Hommel (1972, 403–5, 415–17); for the second, see Guizzi (1968, 113).
10 Beard (1980, 15–16).
11 See Rose (1926, 442–3), who relates the virginity of the Vestals to this notion.
12 Cf. the *kanephoroi* for Athena, or the *arktoi* for Artemis Brauronia (Thuc. 6.56–8, Arist. *Const. Athens* 18, Ar. *Lys.* 641–5).
13 One of the purposes of this paper is to follow Beard's recently expressed desire (1995) to see how Vestal virginity functioned within the play of gender at Rome. Her wish to subject these categories themselves to analysis is a major concern of most feminist anthropology. For cross-cultural examples, see below.
14 Staples (1998, 129–30, 135, 137, 143).
15 As Brelich (1949, 9) points out, 'We know nothing of a cult of Vesta that is older than the public Roman cult, whether it is at Rome or elsewhere'; cf. Wilamowitz-Moellendorf (1931, 1: 158); so too Koch (1958, 1762). The cult of Vesta was *sacra publica*, rites performed for the Roman people as a whole, rather than *sacra privata*, private or household rites. Further features of public cult are that the temples or buildings stood on public land that had been made sacred (*locus sacer*) by the Roman people (or later the emperor) and that the cult was funded from the state treasury. For this distinction, see Beard, North, and Price (1998, 251); Rüpke (2001, 26–31).
16 Dumézil (1970, 1: 315): 'The continuous fire of the *aedes Vestae*, the *ignis Vestae*, is indeed the hearth of Rome, and hence one of the guarantees of the city's being rooted in earth, of its permanence in history.' Cf. Koch (1958, 1737).
17 Dion. Hal. 2.66.1; Wissowa (1925, 247–53).
18 See Wissowa (1912, 158) and (1925, 247–8); Koch (1958, 1766) for examples.
19 E.g., Livy 5.52.6–7.
20 Hor. *Odes* 3.5.11–12; Verg. *A.* 1.292.
21 Gell. *NA* 1.12.14: 'sacerdotem Vestalem, quae sacra faciat, quae ius siet sacerdotem Vestalem facere pro populo Romano Quiritibus' ('As a priestess of Vesta, to perform the rites that it is right for a priestess of Vesta to perform for the Roman people, the citizens').
22 Cic. *Font.* 48, Hor. *Odes* 1.2.26–8, Gell. *NA* 1.12.14, Symm. *Ep.* 10.3.14, Cic. *Haur.* 37: 'pro populo romano Quiritibus.' Cf. 'Expositio Totius Mundi' in *Geographi Latini Minores*, ed. A. Riese (1878; rpt. 1964), 120.12–13: 'quae sacra deorum pro salute, civitatis secundum antiquorum morem perficiunt' (dating to c. 350–3 CE, ibid. xxx).
23 *Leg.* 2.8.19–9.22.
24 Dion. Hal. 2.66.5, Lact. *Inst.* 3.20.4, cf. Ov. *Fasti* 6.254.

25 *pignus imperii Romani*: Fest. 296L; see Wissowa (1912, 159). Livy 28.11, Serv. *Aen.* 7.188. Porcius Latro (Sen. *Cont.* 1.3.1) also called Vesta the *Romani imperii pignus*.
26 Dion. Hal. 2.67.5.
27 *Odes* 3.30.8–9: 'dum Capitolinum / scandet cum tacita virgine pontifex.'
28 So rightly Swartz (1941, 42 and n. 148); Koch (1958, 1735–6). Cf. Dion. Hal. 2.66.1.
29 See Peristiany (1965), Schneider (1971), Schneider and Schneider (1976), Davis (1977), Pitt-Rivers (1977, esp. 126–71), Brandes (1980), Gilmore (1987). For critical surveys, see Brandes (1987), Giovannini (1987).
30 Giovaninni (1981).
31 The fear of women's unquenchable lust is of course an ancient one; see, e.g., Hes. *WD* 695–705, *Theog.* 590–612; for two catalogues, see Prop. 3.19, Ovid *AA* 1.275–342. For a Mediterranean anthropological perspective, see also Mernissi (1975, 4, 10, 16); Fallers and Fallers (1976, 258–9).
32 Giovaninni (1981, 412). See also the pioneering analysis of Hastrup (1978). This symbolism is not, of course, confined to Mediterranean societies. A well-known example is the Samoan *taupou (taupo)* described by Mead and others. The *taupou* was a girl of high rank whose virginity was religiously preserved in order to exchange her in marriage with another village (the system was already passing in Mead's day). 'The prestige of the village is inextricably bound up with the high repute of the *taupo* and few young men in the village would dare to be her lovers. Marriage to them is out of the question, and their companions would revile them as traitors rather than envy them such doubtful distinction' Mead (1928, 100). For later treatments (and the controversy engendered), see Holmes (1987, 79–80, 97, 100–1); Shankman (1996).
33 Douglas (1970, viii–ix).
34 Turner (1969, 98).
35 See, inter alia, Fowler (1922, 47–67).
36 Tambiah (1985, 60, drawing on Austin's *How to Do Things with Words* (1962).
37 Frazer (1911, 1: 52).
38 Gell. *NA* 1.12, Gaius 1.133, Fronto 149 (Naber); cf. Sen. *Cont.* 1.2. See Gardner (1986, 22), Staples (1998, 138–40). This does not appear to be the case for all priests: see Morgan (1974); but cf. Sen. *Cont.* 4.2, Dio. Hal. 2.21.3, Plut. *QR* 73; Wissowa (1912, 491 n. 3).
39 Mauss (1972, 12). Cf. Giovannini's remarks on *la Virgine* as synecdoche for the family, quoted above.
40 Cf. the analyses of Beard (1980) and Cornell (1981, 27); cf. Giovannini (1981, 416).
41 Staples (1998, 130, 143).
42 Pomeroy (1975, 210).

43 For a full description, see Guizzi (1968, 159–200). My analysis differs from that offered by Staples (1998, 138–43).
44 Gardner (1986, 25). Cf. Hallett (1984, 126–7), though I do not accept the suggestion that the lack of *patria potestas* and *tutela* is a regal survival.
45 See Cowie (1978) and the succinct statement by Arthur (1984?, 24).
46 The anthropological idea of the exchange of women (first articulated by Lévi-Strauss 1949/1969) has had a profound effect on feminist anthropology: Rubin (1975), Lerner (1986, 46–9); Strathern (1988, esp. 311–16); [Joplin] Klindienst (1991, 40–2); and literary theory: Irigaray (1985). It has had little impact on Roman studies, where exchange is viewed narrowly in terms of 'politics.' Dixon (1992, 42–3) rightly draws attention to the suspicion that arises from the exchange of women but explains their marginality primarily in economic terms.
47 *XII Tables apud Gaius* 1.144–5, 3.114; Paul. 70; Gell. *NA* 1.12.9; Plut. *Numa* 10; cf. Ambr. *De virg.* 1.4.15, *Ep.* 1.18.11.
48 Plut. *Numa* 9–10, Dio. Hal. 2.67.3, Livy 28.11.6, *Obsequ.* 8, Fest. 94L, *Lyd. de mens.* frg. 6 (180.4W). For discussions see Koch (1958, 1741–2); Guizzi (1968, 113, 143–4); Mommsen (1887, 2: 54–7) and (1899, 18–20, 21 n. 2); Cornell (1981, 30); Staples (1998, 152, 183 n. 39); contra Wissowa (1912, 158 n. 7).
49 Gardner (1986, 5–80) for an overview of the law of status.
50 This is not to say that despite her legal and religious status, a Vestal would not have felt emotionally part of her birth family, still tied by affective bonds to father, mother, and siblings, or that she could not be acted upon as a member of that family, both by friends (cf. Cic. *Font.* 26–8), and political enemies (so the cases of Licinia and Fabia). Likewise, since her term of service, though long, was limited, considerations of the benefits accruing to her agnatic family might have played a part. See Hallett (1984, 83–90); Gruen (1968, 127–32); Herrmann (1964, 42–3); Staples (1998, 144).
51 Labeo quoted by Gell. *NA* 1.12.18.
52 Will: Gell. *NA* 1.12.9, Cic. *Rep.* 3.10, Gaius 1.145, Plut. *Numa* 10; cf. Sozom. 1.9. Witness: Gell. *NA* 7.7.3, Tac. *Ann.* 2.34 (cf. 11.32), Plut. *Numa* 8 and cf. Cic. *Font.* 21.46, Suet. *Caes.* 1.
53 Beard (1980, 15, 17–18). Cf. Dumézil (1970, 2: 587).
54 So rightly Koch (1958, 1734): 'Als freie Persönlichkeit besitzt die Vestalin sodann das *ius testimonii dicendi*'; Staples (1998, 143). The same is true of the right to make a will. The lictors who accompany the Vestals (Plut. *Numa* 10.3: an ancient right; Dio 48.19.4: first in 42 BC) are not a specifically masculine privilege but an extra-legal honour accorded several functionaries. See Staples (1998, 145).
55 Cf. Durkheim's definition of the totem (1915, 123): 'The species of things which serves to designate the clan collectively,' and his analysis of the symbolic value of the totem (235–72).

56 In Greek mythology famous examples are Achilles' heel, Nisus's purple lock of hair, Meleager's log. See Faraone (1992) for a survey.
57 See n. 18.
58 Dessau 4932: 'cuius egregiam morum disciplinam et in sacris peritissimam operationem merito res publica in dies feliciter sensit.'
59 Pliny 4.11.7: 'me Caesar incestam putat, qua sacra faciente vicit triumphavit!'
60 Burkert (1983, 64).
61 Girard (1977).
62 See the special volume of *Helios* Golsan (1990) devoted to Girard; see also Golsan (1993), Hamerton-Kelly (1987), Dumouchel (1988), McKenna (1992), and Reineke (1997, 128–60).
63 Homer, Hesiod, and especially Greek tragedy show a heightened awareness of this. Girard curiously does not discuss the *Oresteia* and only mentions Aeschylus in passing (1977, 46). For the Roman sources (e.g., Livy 1.2; Dion. Hal. 9.40–1), see text.
64 Girard (1977, 39, 52).
65 Ibid. 4.
66 Ibid. 30–1. Girard's schema closely resembles Victor Turner's analysis of 'social dramas' as consisting of four stages: (1) *'breach* of regular norm-governed social relationships between persons or groups within the same system of social re-lations,' (2) 'a phase of mounting *crisis,'* (3) *'redressive action'* in the form of the 'performance of public ritual,' (4) either *reintegration* or schism. See Turner (1974, 40–1).
67 Girard (1977, 13).
68 Ibid. 83.
69 Seneca's *Cont.* 1.3, though a fictional case only loosely based on the laws surrounding the Vestal Virgins, is a clear demonstration of this point.
70 The only recorded protest comes from Cornelia as she is led to death. However, it is clear that the accused Vestal could speak in her own defence at her trial before the Pontiff; see Macr. *Sat.* 1.10.5.
71 4.11.8: 'nescio an innocens, certe tamquam innocens ducta est.' This unquestioning assumption of guilt is something that Pliny shares with many modern historians (see below).
72 Girard (1977, 41).
73 Dion. Hal. 2.67.4; Plut. *Numa* 10, QR 96, *Ti. Gr.* 15.6; Dio. apud Zonar. 7.8.7; Cato frg. 68M; Cic. *Har. Resp.* 13; Pliny 4.11.6–11.
74 Girard (1977, 13).
75 Ibid. 39.
76 Ibid. 12.
77 Including plebeians. Difficulties in recruiting led Augustus to make daughters of freedmen eligible: Dio 55.22.5.

78 Girard (1977, 77).
79 Ibid. 104–6. See also Girard's remarks at (1986, 15). Cf. the increase in sacred value (*kapu*) when a Hawaiian king married his sister: Radcliffe-Brown (1979, 50).
80 See also Bremmer (1983).
81 Girard (1977, 12). The blindness to the role of women continues in many of his explicators. There is a near total absence of women in, e.g., Hamerton-Kelly (1987), Dumouchel (1988), and McKenna (1992).
82 See, however, his remarks on Dionysus and Euripides' *Bacchae* (1977, 141–2): 'Like the animal and the infant, but to a lesser degree, the woman qualifies for sacrificial status by reason of her weakness and relatively marginal social status. That is why she can be viewed as a quasi-sacred figure, both desired and disdained, alternatively elevated and abused.' See also the recent interview in Golsan (1993, esp. 141–3).
83 Brief remarks at Hamerton-Kelly (1987, 86–8, 94).
84 Not so, of course, in a variety of cultures, but this is exactly the case for virilocal and patrilineal Rome. See Parker (1998, 154–5).
85 Girard (1977, 12–13).
86 So for Verginia, one of the founding legends of Rome (Livy 3.4–54).
87 Bellum inde Veiens initium, et Volsci rebellarunt. sed ad bella externa prope supererant vires, abutebanturque iis inter semet ipsos certando. accessere ad aegras iam omnium mentes prodigia caelestia, prope cotidianas in urbe agrisque ostentia minas; motique ita numinis causam nullam aliam vates canebant publice privatimque nunc extis nunc per aves consulti, quam haud rite sacra fieri. qui terrores tandem eo evasere ut Oppia virgo Vestalis damnata incesti poenas dederit.
88 Girard (1977, 33).
89 For the tone and logic, cf. the narratives in Dion. Hal. 2.68.3, 8.89.3–5 and 9.40.
90 Cornell (1981, 28); cf. Herrmann (1964, 52–3); Hallett (1984, 88 n. 32); Fraschetti (1984, 101); Mustakallio (1992, 56); Staples (1998, 129, 143, 136).
91 Girard (1977, 261).
92 Mayer (1970, 60). For cross-cultural data, cf. the Amba of western Uganda, who view witches as a secret association within the village, operating as a fifth-column, attacking only fellow villagers, but sharing reciprocal cannibal feasts with the witches of enemy villages (Winter 1963). So too the Kuma of New Guinea suspect witches of aiding enemy groups (Reay 1959 136); while the Abelam of New Guinea believe that sorcery is performed by a traitor in one's own village working with an enemy sorcerer (Forge 1970, 257–75, esp. 262–3 and cf. xxvii).
93 Cf. Douglas on 'internal traitors' (1970, ix, cited above) and Levine (1982, 271).
94 So L. Cantilius with Floronia (Livy 22.57.3), yet no one is accused with Opimia.

Veturius (Vetutius) with Aemilia (Oros. 5.15.20–2, Plut. *QR* 83), Valerius Licinianus and Celer with Cornelia (Pliny 4.11), Maximus with Primigenia (Symm. *Ep.* 9.147–8). Fest. 277 L: a general statement that the man who makes a Vestal unchaste (*incestavisset*) is beaten to death. Even when the existence of a man is mentioned his name is seldom given: two men with Oppia (Dion. Hal. 8.89.4) and Orbinia (Dion. Hal. 9.40.3), one with Capparonia (Oros. 4.5.6–9), unknown numbers of *corruptores* and *stupratores* with Oculata and Varronilla (Suet. *Dom.* 8.3–5).

95 So for example the cases of Antonius, Crassus, and Catiline; and cf. Elagabalus. These, however, are not my concern in this paper. See Rawson (1991, 149–68); Gruen (1968, 127–32).

96 So Postumia (Livy 4.44.11–12) was accused but acquitted merely for dressing too well and being too clever ('propter cultum amoeniorem ingeniumque liberius quam virginem decet'), while Minucia is buried alive on exactly the same grounds (Livy 8.15.7). Aemilia (178 BC) is accused only on the evidence of the sacred fire being allowed to go out (Dion. Hal. 2.68.3–5, Val. Max. 1.1.7, cf. Livy. Per. 41, *Obseq.* 8); cf. the case of 206 (Livy 28.11.6). Tuccia (Dion. Hal. 2.69.1–3) is accused without even this. No man is mentioned at all for Minucia, Opimia, Sextilia (Livy *Per.* 14, Oros. 4.2.8), or for Aurelia Severa, Pomponia Rufina, and Cannutia Crescentia, executed by Caracalla. See Appendix.

97 Only the mythical Rhea Silva is pregnant (Livy 1.4). Nero is accused of raping a Vestal but no further mention of her is made. The event is used to demonstrate his sexual insatiability and impiety rather than as evidence of an impending crisis (Suet. *Nero* 28.1). Thus the lack of virginity in a Vestal is of importance only when a victim is needed. The account in Dio 77.16 fuses two accusations: that Caracalla raped a Vestal and that he put four Vestals to death for unchastity.

98 Giovannini (1981, 422, 419).

99 Cf. Mayer's remarks (1970, 52) on the Gusii, a western Kenyan Bantu tribe, and Levine (1982) on the Nyinba, a Tibetan-speaking group in Nepal.

100 For Horatia, see Livy 1.26, Dion. Hal. 3.7: cf. the brother's words to his murdered sister: 'sic eat quaecumque Romana lugebit hostem' ('so may she fare, whatever Roman woman grieves for an enemy') with his father's approval and ultimately that of all Roman men. For Tarpeia, see Prop. 4.4, who makes the lust, rather than feminine greed, the reason for her betrayal; so Antigonus of Carystus, and the poet Simylus (Plut. *Rom.* 18). See Ogilvie (1965, 74–5) and Burkert (1979, 76). For Sempronia, see Sall. *Cat.* 24–5. An analysis of the adulteress/traitoress/poisoner requires a separate paper. See Currie (1998).

101 Livy 8.15.7, Cic. *Mil.* 59, Schol. Bob. Cic. 90S, Val. Max. 6.8.1. Cf. Pliny

Panegyr. 42.3–4, Livy *Per.* 77, Dio 55.5. See Cornell (1981, 34–5) and Buckland (1908, 90–1). Cases involving evidence from slaves (see Appendix): Orbinia in 472 BC (Dion. Hal. 9.40.3), Minucia in 337 (Livy 8.15.7); Aemilia, Licinia, Marcia in 114 (Plut. *QR* 83, Dio frg. 87.5 B). Note the execution of the *conscii servi* (that is, the slaves who failed to report the crime) with Caparronia in 266 (Oros. 4.5.6–9); see discussion by Guizzi (1968, 145–9). Significantly, the Lex Julia expands this to adultery by means of a fictitious sale to the state; Wiedemann (1987, 27). For *incestum*, see below. Cf. Mayer's remarks (1970, 61–2).

102 Cic. *Leg.* 2.19, 22; Tac. *Ann.* 1.73 (Tiberius: *deorum iniuriae dis curae*); *Cod. Just.* 4.1.2. See Koch (1958, 1747; Mommsen (1887, 2: 50–54) and (1899, 36–7) (on *Sacraldelict*); Wissowa (1912, 380–409, esp. 388–9); Nock (1972, 2: 531).

103 As Cornell (1981, 29) points out, 'offenses against the gods, which involved the community as well, such as sacrilege ... were subject to the normal process of criminal law.' Further, even purely religious matters could come under non-religious law. See Cornell (1981, 36–7: e.g., the censors could degrade a man for impiety (Cato frg. 72M).

104 So Mommsen (1899, 18).

105 Koch (1958, 1749) and (1960, 1–4); cf. Guarino (1943, 177).

106 See Fantham (1992).

107 See Guizzi (1968, 143–4 and nn. 6–7); Ogilvie (1965, 349). For the etymology and meaning, see Fest. 95L, 277L (s.v. *probrum*), Gaius 1.59, 64.

108 The laws relating to adultery are notoriously confused, but only the law attributed to Romulus (Dion. Hal. 2.25.6 = *FIRA* 3) makes any mention of a trial (held by the accused's husband and her father's relations). For the trials after the Bacchanalia of 186 BC (Appendix), see below. The Lex Julia refers not to trial, but to summary execution by the father of a daughter caught in the act of adultery. See Rotondi (1912, 443–7); Richlin (1981); Beard (1980, 15 and n. 20) (citing Volterra 1948); Cantarella (1976); Cohen (1991). No other crime specifies burial alive and the only analogue is the execution of Antigone in Sophocles.

109 Wissowa (1923–4, 201–14, esp. 207–8); Nock (1972, 1: 254); Ogilvie (1965, 74, 349); Staples (1998, 133–4).

110 Cornell (1981, 31).

111 Cornell (1981, 31) cites Livy 28.11.6–8 for a hard and fast distinction between the prodigies and the act that produces them: 'id [a Vestal allowing the fire to go out] quamquam nihil portentibus dis ceterum neglegentia humana acciderat, tamen et hostiis maioribus procurari et supplicationem ad Vestae haberi placuit.' Livy does not, however, mean that all such events are human mistakes rather than portents, but it was so in this particular case. In fact, the

proof (within the belief system) that this was *error* and not *incestum* is the very fact that the Vestal was merely scourged and not killed; cf. the case of Tuccia (c. 230 BC; Appendix). Likewise, Livy 22.57.2: 'territi etiam super tantas clades cum ceteris prodigiis [N.B.] tum quod duae Vestales eo anno, Opimia atque Floronia, stupri compertae' shows that their crime was indeed accounted a *prodigium*, while 22.57.4 – 'hoc nefas cum inter tot, ut fit, clades in prodigium versum esset' – does not show 'that such offenses were *not* normally considered prodigies' (Cornell 1981, 32), but rather, that Livy considered himself less credulous than others.

112 For sacredness and pollution as the characteristics of things that cross classificatory boundaries, see Douglas (1966, esp. 41–57). For the application of this to the sacred character of the Vestal Virgin, see Beard (1980, 20–2).

113 One can also compare Turner's remarks on the way in which twins in many cultures are either 'permanently assigned a special status' or else one or both of the twins are killed (1969 48–9): 'This may be regarded as another instance of a widely prevalent social tendency *either* to make what falls outside the norm a matter of concern for the widest group *or* to destroy the exceptional phenomenon. In the former case, the anomalous may be sacralized, regarded as holy ... Here the anomaly, the "stone that the builders rejected", is removed from the structured order of society and made to represent the simple unity of society itself, conceptualized as homogeneous, rather than as a system of heterogeneous social positions.'

114 See Staples (1998, 151–2) for a different explanation.

115 Koch objects that the Vestal cannot be considered a *prodigium* for this reason (1958, 1748). So too Cornell (1981, 35).

116 Girard (1977, 83), quoted above.

117 Mustakallio (1992).

118 Cf. the comments of Fraschetti (1981, 58). E.g., Dumézil (1970, 2: 450): 'crime' for the Vestals, vs. 'quadruple murder' for the Greek and Gaulish couples; Cornell (1981, 28): 'punishment' vs. 'human sacrifice' and writes, 'A confirmed instance of *incestum* was an extremely rare occurrence,' without asking by whom and how confirmed. Marshall (1985, 196) thinks Licinia and Marcia's brief escape from death was due to 'an obvious coverup.' Mustakallio (1992, 63) is even able to tell us the season of the 'crimes': 'We may suggest that Orbinia, Sextilia and even Caparronia had committed their incest crimes in spring time, thus contaminating the fertility and purification rites of this period.' Even Staples (1998, 134) merely states that the 'execution of Vestals ... coincides with two of the three known instances of human sacrifice ever recorded in Rome.' Porte (1984, 233) is almost alone in calling both 'sacrifices humains.' Radke is also explicit (1975, 1129): 'Sie entsprechen weder der

Königin noch Königs- oder haustöchtern, sondern wurden ... Mädchenopfer bereitgehalten, wofür Bruch sexuallen Tabus als Motiv galt.'
119 Wissowa (1923–4, 24, 209).
120 Livy 27.37.6. For other examples, MacBain (1982, 127–33).
121 Cornell (1981, 36); Briquel (1984, 226); Dion. Hal. 4.62, Zonar. 7.11, Val. Max. 1.1.13; cf. Cic. *Rosc. Am.* 71–2.
122 Girard (1977, 79).
123 Pomeroy (1975, 211), Rose (1970), Staples (1998, 133).
124 The comparison is made by Wissowa (1923–4, 211).
125 Girard (1977, 287); Plut. *Numa* 10, Dion. Hal. 2.67.4, 8.89.5, 9.40.3, Pliny *Ep.* 4.11.
126 *Pomerium*: Serv. *Aen.* 11.206, Dion. Hal. 8.89.5; sacrifices: Plut. *Numa* 10, *Quaest. Rom.* 96; Dion. Hal. 2.40.3 on Tarpeia, citing Piso.
127 For an overview, see Versnel (1976, esp. 405–10) with previous literature. Versnel makes a distinction (which the Romans did not) between the *consecratio* of the general and his *devotio* of the enemy troops. He does not deal with the aftermath of the rite.
128 For the details of the ceremony, the oath, and the expiatory purpose, see Livy 8.9.4–10.12.
129 Quint. 7.8.3f., Tac. *Ann.* 6.19, Livy *Per.* 77, Val. Max. 6.5.7, Plut. *Sulla* 10, Sen. *Dial.* 3.16.5. Radke (1965, 311; 1972, 432) is misled by Hor. *Odes* 3.30.8 (quoted above) and the fictitious case of Sen. *Cont.* 1.3 into thinking that this was a punishment for the Vestal Virgins.
130 For cultic practice and the reinforcement of women's social roles, see Cantarella (1987, 150–5).
131 For the ritual significance of poisoning as a charge, see Girard (1986, 16–17) and Levine (1982, 265) (on the Nyinba).
132 Instead, Herrmann (1964, 47–8) sees an early attempt at 'women's liberation' culminating in murder. Bauman (1992, 13–14, 17–18, 20–1) sees a protest against *manus* marriage, taking 'the form of a criminal conspiracy directed not only at their husbands but at public figures in general.' The resemblance to the African poison oracle should not need to be pointed out but apparently does. Any other discipline, historical or anthropological, examining a year of plague during which 170 women are charged with poisoning and then executed, would smell a rat. What is most disturbing here is the lack of the barest con-sideration of the possibility that these women were innocent, a failure of the historian's minimal obligation to question the sources. Given a choice between seeing a vast murderous conspiracy of wives, or acknowledging the use of ritual scapegoats, some have chosen the former.
133 See Münzer (1923, 1721); Gagé (1963, 262–4) (for doubts as to historicity);

Monaco (1984). Cantarella (1987, 126) gives the number as 160, Pomeroy (1975, 176) as 116.
134 See Palmer (1974, 122–5, 132–4).
135 Bauman (1992, 17 and 223 n. 15) assumes they were guilty of prostitution; Gardner (1986, 123) of no more than drunken high spirits. I see no reason to assume they were 'guilty' of anything.
136 See Palmer (1974, 135–6); Culham (1982).
137 Bauman (1992, 25), though covering the first event, fails to note the second. Gruen (1990, 40) does not comment on implication of women in the purification.
138 See Herrmann (1964, 58–9); Gallini (1970, 71–2); Beard (1995, 171).
139 For the poisoning trial and the Bacchanalia of 186, see Herrmann (1964, 68–79); Gallini (1970, 11–52); Pailler (1988), (1990); Rousselle (1989); Gruen (1990, 34–78); Bauman (1992, 35–40).
140 See Herrmann (1964, 78); Gallini (1970, 45); Bauman (1992, 38) is right to argue for the inclusion of women.
141 Bauman (1992, 38) wonders if the surviving members of the Bacchic cult were not indulging in 'a fund-raising programme' by murder; again, the idea of a witch-hunt does not occur.
142 Bauman (1992, 38) speculates that Publilia was 'a Bacchanalian sympathizer who killed for the cause.'
143 Bauman (1992, 52–8).
144 For an excellent introduction, see Briggs (1996).
145 See Hallett (1989); Dixon (1992, 42–3) (purely in economic terms); Saller (1994, 76–88); Parker (1998, 154–5), for overviews of this conceptual difficulty. The most obvious sign of this lifelong possession is the fact that a woman retained her father's gentile name; Hallett (1989, 67): 'Roman society thus labeled her the daughter of her father for purposes of lifelong identification'; see also Kajanto (1972, 13–30); (1977, 184); Pomeroy (1975, 152, 165) and (1976, 225–6). Even in the case of (increasingly rare) *manus* marriage the new *materfamilias* did not lose all connection with her natal family. She was transferred to her husband's *familia* (Gel. 18.6.9, Serv. A. 11.476) for purposes of property transfer (especially intestate succession); she stood *filiae loco* (*Tit. Ulp.* 23.3) but she was not part of her husband's *gens* (see Ulpian's careful definition: *D.* 30.16.195.2). As Treggiari (1991, 30) writes: 'She was not a daughter but in the position of a daughter.' That is, her *pater* remained her *pater* (though she was no longer *in patria potestate*), her *mater* remained her *mater*, and so on. The most vivid proof of these agnatic ties, besides the fact that the wife *in manu* did not change her gentile name, is that a father retained the right to kill a daughter taken in adultery even after he had transferred her to the *manus* of her husband (*Coll.* 4.2.3 from Paulus = *FIRA*

2.553; but not over a daughter freed by *emancipatio*: *Coll.* 4.7.1): 'Secundo vero capite permittit patri, si in filia sua, quam in potestate habet, aut in ea, quae eo auctore, cum in potestate esset, viro in manum convenerit, adulterum domi suae generive sui deprehenderit isve in eam rem socerum adhibuerit, ut is pater eum adulterum sine fraude occidat, ita ut filiam in continenti occidat.' See Treggiari (1991, 282) for texts and analysis.

146 Purcell (1986, 95); Edwards (1993, 51–2); Santoro L'Hoir (1992, 41–2); Wiedemann (1987, 25–6); Parker (1998, 154–5, 164). See also the bibliography cited in n. 27.

147 Noy (1991), Watson (1995).

148 See Rosaldo (1974, 32–4) for an overview. Gluckman (1956, 98) (Zulu); Middleton and Winter (1963, 14–17) (E. Africa); Beidelman (1963, 86–7) (Kaguru, a Bantu-speaking people of Tanzania); Winter (1963, 278, 287–8) (Amba, mentioned above); Epstein (1967, 135–54, esp. 150) (Mysore); Harper (1969 (Brahmins in S. India); Hunter Wilson (1970, 252–63, esp. 261) (Mpondo, Bantu-speaking people of S. Africa); Marwick (1970, 280–1) (South-Eastern Bantu). See also Giovannini (1981) (Sicily).

149 Ziegler (1957): 'for poisoning, or for substitution of children or keys,' producing a harsh zeugma. There is no reason to doubt the text, unless one has already decided that it cannot be saying what it says.

150 Cf. the famous remarks of Metellus Macedonius on the burdensome necessity of wives in order to procreate: Suet. *Aug.* 89.2, Livy *Per.* 59, Gell. *NA* 1.6.

151 See n. 81.

5

'Only Virgins Can Give Birth to Christ': The Virgin Mary and the Problem of Female Authority in Late Antiquity

KATE COOPER

Stretching out her hands, she prayed thus to the Lord, 'Lord God, you who healed me of leprosy by the prayers of your martyr Agnes and graciously showed me the path of your love, and moreover preserved the marriage-bed of the virgin your mother, where you the Son have shown yourself to be a Bridegroom, you born of Mary and you true progenitor of Mary, you having suckled at her breast and you in turn feeding the whole world ... I ask, Lord, that you win over these daughters of Gallicanus ... that they may seek to attain entry to your celestial bed-chamber.'[1]

The sixth-century *Passion of Gallicanus*, a Latin romance purporting to record the martyrdom of a Christian general of the fourth-century pagan emperor Julian the Apostate, records the prayer of Constantia, daughter of Constantine the Great and virgin of the Church.[2] Beseeching Jesus, son of Mary, to move Artemia and Attica, the general's daughters, to dedicate themselves as virgins of the Church, Constantia illustrates the firm belief of Christians at the end of antiquity that human relationships echoed or reflected the mysterious workings of the heavenly realm. According to this view, the Virgin Mary stood as an intercessor before God for the interests of women, and among women virgins enjoyed a special, though not exclusive, claim to her protection.

We also see in Constantia's prayer a number of other important themes which will concern us in the present study. First, the heavenly sphere was punctuated by relationships of patronage and intercession. The intercessory role which women of the imperial family were understood to play was not unlike that played by the Virgin herself. Second, the intercession of Mary and other female saints – such as the virgin martyr Agnes – was understood to reach across the divide between heavenly and earthly spheres and thus to contribute to the spiritual wherewithal on which their earthly counterparts,

Christian women, could draw. Finally, there is compelling evidence that meditation on – and imitation of – both Mary and the other female saints was considered central to women's spiritual life, serving in addition as a resource which women could invoke on behalf of their own spiritual power as women of God. Dozens of lives of female saints and *passiones* of female martyrs produced at the end of antiquity attest to a widespread interest in holy women, and many of these texts include, as does the *Passion of Gallicanus* itself, some indication of how late Roman women could invoke the power of 'their' saints even as they sought to imitate their virtues. It is only in the last generation that scholars have begun to assemble the mosaic of glancing references attesting to this nexus between Christian women and their heavenly champions.

Still paradoxically little understood among the female saints who played such a central role to Christian spirituality at the end of antiquity is the best known of them all, Mary, mother of Jesus. Known since the third century as *Theotokos*, the one who gave birth to God, Mary is by far the most discussed of the female saints in the ancient sources, but several factors have kept her from centre stage where the study of female spirituality is concerned. Perhaps most significant is the fact that historical theology has long treated the ancient sources on Mary as of interest predominantly for their Christological implications. Even more surprisingly, feminist theology and gender studies have shown little interest in Mary and her cultural history. What these approaches have in common, however, is that they are rarely accompanied by sustained attention to the evidence for how ancient women themselves understood Mary and her cult. This neglect, the present essay will suggest, threatens to distort our understanding of late Roman women and their contribution to late Roman Christianity.

Many factors have contributed to the neglect of Marian piety among late Roman women as a subject of study. In addition to general factors such as the strength of Protestant, non- and post-Christian sensibilities in gender-focused scholarship, two more specific factors seem to have been significant. The first is the historiographical tradition surrounding the idea of the Divine Feminine. While Jung had made a great case for the Virgin Mary as an expression of the Divine Feminine in the 1950s, by the 1970s feminist writers came to view this notion with suspicion. Already in 1968, Mary Daly argued in her *The Church and the Second Sex*[3] that far from being an unequivocal boon to women, the projection of the Virgin as a female icon of religious authority could also serve a negative function, as a compensatory licence for misogyny against real historical women, a position echoed by Marina Warner's *Alone of All Her Sex*.[4] While a number of feminist writers sought to develop the idea of an icon of female authority in early Christianity, either through the figure of Sophia or through the figure of Mary Magdalene as an early recipient of the Kerygma, the Virgin Mary was viewed with suspicion by the scholarly parties who would in theory have been most likely to be interested in her.

A second factor has been how scholars have understood the problem of women's agency. Where women and gender were concerned, the relationship between rhetoric and reality was often characterized by paradox. Despite the sometimes overwhelming misogyny of the early Christian tradition, in late Roman society women could exercise enormous power in certain, especially elite, contexts. Even while women were barred from the clerical and many other institutional roles, their active and demanding presence as agents within and beyond the Church needs to be fully realized in our imaginations if we are to understand late antiquity accurately.[5] This now is a truism, but it did not go without saying a decade or two ago.

Though women were clearly not the only people to take an interest in the *Theotokos*, it is now fairly clear that the interest taken in her by women of the patronage class was important if not decisive at turning points in the development of her cult. What this adds up to, among other things, is a warning that, like the late Roman bishops, the present generation of scholars will have to take an interest in the *Theotokos* if we are to understand late Roman women.

'Has God a Mother?'

According to the fifth-century historian Socrates of Constantinople, the Christological controversy which convulsed the Christian churches in his day opened in earnest when Nestorius, Bishop of Constantinople, defended a visiting priest who had preached against the increasingly widespread term *Theotokos* as a description of the Virgin Mary.

Nestorius had an associate whom he had brought from Antioch, a presbyter named Anastasius; for this man he had high esteem and consulted him in the management of affairs. Anastasius, preaching one day in church, said 'Let no one call Mary *Theotokos* ['god-bearer']: for Mary was but a human being, and it is impossible that God should be born of a human being.' This caused a great sensation and troubled both the clergy and the laity, as they had been heretofore taught to acknowledge Christ as God and by no means to separate his humanity from his divinity on account of the economy of incarnation.[6]

Only decades after the Council of Constantinople in 381 had established what was meant to be an enduring theological settlement on the nature of the Trinity – the relationship among the Father, Son, and Holy Spirit – a further crisis emerged whose central question was whether the Son was fully human or fully divine. Although Nestorius was deposed as Bishop of Constantinople and condemned at the Council of Ephesus in 431, the problem of how to understand the Incarnation, with its implications for the relationship between Christ's humanity and his divinity – the so-called Two Natures – was never definitively resolved. Over a millennium later, the Eastern Churches are still in schism over it.

That the dispute over whether the Virgin Mary should be called *Theotokos* was the trigger for the controversy is not in doubt, yet an attempt to understand the Mariological aspect of the debate has played a surprisingly small role in the scholarship on the controversy. On the historian of theology's usual reading, the *Theotokos* epithet was controversial because of its Christological implications. As Frances Young puts it, in what has become the standard introduction to the problem for English speakers, the core of the controversy resided in 'two different answers to the question, "Who was the subject of the incarnate experiences of Jesus Christ?"'[7] It is useful to remember here that in the early fifth century, despite the agreements made over the persons of the Trinity at Constantinople in 381, questions about the person of the Son as basic as whether the Son of God referred by the Bible was in fact the same being as the historical Jesus, born from the line of David,[8] were still not fully resolved. Christian theology was, in many respects, still in its infancy.

Also in its infancy was the problem of the divine feminine, which the traditional religions of the Roman Empire so often emphasized. At the Council of Ephesus Nestorius was deposed from his position as Bishop of Constantinople for having made statements such as the following: '"Has God a mother? If so we may excuse paganism for giving mothers to its deities ... No, Mary was not *Theotokos*. For that which is born of flesh is flesh. A creature did not bring forth him who is uncreated; the Father did not beget by the Virgin a new God."'[9] But the anxiety about the *Theotokos* has been viewed by historians as turning on the problem of Jesus as Logos, the divine Word of God, already existing in the beginning when God created the world according to the first chapter of the Gospel of John.

According to Nestorius's reasoning, the name *Theotokos* implied that the Logos, having been born, also suffered the crucifixion, and that this manner of mixing the distinct natures of the divine Logos and the human Christ (Nestorius offers the term *Christotokos* as an acceptable substitute) was tantamount to Apollinarianism, Arianism, or indeed to paganism.[10] Cyril of Alexandria, Nestorius's principal though not only opponent, took the view that with his Birth the Logos had taken on a new condition of existence. Young summarizes Cyril's position thus: 'It was the Logos who was incarnate, and there is only one Lord and Christ and Son. He admits that two Natures are involved, but their union, he says, is hypostatic, because the Logos united Manhood to himself "in his own *hypostasis*."'[11] Cyril's view depends on the doctrine of *communicatio idiomatum* – 'communication of properties' – which J.N.D. Kelly defined as the idea that 'in view of the unity of Christ's Person, His human and divine attributes, experiences, etc. might properly be interchanged.'[12] Although this idea was developed by Athanasius, it in fact drew on usage going back at least as far as the early second-century martyr-bishop Ignatius of Antioch, who talks about 'the suffering of my God' and 'God ... [who] was conceived of Mary.'[13] What bothered people like Nestorius about people like Cyril was the danger that the Alexandrian 'Word-Flesh' notion of the Son was not, in fact, sufficiently enfleshed – that they read the *communicatio idiomatum* as meaning that the Word wins out over the Flesh, with the result being a Gnostic, docetic Jesus who did not *really* suffer.

What makes the Christological controversy especially difficult to understand is that neither of the men viewed as the key players – Nestorius or Cyril – seems to have had a stable position to argue in the negotiations across the twenty years between Ephesus and Chalcedon. Historical theologians have worked admirably to account for how each of these men could shift his ground so significantly in matters of Christology without betraying his initial position entirely, but on the face of it it is difficult to reconcile the intensity of the conflict with the fact that neither figure seems to have been fully committed to the view he was arguing for. Indeed, a school of thought has grown up which suggests that the altercation leading up to the Council of Ephesus should be explained as a misunderstanding of terminology for two essentially similar positions.[14] This is where the gender historian notices that unlike their Byzantine predecessors, by and large the modern historians and theologians have been looking only at the men.

The present essay, by contrast, will point to the influential women of the imperial family who seem to have played an important role in theological debates of the day, and particularly to the Empress Pulcheria (d. 453). At face value, Pulcheria, too, looks as if her theology were as unstable as that of Cyril and Nestorius – at least her Christology looks that way. She was fiercely anti-Nestorius at the Council of Ephesus in 431, but at Chalcedon two decades later she espoused a position on the two natures of Christ that was far more reminiscent of Nestorius's views than those of her old ally Cyril. What did not change, however, was her vision of Mary as *Theotokos*, the woman who confers human birth on the Logos. It can be argued that Pulcheria's Mariology was the one theological constant in the whole controversy and, indeed, that it was the hinge on which the controversy turned. Put bluntly, on this reading it is not Nestorius's *Christology* per se that was rejected at Ephesus, but more precisely his *Mariology*.

Our reading follows the suggestion made by Vasiliki Limberis a decade ago that the coalition between Pulcheria and Cyril was a marriage of convenience. While Cyril was interested in Christology per se, he only attained the support of the Empress insofar as his concerns overlapped with her interest in developing the cult of the Virgin Mary as a form of imperial civic religion. Theologians and historians of theology have tended to assume that serious people dealt with the 'real theological issues'[15] of Christology at the Council of Ephesus while the Empress was running what amounted at best to a theological side show, one whose significance was fundamentally 'political' rather than 'theological.' But if the fifth-century Church was far more dependent on female patrons and their concerns than has generally been recognized, this does not mean that its concerns were 'political' rather than 'theological.' Rather, it means that Mariological debate was central to fifth-century theological developments and that the theological concerns – and contributions – of late Roman women must be taken seriously by historians and theologians alike.

Mariology versus Christology: Putting the Women First at Ephesus

Kenneth Holum noted a quarter-century ago that the centrality of Pulcheria is not in dispute in the ancient sources: 'A tradition on both sides of the question said that it was she who brought down Nestorius.'[16] For Holum, the conflict between Pulcheria and Nestorius developed a tradition of tension between the bishop of Constantinople, who sought to strengthen the church hierarchy and to make his see independent from lay meddling, and the imperial family, who viewed the church's principal role as that of sacralizing their rule and protecting the Empire. The classic instance of this tension was the altercation a generation earlier between Pulcheria's mother Eudoxia and John Chrysostom, an earlier Bishop of Constantinople who was widely believed to have been deposed due to the enmity of the Empress.[17] The imperial women seem to have acted as focal points for this tension. Holum saw the fact that the Council was held at Ephesus, a city whose ancient cult of the virgin goddess Artemis had already given way to a thriving cult of the Virgin *Theotokos*, and that the council itself was held in the great basilica dedicated to the Virgin, as a sign of Pulcheria's behind-the-scenes engineering against her brother's public support for Nestorius.[18]

Rather than detailing all of the evidence cited by Holum, or the subsequent debates over his hypothesis,[19] I would like to highlight a context for Pulcheria's patronage which Leslie Brubaker has called the 'matronage' tradition.[20] Brubaker's own contribution was to demonstrate that the aristocratic and imperial women of Constantinople built up a distinctive tradition of patronage in which women of later generations commemorated the achievements – and indeed the patronage – of their female forebears. The iconic act to which female patrons returned again and again in memory was the Empress Helena, the mother of Constantine the Great, and her founding of a shrine to the Nativity at 'the place where the *Theotokos* gave birth'[21] in Bethlehem. Thus the imperial mother and the Mother of God were bound in a reciprocal relationship of patronage, and this was something that later imperial women could not afford to forget.

Socrates himself seems to have meant to highlight this tradition. Following the passage cited above, Socrates clarifies that Nestorius was not in fact a proponent of docetism as some people believed but that his error arose from his ignorance of Church history: he repudiates a term, *Theotokos*, which had been established in ecclesiastical usage by Eusebius and Origen.[22] To illustrate his point he gives a direct citation from Eusebius's *Life of Constantine*: 'And in fact Emmanuel submitted to be born for our sake, and the place of his nativity in the flesh is by the Hebrews called Bethlehem. Wherefore the devout Empress Helena adorned the place where the *Theotokos* gave birth with the most splendid monuments, decorating that cave with the richest ornaments.'[23] There is every reason to believe that the champion of the term *Theotokos* in Socrates' day, the Empress Pulcheria, was conscious of the resonance between her role as patroness to the Virgin's cult and that of her illustrious predecessor Helena.

Holum and Limberis saw *Theotokos* piety as incorporating a strong element of popular piety in which Empresses mobilized a following of women from all social classes, and in turn were perceived as speaking on behalf of a constituency. As patronesses with special responsibility for women from the different levels of society, they might have acted as intercessors on behalf of less fortunate women in much the same way the Virgin herself was understood to do. That a strong popular following was attached to the cult of Mary could perhaps be inferred from writings such as the *Panarion* of Epiphanius of Salamis[24] which link Marian cult to heretical groups, but there is still work to be done to understand how class and gender intersected in this context as in so many others. We will see below that Mary would have been received differently as a figure of intercession and identification by different women according to the social location of each.

Women, *Imitatio*, and Spiritual Authority

In the century between Helena and Pulcheria the idea that the virgins of the Church had a special relationship to the Virgin Mary had become central to the ideology of virginity. What might be termed the politics of identification had become central to the emerging cult of the saints.[25] A little-known fifth-century Latin text, the *Epistula ad Marcellam*, records the effort of an anonymous writer to encourage a married woman to participate in an advent retreat at which both virgins and married women would meditate on the Nativity.

It is clear from the letter, which seems to follow up on an earlier invitation, that the married recipient had tried to give her excuses, noting in particular that this kind of retreat was really more appropriate for virgins of the Church:

But perhaps you will say, why do you trouble me with a vain promise of hope? Only virgins can give birth to Christ. But I do not wish that you restrict the grace of God to the narrow confines of a single person. Look at where the apostle says to sinners and prevaricators, 'Until Christ is formed in you.'[26]

Even as he or she attempts to disagree, the anonymous writer makes it clear that one of the criteria fifth-century women were using in choosing devotional practices was whether they could as individuals identify with the divine or saintly figures to whom meditative attention was directed.

Another text, the *Handbook for Gregoria*, a sixth-century devotional manual for married women, shows a somewhat different approach to breaking the hold of virginity as the devotional *sine qua non* for women. 'Gregoria,' the text's addressee, is exhorted to model herself after the legendary martyr Anastasia, a married woman whose husband, a pagan official, imprisoned her when he discovered that she was circulating freely in the city dressed as a widow and engaging in acts of Christian charity. The *Passio Anastasiae* shows a self-consciousness about the issue of the female reader, presenting in its first section a correspondence between Anastasia, imprisoned in the marital home, and her spiritual director, Chrysogonus, who counsels her to have courage during her hidden trials.

It is certainly no accident that it is Anastasia whom the anonymous author of the *Handbook for Gregoria* selected as a devotional model for married women. The *Handbook* offers a metaphor of daily life as an enactment of the sufferings of the martyrs, and Anastasia in particular, as a key to the laywoman's problem of finding Christian meaning in her own experience. The anonymous writer addresses the martyr Anastasia as serving as a bridge for *imitatio*, both imitating Christ and herself serving as a model for the imitation of women who could hope to identify with her. Since Anastasia's feast day took place on 25 December, she was seen as an especially important link for married women to Mary and to the Incarnation:

Justly Christ took you up into the heavens on the same day on which he himself descended to earth, and he permitted the anniversary of your martyrdom to occur on the same day as the nativity of his assumption [of the flesh], because you, by suffering martyrdom, offered to many what he offered to all by being born. And just as, having despised majesty, he took on the form of a servant, so that he might assist us all, so you yourself, having despised the glory of nobility, took on an ignominy of person, so that you might be imitated by others, and so that you might provide a model of Christian endurance for all. You will receive everlasting glory as much because you set an example for the edification of all matrons (*pro adeificatione omnium matronarum*) as because of your own martyrdom.[27]

In the *Handbook for Gregoria* the Incarnation is explained in terms which invite the lay female reader to imagine the incarnation through the lens of Anastasia, a bridge through whom she too can engage in a form of *imitatio Christi*. At the same time, the reader is repeatedly reminded that when she faces the discouragement of daily life she should compare herself to the martyrs – such as Anastasia – who in their courage sacrificed themselves for Christ, meditating in the meanwhile on the figure of the *miles Christi*, who fights the spiritual battle for virtue against the vices.

The notion of the Christian life as *imitatio* is one whose roots lie deep in the period of the persecutions. The historical martyr her- or himself was expected to engage in *imitatio* – to reenact by his or her own endurance the passion of Christ – a *topos* which reaches back to the letters of Ignatius of Antioch at the turn of the first century. The average Christian, in turn, was to find in the trials of daily life an opportunity to reenact the passion of the martyrs.

While the idea of spiritual warfare had existed in the Latin west since Tertullian,[28] it was through Ambrose – and thus, indirectly, through the influence of Origen – that it gained an important place in Latin preaching and exegesis. From the allegorization of the scriptures, an application of the allegorical method to the experience of the individual was perhaps the next logical step. Ambrose's innovation was to introduce the struggle of the Christian martyrs as an *exemplum* to guide 'average' Christians as they faced the struggle within the soul.

In his *Expositio in Psalmum 118*, Ambrose turned from discussing the martyrdom of Saint Sebastian – on whose feast day the *expositio* was delivered[29] – to address the reader:

But what is worse, not only the visible but also the invisible are persecutors, and there are more of these by far ... For who can be exempted, when the lord himself suffered the temptations of persecution? Avarice, ambition, extravagance, pride, and fornication all attack the soul.[30]

Ambrose went on to specify that because each Christian would continuously be called to witness for Christ, he or she must take special care to show allegiance to Him in every action.[31]

Writers and preachers following Ambrose took care to draw a connection between the prowess of the historical martyr and the experience of ordinary Christians wherever possible. The martyrs themselves were figured as taking part in the spiritual wrestling match with the vices with which the faithful were presumed daily to struggle.[32] Equally, Christian audiences were encouraged to identify their own struggle with the vices with the more patently heroic struggle of the martyrs against an earthly persecutor:

Beloved, if you wish we should have a share in the heavenly seat, as God promised to the victors, let us in the first instance imitate the faith of the wholly martyr confessing, and let us follow his path in virtue, nor should we be afraid in the love of God to set our hearts against the bloody hands of the persecutor ... for it is not beyond you to be a victor daily in any respect, if you will only reject the desires of the flesh.[33]

Such exhortations served to strengthen the sense of Christian identity among the faithful. They accord precisely, as it happens, with the shift noted by Charles F. Altman in a 1975 article from 'diametrical' to 'gradational' models in hagiographical writing from the fourth century onwards.[34] On the whole, according to Altman, the *passiones* of the pre-Constantinian period served to pose a diametrical opposition between the forces of good and evil, while the *vitae* of the post-Constantinian period place stress on development and transformation within an individual and the possibility that others may be transformed by contact with the individual in question.[35]

André Vauchez has suggested that the prevailing standpoint of hagiography before the twelfth century was to stress the supernatural power of the saint to the exclusion of the possibility of *imitatio*. The result of this was to situate the invention of the saint's life as a *règle de conduite* for the laity as a by-product in the aftermath of the Gregorian reform, and there may be some truth to this.[36] Vauchez's proposal might superficially seem to be confirmed by twelfth-century citation of patristic *auctoritates*,[37] but the presence of such citations is misleading. To put it simply, almost any position on *imitatio* could be defended by recourse to the fathers.[38] This was not mere sophistry: different aspects of tradition were brought forward in different pastoral contexts. What made the difference was an assessment of the consequences for the well-being of the faithful, which would be governed by context and by an assessment of the individual or circumstance in question.

But certainly both the ascetics and the laity of the fifth and sixth centuries saw saints as something to be imitated even while also being venerated. Already at the end of the fourth century, *imitatio* could be a volatile and powerful tool in the hands of the laity. The Empress Pulcheria's use of patronage for the cult of the Virgin Mary as a vehicle for consolidating her own imperial power is a case in point.[39]

Narrative and Agency

Our own view of how readers and viewers interact with texts and spectacles has changed dramatically over the last generation, and this has repercussions for our understanding of how women in late antiquity could engage and identify with the figures of the saints. Theories of the gaze in early postmodern feminist film criticism called attention to the unpredictability of the identification process. I am thinking here particularly of Laura Mulvey's 1975 article, 'Visual Pleasure and Narrative Cinema,'[40] where female characters were seen not as points of identification for the female viewer but rather as an 'erotic object for the characters in the story and erotic object for the spectator.'[41] Later theorists, such as Janice Radway, who undertook fieldwork on readers of romance novels, or Jonathan Culler, whose 1981 essay 'On Reading as a Woman'[42] undermined the idea of the reader straitjacketed to a response 'required' by a text where gender was concerned. A single text can be alternately hegemonic or empowering for the same reader, depending on the context in which the reader encounters it and on the reader's own strategy in approaching the text. Whether there were specific issues where ancient or medieval readers read *religious* texts is an open question, especially since we can never be sure how, if at all, ancient and medieval people, whose sense of 'self' was so profoundly different from our own, perceived what they read or otherwise encountered. Nonetheless there is something to be learned from looking at how nineteenth- and twentieth-century human beings have been understood to map their religious experience in narrative terms.

At the turn of the twentieth century, William James argued, in his *Varieties of the Religious Experience,* that narratives of religious conversions are characterized by a 'peak experience' that marks the turning point after which one cosmic paradigm is exchanged for another and the sense of self is transformed. But while James saw this 'peak experience' as a fact of experience, it is in fact a product of *language*, of retrospective re-construction of experience, a point which is not yet fully understood. Paula Fredriksen looked at this problem in her article on the conversion narratives of Paul of Tarsus and Augustine of Hippo,[43] and Susan Harding's 1990 fieldwork-based account of conversion among American 'born-again' Christians[44] saw conversion as fundamentally a process of exchanging one language for describing experience in favour of another. This idea of narrative and language as central to the religious impulse is of course as compatible with Durkheim's idea of 'God' as 'Society' as it is with Wittgenstein's idea of the 'language game.' It is surely at the heart of the problem of the *exemplum* in late Roman and early medieval religion.

Comparative material can shed light here. For example, the debate on the function of *sati* in the context of Hindu fundamentalism has stressed the important difference between a martyr-heroine's function as a social icon and her possible effect on actual female members of the religious community of which she is a part. This is a point similar to that made by Marina Warner with regard to the Virgin Mary a generation ago. Part of this depends on how we assess the power relationship between writer and intended reader. This is important, because the issue of empowerment would work very differently for a woman who was being addressed by a social inferior – as would have been the case for a religious or literary patroness – than for other, lower-status women, who might encounter a text at a later stage, perhaps long after its production.

I have argued elsewhere[45] that the idea of 'invisible martyrdom' which is present in the anonymous sixth-century *Handbook for Gregoria* offers to the reader the reassuring idea that however she may have failed in the competitive late Roman game of self-representation in the earthly community, her seemingly unrecognized performance of a heroic Christian identity will have gone recorded by the all-seeing eye of God. Even taking into account the caveats expressed above about ancient and modern ideas of selfhood, it may be worth borrowing from postmodern psychology a critical language for talking about this phenomenon. Though I would hesitate to assign modern or postmodern ideas of pathology to ancient or medieval experience, I think it may be relevant at least heuristically to look in religious texts for a pattern of offering enabling narratives by which the reader can construe meaning, specifically pattern and coherence, agency, recognition, and identity, from the confused sequence of lived experience. An approach drawing on the literature of narrative psychology[46] would stress the centrality of the enabling narratives which women and men construct in order to give meaning, shape, and validation to experience. In the fieldwork case study provided by Michelle L. Crossley's *Introduction to Narrative Psychology: Self, Trauma, and the Construction of Meaning*, 'Belief in God' is assigned to the psychological 'themes' of recognition and agency.[47] If this is the case, it allows us to frame the problem of agency in these texts in a somewhat different way from the 'empowerment'-versus-'silencing' polarity that has characterized some writing about Christian literature for women.

We can begin to imagine that where a text directed a woman reader's self-understanding toward a paradigm of self-sacrifice, this could have simultaneous and conflicting implications. It could serve a patriarchal social function of encouraging forbearance while at the same time offering the female reader an empowering language of self-interpretation. Not only could this language be used rhetorically to present her actions in the best possible light, but it could also be used internally to interpret her own experience in a way that lent meaning to setbacks. Since the relationship between action, audience, and self-perception is always volatile, even an apparently misogynistic language could furnish a vehicle for enhancing a woman's claim to the validity of her own agency. But we can begin to understand how a female reader – or a female writer or literary patron – might have warmed to a language linking femininity and sacrifice as offering positive, if also ambiguous, rhetorical possibilities.

We began with the Roman princess Constantia, and her invocation of Agnes, Mary, and Jesus as the intercessors through whom God would receive, and act upon, her prayer, made in turn on behalf of young women bound to her through a chain of human relationships. In concluding, we return to consider the layering of interdependence and reciprocal agency – the chain of human and divine relationships stretching to heaven and back again – which this brief episode evokes. When the fifth- or sixth-century author of the *Passio Gallicani* invoked the memory of Constantina/Constantia, he or she probably had little to go on in terms of narrative tradition. Surely, however, the Roman community for whom the text was written knew the dramatic fourth-century mausoleum centred on Constantina's sarcophagus, along with the nearby basilica of Agnes, which the historical Constantina herself as patroness had dedicated.[48] As daughter of the deceased emperor Constantine and cousin of the pagan emperor Julian in whose reign the story was set – although in fact she died before Julian became Augustus – Constantia serves in the text as an icon of lay and female authority but also as a representative of the authority of the imperial family. We must remember that in a society where family and class so predominated as structures of identity, women frequently stood as the pivotal figures in an alliance, often with life-or-death consequences for the men involved. Certainly, where attempts to claim legitimate authority were concerned, women were still at a disadvantage compared with men, and poor women still at a disadvantage compared with the rich. But in many respects the centrality of kinship worked to women's advantage.

Finally, we should remember that the Christian literature of female spirituality was necessarily addressed to a disarmingly wide readership, ranging from the emperor's household in the capital cities to the slaves and artisans of the distant provinces, where illiterate Christians could listen to another member of the community rather than read independently.[49] By elevating a carpenter's wife from Palestine to serve as Queen of Heaven, the fourth- and fifth-century Church sought to unite the women of the Empire into a collectivity whose shared identity as Christians could outperform the allegiances of family and class, race, and province. This collectivity, in turn, could offer a platform for the authority of elite women, such as Pulcheria, who acted to defend the pious traditions that had come to be identified with the women of their generation. In championing the cause of Mary, Pulcheria was seen to speak to the interests of women drawn from a wide social spectrum. In the end, her attempt to mobilize an ideal of shared feminine piety cutting across the allegiances of class and province would have the effect of enhancing not only her own authority, but that of the Empire itself.

NOTES

1 Anonymous (1477 [1910], 570): 'expandens manus ad dominum sic oravit, Domine deus omnipotens qui me orationibus tuae martyris Agne a lepra mundasti et semittam mihi amoris tui propitius ostendisti porro virginis tuae matris thalamum reserasti, ubi sponsus tu filius manifestatus es, tu genitus ex Maria tu genitor probatus Mariae, tu eius lactatus huberibus tu etiam omnes saeculum nutriens ... Peto itaque domine ut has Gallicani filias lucreris ... ut ferventes as thalamum illum tuum caelestem pervenire studeant.' On this passio and related texts, see Leyser and Pilsworth (forthcoming).
2 In fact, Constantine's daughter was called Constantina, while he had a sister and niece called Constantia; see Jones et al. (1971, 222).
3 Daly (1968).
4 Warner (1976).
5 Clark (1990, 253–73).
6 Bidez and Hansen (1995, 38).
7 Young (1983, 180).
8 Young (1983, 196): Diodore of Tarsus, for example, was accused of asserting that they were not.
9 Nestorius, First sermon, cited in Loofs (1905, 252), and discussed in Holum (1982, 155).
10 Young (1983, 219) characterizes the view of Nestorius thus: 'To attribute birth and suffering and death to the Logos is to fall into pagan thinking and follow the heresies of Apollinarius and Arius.'
11 Young (1983, 217).
12 Kelly (1977, 143).
13 Ignatius, *Letter to the Ephesians* 18, 2 (*PG* 5, col. 660); Ignatius, *Letter to the Romans* 6, 3 (*PG* 5, col. 694).
14 For discussion see Young (1983, 228), and literature cited there.
15 Young (1983, 228), arguing against the position sustained by Sellers and others that the controversy was caused by political rather than theological differences.
16 Holum (1982, 163).

17 On the sources for Chrysostom and Eudoxia, see Cooper (1996, 17–19), and literature cited there. On the complex evidence for Pulcheria and Nestorius, see Cooper (1998, 31–43).
18 Holum (1982, 164).
19 For discussion of Holum's view and subsequent critiques, see Cooper (2004) and Price (2004, 31–8).
20 Brubaker (1997, 52–75). See also Clark (1990) and Harrison (1989).
21 Socrates, *Historia Ecclesiastica* VII. 34. 11 (ed. Hansen, 383, tr. Zenos, 172).
22 Pelikan (1996) on the history of the term.
23 Eusebius, *Life of Constantine*, 3.18 (*PG* 20, cols. 1101–4).
24 Benko (1993), esp. chap. 5, 'The Women Who Sacrificed to Mary: The Kollyridians'; Burrus (1991, 229–48).
25 The next three paragraphs summarize material discussed in greater detail in Cooper (1998, 36–41).
26 Morin (1928, 398); the biblical citation is from Galatians 4.19.
27 *PLS* 3, col. 227; my translation.
28 E.g., Tertullian, *De Spectaculis*, 29.
29 *Expositio psalmi* CXVIII 20, 44 (*CSEL* 62, 466): 'Utamur exemplo Sebastiani martyris, cuius hodie natalis est.'
30 *Expositio psalmi* CXVIII, 20, 45 (*CSEL* 62, 466–7): 'Sed quod peius, non hi solum persecutores sunt qui videntur, sed etiam qui non videntur, et multo plures persecutores ... Quis enim exceptus potest esse, cum ipse dominus persecutionum temptamenta toleraverit? Persequitur avaritia, persequitur ambitio, persequitur luxuria, persequitur superbia, persequitur fornicatio.'
31 See, for example, *Expositio psalmi* CXVIII, 20, 47 (*CSEL* 62, 468): 'Quod est amplius, non sermonis tantummodo, sed etiam operis testimonium praebuisti. Quis enim locupletior testis es quam qui confitetur dominum Iesum in carne venisse, cum evangelii praecepta custodit? Nam qui audit et non facit, negat Christum; etsi verbo fatetur, operibus negat.'
32 Victricius, *De laude sanctorum*, 6 (*PL* 20, col. 1447): 'Quid est enim aliud martyr nisi Christi imitator Domitor rabidae voluptatis? Calcator ambitionis, et mortis ambitor, contemptor divitiarum, compressor lasciviae, intemperantiae persecutor? Cui numquam sceptrum prudentiae avaritia praeripuit, aut cupiditas vindicari. Per hos virtutum gradus unde descenderat salvator ascendite.'
33 Valerianus of Cimiez, *Homilia* XV *De bono martyrii*, 5 (*PL* 52, 740): 'Si vultis ergo, dilectissimi, ut sit nobis in coelesti sede portio, quam victoribus Dominus repromisit, imitemur primo loco sancti martyris fidem in confessione, et sequamur viam ejus in virtute, nec dubitemus in amore Domini cruentis lictoris manibus pectus opponere ... non deest autem in quo possis quotidie vincere, si volueris carnis desideriis repugnare.'
34 Altman (1975, 1–11).

35 Altman implies obliquely that the shift can be accounted for by the changing social function of hagiographical narrative as the Church itself is transformed progressively from an embattled group of 'outsiders' to a normative cultural institution. For the present discussion, it will suffice to acknowledge the wider problem of the social function of *imitatio*.
36 Vauchez (1991, 164).
37 Discussed by Brasington (1992, 135–52).
38 For example, the frequently cited opinion of Gregory the Great, explaining to his interlocutor in the *Dialogues* that not all qualities of the spiritually great are to be imitated: 'The freedom of their life must not be taken as an example by the weak, lest, while someone presumes that he is similarly filled with the Holy Spirit, he should disdain to be a disciple of a man and become the master of error ... Thus Moses was taught his mission in the desert by an angel, not instructed by a man. But these things, as I have already said, must be venerated – not imitated – by the weak [*sed haec, ut praediximus, infirmis veneranda sunt, non imitanda*].' Gregory the Great, *Dialogues* 1.16–17 (*SC* 251, 22); Brasington (1992, 143), discusses the importance of the citation for medieval debate over legal precedent. What becomes apparent, if we compare the citation from Gregory with its converse ('an intention of imitating them, not ... of actual worship') formulated by Augustine in his altercation with the Manichaeans, is that the attitude to *imitatio* varied, depending on a variety of factors.
39 Cooper (1998, 31–43).
40 Mulvey (1975, 6–18).
41 Jill Nelmes (1999, 277).
42 Culler (1982, 43–64).
43 Fredriksen (1986).
44 Harding (1987, 167–81).
45 In Cooper (1996) 'The Imprisoned Heroine.'
46 A term which, to my knowledge, first appears with Sarbin (1986).
47 Crossley (2000, 96).
48 On the dedication, see Curran (2000, 128).
49 On reading aloud in early Christian communities, see Gamble (1995).

6

Virgo Fortis: Images of the Crucified Virgin Saint in Medieval Art

ILSE FRIESEN

Postmodern feminist artists have thrust the unsettling image of the crucified woman into the contemporary public consciousness, a deliberate and provocative challenge to the most androcentric religious sensibilities. British sculptor Edwina Sandys's *Christa* (1975) depicts a naked woman pinned on a cross. Other, more confrontational, works by Barbara Kruger and Sue Coe exploit the form of the crucifix as a metaphor for misogyny and sexual assault.[1]

Although such images, which allow for what Jerry Meyer identifies as a 'diverse expressive, political and social commentary,'[2] seem to be a radical departure from the traditional crucifix, they share an antecedent in what was once one of the most popular saints in Europe. In this essay I explore the origins and popularity of St Wilgefortis, the female crucifix whose cult rivalled at one time that of the Virgin Mary and whose most noticeable feature is her luxuriant beard.

In his pragmatic assessment of the history of the female crucifix, Erwin Panofsky speculated that the image of St Wilgefortis evolved from a depiction of the crucified Christ in which his body is fully covered by a long gown which is gathered by a belt. This type of robed crucifix follows an oriental or Syrian-Palestinian tradition and may well have been read as a female figure by viewers more familiar with the Hellenistic or Western crucifix, which is unclothed.[3] The most famous example of this type of draped (male) crucifix is the so-called Volto Santo (literally 'Holy Face'), preserved in the Cathedral of Lucca in Italy. A monumental, larger-than-life-sized wood carving, it was one of the most venerated images of the Middle Ages. From the twelfth century on, the Volto Santo was the focus of pilgrimages and the object of vows and votive offerings of precious garments, jewellery, and shoes, which gradually came to constitute the 'wardrobe' of the statue for festive occasions.⁴ Already by the end of the twelfth century, various copies of the Volto Santo had been produced throughout Italy. Since some of these copies portrayed the statue as wearing additional clothing, these images contributed to the spread of a rather strange legend which concerned a bearded virgin on a cross. Apparently, the Volto Santo came to be misinterpreted as depicting a crucified woman because of the statue's long and festive robes.

It is of course impossible to know the specific process by which the image of the bedizened crucifix was read as female, but obviously the idea appealed to the popular imagination and may have resonated with preexisting legends and cults. Were there already stories in circulation about bearded virgins? Did the image tally with permutations of ancient stories of the bearded goddess Aphrodite? Certainly by the Middle Ages there was a philosophical understanding that virginity could be associated with transvestism. The Alexandrian philosopher Philo wrote that women could attain the superior masculine qualities of rationality by taking the active male role, best attained by remaining a virgin.⁵ It is only a short step from this to the idea that virgins have a predisposition towards transvestism; control of libido is associated with masculinity in this conceptual system.⁶ Early and medieval Christianity abounds with transvestite saints. St Margarita-Pelagius, to name but one of the earliest examples, avoided marriage, dressed as a male, and lived as a hermit.

Legends, carvings, paintings, and prints depicting this venerated virgin were created and circulated throughout Europe from about 1400 on. She was referred to as Wilgefortis or Liberata in Italy, Ontkommer in the Netherlands, Uncumber in England, and Kümmernis in the German-speaking countries. The bearded female saint is depicted in a woodcut by the Augsburg artist Hans Burgkmair in the early sixteenth century. In most editions of the print, the full text of her legend has also been added, adjoining the image to the left.⁷ The woodcut carries a double title, with the result that the crucified person can be regarded either as the Volto Santo or as Kümmernis.⁸ The artist informs the viewer in the text on the margin of the print that this virgin saint's cult had originated in Steenbergen in Holland around 1400.⁹ According to the lengthy text on Burgkmair's woodcut, and other sources, Kümmernis had been the beautiful and wise daughter of a heathen Portuguese king. She had refused to submit to marriage to a Sicilian prince, and for this her father had her imprisoned. Christ, in fact, was supposed to have visited her in the dungeon, and she had subsequently prayed to be transformed into his likeness so that her appearance would not please any man but only her crucified Lord, whom she called her true spouse. In some versions, her prospective husband did in fact glimpse her hirsute face under her veil and called off the engagement. The outraged father had her crucified, whereupon she died a martyr's death. Burgkmair concluded his text with the statement that whoever called upon this virgin 'Kumini' in afflictions or grief ('Kummer') would be helped by her. Consequently, she acquired the symbolic name of 'Kümmernis,' which means that she not only embodied grief but could also help to overcome it.

The saint was often associated with her discarded right shoe, which had fallen onto the altar table below her or onto the ground. The account of the gift of a shoe originated in the twelfth century and was originally connected with the Volto Santo. This motif was later transferred onto Wilgefortis or Kümmernis, who was said to have deposited one of her shoes in order to reward a poor and pious fiddler who played in front of her. Burgkmair's text also includes the story of the fiddler who had encountered her in her last hours; he was supposed to have played so fervently that she dropped him a golden shoe as a reward for his compassion and piety. The text goes on to note that when he carried this gift to a goldsmith in order to sell it, he was suspected of theft. Faced with his impending execution, he asked to be brought before the image once more. After placing the shoe back on the foot he played again, and the image thereupon dropped the second shoe. This, the first miracle of the bearded virgin martyr, convinced the authorities of the man's innocence, and he went away happily, 'thanking God and Saint Kuemmernuss.'[10] The symbolism of the shoe encourages us to associate St Kümmernis with fertility. Many European wedding ceremonies included throwing shoes at the bride and groom, a custom which persists in the practice of tying old shoes to the car which carries the bride and groom to their honeymoon. Fairy tales such as Cinderella associate shoes with marriage, and indeed the shoe, a container with an opening, has been interpreted as a female sexual symbol.

Through the medium of the woodcut, the virgin saint, having renounced her sexuality for the sake of a martyr's death, was proclaimed as a model of virginity, worthy of imitation by other women. She was hailed as exemplifying the fact that God could bring about wonderful things in his saints: 'Mirabilis deus in sanctis suis,' as Burgkmair put it. Burgkmair's reference to 'Stouberg' most likely referred to the town Steenbergen in North Brabant, a site which had emerged since the fifteenth century as the centre of the cult surrounding the crucified virgin. Unfortunately buildings associated with Catholicism were destroyed by the Calvinists, so it is impossible to determine the extent of the cult of Kümmernis in this area. Since neither a tomb nor any relics nor any historical records concerning this saint have ever been found, scholars have concluded that she is an entirely fictional and legendary medieval creation. This conclusion, however, raises as many questions as it purports to answer. Why would the cult of such a fictional person become so widespread and intensive that even crucifixes of Christ were adapted, recarved, or dressed with additional and fashionable clothing in order to resemble a woman's appearance? Why did she pose such a threat to the Catholic Church and why was she seen as competing with officially sanctioned cults of other saints? Many of her pilgrimage sites in Germany and Austria, for example, were later forcibly abandoned in order to conform to cults of the Virgin Mary and other, more established, male or female saints. Many of her images were removed or else deliberately destroyed, either by burning them, by whitewashing the church walls which had borne her likeness, or by confining her statues to inaccessible storage places.[11]

As we have noted, the simple explanation proposed by historians has been that the cult of a female crucifix was nothing but an ignorant misunderstanding of images of the robed, crucified Christ. This explanation, however, does not account for the phenomenon of widespread veneration and profound popularity of this virgin. A mere misunderstanding could surely not have created a cult that flourished for at least five hundred years throughout Europe, nor does it explain why the name of this strange and controversial saint appeared repeatedly in so many different versions and languages. Her most significant names were, in fact, not common names at all but, rather, symbolic expressions of basic human experiences: Kümmernis, the embodied figure of grief who also triumphed over it; Liberata, the liberated one; Ontkommer, the one who escaped bondage; Uncumber, the one who liberates women from cumbersome men and especially troublesome husbands; and Wilgefortis, a name most likely derived from 'Virgo fortis,' the strong virgin.

It is possible that this powerful virgin may in fact have been a primeval and cross-cultural personification of mythical proportions, substantially older than either Christian art or other forms of Western culture. It has been suggested that images of the crucified Christ might have been adapted or otherwise integrated to merge with ancient images of female figures. Wilgefortis may, indeed, have been an archetypal figure, symbolizing the predicament of human life, which was understood as centring around suffering, giving life, and enduring death. In this connection, her image can be thought of as having embodied a prehistoric, bisexual power of fertility. Some of her peculiar features, such as the combination of male and female genders, were expressed in ancient art and mythology, beginning with the ancient Egyptians and Classical antiquity, particularly with regard to myths of a 'Venus Barbata,' the bearded Venus.[12] It has also been suggested that Wilgefortis may have been an ancient, androgynous divinity who was suppressed once patriarchal religions were established and who was only much later reinterpreted as an embodiment of the Christian ideal of virginity.[13]

In Germany, centres of this virgin's worship could be found in all regions, but especially in the Bavarian towns of Burghausen and Neufahrn. Relevant shrines and pilgrimage sites have also been recorded in Switzerland, Austria, Poland, Slovenia, and Bohemia, where she was known as 'the Flemish saint.' In Austria alone, sixteen pilgrimage sites of Kümmernis have been recorded, ten of these in Tyrol. She has also been represented in Italy and Spain, and images of her were even taken by German immigrants to Brazil, where, according to a Catholic *Hauskalender*, her feast day, 20 July, was still being observed as recently as 1936.[14]

Her great popularity was based on the fact that she was thought to be helpful in curing all kinds of afflictions. She was especially, but not exclusively, a women's saint and was called upon in sexual dilemmas, cases of infertility or illnesses of the reproductive organs, or in situations of violence, such as rape. She was also a patron saint for people who were imprisoned or for soldiers who were engaged in war. In particular, people who were close to dying, as well as those who were caring for the terminally ill, prayed to her for a peaceful death without agony. Because of the legend of her generous gift to the poor fiddler, she also became the patron saint of musicians and minstrels. Her beneficial intercession even extended beyond humans to encompass pets and livestock. She was also said to be helpful during droughts, bad harvests, floods, and even periods of high inflation.[15]

A total of about one thousand examples of this remarkable type of female crucifix have survived.[16] The oldest examples are large sculptures which were created with reference to the Volto Santo. A significant number of medieval images were either deliberately or unintentionally ambiguous with regard to the true gender of the crucified figure. Some of these images are consequently referred to by various titles, not only within local communities but also in several collections and catalogues. An example of this phenomenon concerns a Romanesque wood carving of a crucifix from Uznach near St Gallen, now housed in the Schweizerisches Landesmuseum in Zurich. It is a large wood statue whose left arm is missing and whose right arm has been restored, with traces of various previous colours still apparent on the robe and mantle. For stylistic reasons it has been dated to the eleventh century and is thus the oldest work of art in the museum. In the museum catalogue, it is simply referred to as a crucifix, but there is also reference to the fact that this robed crucifix was 'later' often reinterpreted as representing the virgin saint Kümmernis.[17] The carving of the folds may, in spite of its Romanesque rigidity, suggest an ascetic female body, at least in the eye of some beholders; it becomes clear from this example how easily a robed crucifix could be 'misunderstood,' thereby making a confusion of genders possible and even likely.

One of the oldest medieval wood carvings in Bavaria is a crucifix which is displayed in the pilgrimage church of Neufahrn near Freising (see figure 1).

Figure 1 'S Wilgefortis Sive Liberata' from the altar of the Church of Neufahrn, Bavaria, 1661

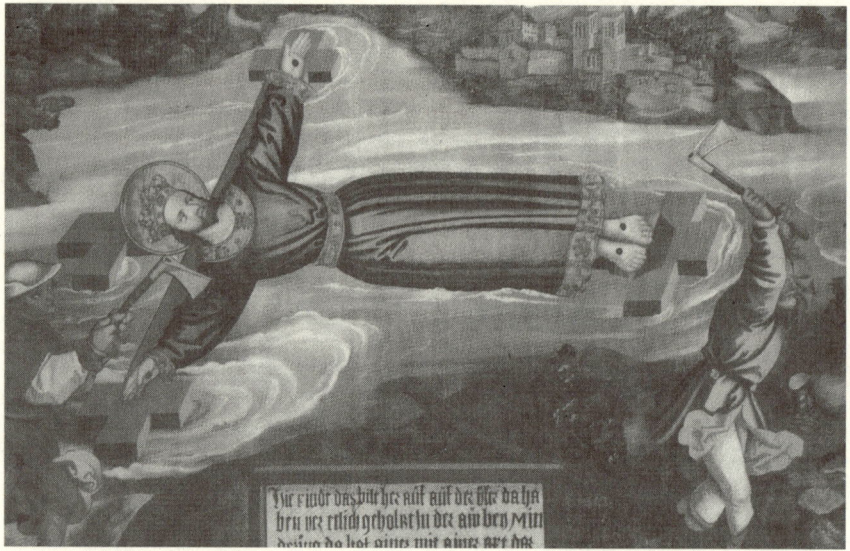

Figure 2 Altar panel 1 from the Church of Neufahrn, Bavaria

This local *Gnadenbild*, or image of grace, is thought to be a Romanesque replica of the Volto Santo and has been dated to the twelfth century. It was badly damaged in a fire in 1580 and was later restored and frequently repainted. This Bavarian crucifix is to this day the centre and focus of the Baroque high altar, where it is surrounded by adoring angels and carries the inscription 'S. Wilgefortis Sive Liberata V.M. 1661 H. Jungfrau u. Martyrerin ohne Kümmernuss bitt fuer uns.'[18] It is not clear at what time this crucifix first became venerated as Wilgefortis. While pilgrimages to Neufahrn apparently began in 1497, people may have originally worshipped Christ in the form of this image.[19]

Seven panels on either side of the altar of this church portray the story of a miraculously bleeding crucifix, which was said to have been found floating on the nearby river Isar and was eventually brought to this pilgrimage site (see figure 2). The panels, created in 1527, constitute unique and intriguing visual documents of this local legend. In the panel paintings, the crucified figure wears a gown gathered around the waist, which could easily lead to a possible misrepresentation of the crucified person as being female.

It should be noted in this connection that Christ, during the course of the Middle Ages, had not exclusively been represented as being male. He was also understood to be a nursing mother, especially on account of his bleeding wounds, which were regarded as nourishment for the faithful.[20] This symbolic merging of genders can already be observed in sculptures and paintings of early Christian art in which the figure of Christ appears to feature delicate breasts.[21]

Saint Ontkommer, as seen in images from the Netherlands created during the fifteenth century, is even more specifically portrayed with female characteristics. These include a delicate bosom, a slender waist, and a sinuous lower body. She is always tied, with ropes around her wrists and ankles, to a T-shaped cross. A tightly pulled rope usually gathers her full skirt in such a way that the folds obscure her feet together with the lower part of the cross. She is frequently depicted alone and abandoned in a valley which constitutes part of a rocky and otherwise uninviting landscape.

The fame and appeal of the crucified virgin were so great that her representations are not confined only to monumental statuary and portraiture but also appear in artworks for private consumption, such as books and textiles. The aforementioned woodcut by Burgmair indicates how deeply rooted her cult was. As far as the Netherlandish variation of the crucified virgin is concerned, it is obvious that the visual references to the Italian origin of the image have become rather faint, particularly in book illuminations from that region. The background behind the crucified virgin, which features either abstract ornaments or else a barren landscape, has no connection with the original altar niche in the cathedral of Lucca, where the Volto Santo is still housed. Neither has the fiddler found his way into the Netherlandish cultural environment. As a result, Ontkommer's shoes have lost their symbolic significance and consequently remain hidden under her long dress.

A Book of Hours, now in the University Library in Liège, consists of a devotional text illuminated by miniatures which was possibly made for a woman because of the feminine endings of some of the prayers; within this book, a very different depiction of Saint Ontkommer can be found.[22] The bearded virgin, holding a large cross, is now seen in the company of several other saints, including Francis, Mary Magdalene, and Dorothy. It is interesting to observe that St Francis, the central figure of the group, is portrayed as youthful and beardless, while St Ontkommer, standing at his side, sports a well-developed and bushy beard which is discreetly, albeit only partly, covered by her cross. Her ample dress, however, leaves no doubt about the true nature of her sex; she exhibits the curvilinear feminine elegance of an aristocratic lady. She carries a book in her right hand, while her left hand holds the cross and a piece of untied rope. Ontkommer is shown here as having escaped from bondage and is therefore visualized in the symbolic context of her name. Thus, both the cross and the rope are portrayed as attributes of her liberating power.

Once the Hapsburgs adopted this strange virgin, along with numerous other saints of the Burgundian court, Ontkommer could be found embroidered on garments belonging to the treasuries of the Golden Fleece, now housed in the Schatzkammer in Vienna. This aristocratic order became the most significant dynastic and religious symbol of the House of Hapsburg. Their treasures included a set of gold, silver, and silk textiles. The 'most costly vestments in the world,' as these Burgundian parament treasures have been called, 'can be regarded as the finest work achieved in the art of European embroidery.'[23] These treasures were first mentioned in an inventory of the order in 1477 but must have originated, at least in part, already in the first half of the fifteenth century. The design of the figures in these textiles, as well as the individual scenes within them, can be connected with the greatest Netherlandish artists working at that time, such as Van Eyck, Rogier van der Weyden, and Hugo van der Goes.[24] These vestments have rightly been called 'a textile All Saints Feast,' originating at a time when Flanders was at the centre of cloth and garment production in Europe. One of the vestments, called a tunicle, displays female saints in three rows: the first saint in the second row on the left can be identified as Ontkommer or Wilgefortis, while other panels portray saints such as Apollonia, Martha, Cecilia, Christina, Agnes, Dorothy, and other, less familiar, individuals who were only of local significance with regard to French and Netherlandish sites. In this connection, Wilgefortis has been described as 'bearded, crowned, with the cross, in a blue dress with red used for the belt and the lining of the sleeves, while the undergarment and mantle is green.'[25] Similar to the previously mentioned miniature depicting her in the Book of Hours, the virgin saint is portrayed as standing upright while holding a large cross. Pieces of rope can be seen dangling from the wood and are grasped by her right hand; these attributes identify her as having escaped from the cross.

Between 1500 and 1515, Hieronymus Bosch painted an altar devoted to St Julia, a work which now belongs to the inventory of the Doge's Palace in Venice. The central panel of this altar portrays the crucifixion of Julia of Corsica.[26] Julia, according to a medieval legend, was a noble maid born in Carthage during the early Christian era; she was sold in slavery to a rich Syrian merchant called Eusebius, who brought her to the island of Corsica. Since she was not willing to make sacrifices to heathen gods, she was crucified by order of the local governor Felix. Monks later rescued her body and brought it to Brescia. In time, she became the patron saint of Corsica as well as of Leghorn (Livorno).[27]

In Bosch's painting, Julia's master, Eusebius, has collapsed to the ground, either because of weakness or because he is drunk. This unflattering detail may indicate Bosch's grim sense of humour, together with his sarcastic view of the nature of man.[28] While Bosch appears to have used aspects of the iconography of the crucifixion here, he ingeniously reverses the genders of the main protagonists. Thus, Christ has been replaced by Julia, while the uncouth Eusebius has assumed the role of the swooning Virgin Mary. There is no proof that Julia, as presented in this painting, is actually intended to represent Wilgefortis or Ontkommer, names which were presumably familiar to Bosch as part of his Netherlandish religious background. He may have painted this triptych during a trip to northern Italy, a region in which St Julia was more popular than St Ontkommer. Consequently, he could have been commissioned to paint this altar for Italian merchants or diplomats who were active in the Netherlands during that time.[29]

It is interesting to note in this context that an Italian art historian, Dino Buzzati, described this work as representing the martyrdom of St Liberata. He was convinced that Bosch was depicting not St Julia, but rather 'Ontcommer, cioe Liberata o "Virgo Fortis."' Interestingly, a book on Venetian painting published in 1771 characterized Bosch's painting as representing the crucifixion of either a male or a female martyr.[30] The crucial detail of this martyr's beard is so delicately indicated that one could easily miss it and therefore believe her to be St Julia. Once the beard is noticed, however, the figure can clearly be identified as St Ontkommer. Bosch was apparently shrewd enough to combine the iconography of Julia with that of Ontkommer, thereby pleasing both Italian and Dutch patrons.

As mentioned above, Bosch was active at a time when the intense piety of the Middle Ages had reached its climax. This piety was based, to a considerable degree, on the acceptance, or even deliberate seeking out, of physical suffering, especially on the part of virgins who had taken religious vows. Some popular images in illuminated manuscripts from that era show Christ carrying the cross while followed by a personification of Love or *Minne*, who is carrying her own cross, which is similar to that of Christ. She is portrayed either as walking closely behind him or else as residing in his heart on the cross itself.[31]

During the second half of the sixteenth century, Wilgefortis was depicted with decreasing frequency due to a temporary decline in her popularity. Humanists such as Thomas More, among others, were highly critical of her because of the gross superstitions which flourished at her cult sites.[32] Also, the fictional nature of her origins, and especially her strange bearded appearance, were no longer considered spiritually uplifting or aesthetically desirable. Only during the Counter Reformation, when some former devotional trends were reactivated, did Wilgefortis regain some of her previous popularity. During the Baroque era, her cult became so widespread, especially among the population of the countryside and in alpine regions, that church authorities felt compelled to discourage these devotions. While contemporary artists have created many daring and provocative visualizations of a female crucified figure, it has to be remembered that such controversial images were already an integral part of the culture of the Middle Ages.

NOTES

1 Barbara Kruger's work *It's Our Pleasure to Disgust You* (1991) depicts a woman in a gas mask pinned to a cross. Sue Coe's *Gray Rape* (1983) shows a woman being gang raped as if she were nailed to the cross. For further discussion and other examples see Meyer (1997).
2 Meyer (1997, 27).
3 Panofsky (1923, 37).
4 While dating from about 1200, the Volto Santo is probably a replica of an earlier image made in 1100 or even earlier. According to a medieval legend, the image had originally been carved by Nicodemus in response to his witnessing of the crucifixion at Golgotha. Angels, in turn, were said to have completed the face of Christ while the artist was asleep. According to this legend, the sculpture was brought to Lucca from Palestine as early as the eighth century. See Haussherr (1962, 136, 153).
5 Philo, *Questions and Answers*, cited in Bullough (1974, 1382).
6 Bullough (1974, 1392) notes that medieval society condoned transvestism in women because it signified their superiority to other women. Male transvestites, on the other hand, experienced a loss of social status.
7 Falk (1946, 64).
8 One cannot help but ask why Burgkmair, a court artist with connections to leading humanists in southern Germany, obfuscated the identity of this image by naming it as both the Volto Santo and Kümmernis. A possible answer lies in the fact that the various traditions concerning a bearded and clothed crucifix had merged in the arena of popular devotion to such an extent that people of the late Middle Ages were not troubled by the sight of either male or female crucifixes. It might also have been politically advantageous for the artist to merge the two images in that the Netherlands had recently been incorporated into the Hapsburg empire; in this way, pilgrimage routes could be redirected to cult sites in the newly incorporated territory. Burgkmair could therefore have seized the opportunity to advertise and publicize a new geographical and political unity by integrating German, Italian, and Netherlandish religious traditions concerning various saints, especially those involving the robed crucifix in both its male and female manifestations.
9 Burkhard (1932, 29).

10 Depictions of the dropped shoe can be found in numerous Central European prints, paintings, and sculptures dating from the Middle Ages to the early twentieth century. For further discussion see Friesen (2001, 35–45).
11 See Friesen (2001, 5–7) for an account of how the author located some of the most arcane of these images.
12 MacLachlan (2002, 369–83).
13 *Lexikon der Kunst*, 3, 180.
14 Schreiber (1937, 33, 34, 61); Gugitz (1985, 83).
15 *Handwörterbuch des Deutschen Aberglaubens* 807–10.
16 Schnürer and Ritz (1934).
17 Baier-Futterer (1936, 6, fig.7).
18 This can translated as 'Saint Wilgefortis or Liberata, Holy Virgin and Martyr without Grief Pray for Us, 1661.'
19 Staber (1955, 55, 94).
20 Bynum (1982).
21 Newman (1993, 121–2).
22 Marrow (1989, 61, fig. 18, nr. 13).
23 Catalogue of the Kunsthistorisches Museum Vienna, *The Secular and Ecclesiastical Treasuries, Illustrated Guide* (1991, 208).
24 Leithe-Jasper and Distelberger (1982, 42).
25 Schlosser (1912, 25, figs. 28 and 29).
26 Bosing (1987, 84).
27 Thurston and Attwater (1956, 367).
28 Linfert (1970, 72, fig. 17).
29 Gibson (1973, 17).
30 Buzzati (1966, 96).
31 Büttner (1983, 59, fig. 48); Hamburger (1997, plate 10).
32 Shinners (1997, 201–2).

7

Amplification of the Virgin: Play and Empowerment in Walter of Wimborne's *Marie Carmina*

JENIFER SUTHERLAND

The men and women who turned to the Virgin Mary for spiritual comfort and guidance in the Middle Ages may have felt that the Mother of God was more approachable than the Father. Certainly this is true of thirteenth-century Franciscan writer Walter of Wimborne. His poetry expresses ambivalence towards the God who 'prius rigidus et quasi seuiens / sub lege fuerat et leo rugiens' (previously under the law was rigid / and like a raging, roaring lion), a God who held in his hand 'ferulam ... et trucem uirgulam' (the whip and savage rod). Walter seems to have been a schoolmaster at Wimborne Minster in Dorset, a member of the college of secular canons who may have studied at Oxford. He likely joined the Franciscans soon after they were established in England at Salisbury, serving as eighth Franciscan lector at Cambridge from 1261 to 1263, and ended his days in a Franciscan house in Norwich.[1] One of his early poems is dedicated to 'infantibus quorum sum flagio' (the little children whose whip I am).[2] Corporal punishment was a routine part of the teaching of grammar, and the personified figure Grammar is often depicted holding a flail. For Walter, and perhaps many others like him, the Virgin Mother may have offered compensation for a premature separation from his own mother as he was sent off to acquire his Latin letters at the end of a rod. The reasons for Walter's particular attachment to Mary are not accessible to us; his poetry, however, affords a look at the ways his devotion to the Virgin moved him to ask difficult questions of his world and his faith.

Walter of Wimborne understood the importance of the Virgin as an image. In his *Moral Treatise on the Four Elements* he tells the following story, popular in his day:

When the leaders of the city of Rome thought to honour its greatness with a visible image, they set about eagerly to have made out of bronze, with exquisite workmanship, the form of a woman, holding an orb in her right hand. The statue being of perfect and exceptional form, certain men alleged that her shins alone were inadequate to support such a mass. The craftsman replied that the shins would do until that time when a virgin gave birth, believing such a thing impossible.[3]

You can see what's coming: 'When the birth of Christ was accomplished, the statue shattered and collapsed.'[4] Walter uses the image of the monumental bronze woman to suggest the complete collapse of the ancient world: the virgin birth was not simply a miracle; it was a revolution. Yet the image of the shattered bronze woman is not removed but replaced, transformed, and so, in some way, continued by Mary. Mary is the centrepiece in the City of God, bronze cast replaced by radiant flesh, her basic humanity enhanced by a wardrobe of images gathered from classical, biblical, and other sources. Walter's use of these images in his last extant work provides valuable insight into the way sexual renunciation functioned in the collective psyche of the later Middle Ages.

Walter's earliest works are satirical poems, filled with classical references, decrying flattery, bribery, and the greed of present times. His middle work, the very long *Moral Treatise on the Four Elements* quoted from above, offers a grab bag of science in the service of allegorical and moral exegesis of scripture. Beryl Smalley, on the strength of these writings, counts him among her 'classicizing friars.'[5] In his later poems in praise of Mary, Walter demonstrates the kind of affective piety and Marian devotion that has been particularly associated with the Franciscan order. All of his works contain themes and elaborations that are part of his order's development yet are unmistakably idiosyncratic. The main focus of the present article is *Marie Carmina*, which A.G. Rigg has argued convincingly to be Walter's final work.[6]

By the thirteenth century the Christian West had developed a vast fund of Marian imagery, much of it a product of popular piety. More than eight hundred years before Walter, in the year 431, a crowd protesting the heretic Nestor's denial of the virgin birth marched through the streets of Ephesus chanting 'Theotokos!' From the icons of the Eastern Church to the interpretive *tituli* of Western church architecture, the God-Bearer was praised in images that became increasingly familiar. Hymns, often in the famous Stabat Mater stanza associated with the Abbey of Saint Victor, were vehicles for Marian epithets. Walter wrote one such hymn himself: 'Ave Virgo Mater Christi.' Each of its 164 stanzas makes some claim for the Virgin based on a more or less conventional image:

Hail, virgin, sweet luminary,
who are gloss and commentary

of scripture's prophetic call,
whose long awaited gloss lays bare
what for so long lay hidden there
underneath the literal.[7]

To call Mary 'gloss and commentary' is by no means to diminish her status. Scriptural commentary gathered together by Fulbert of Chartres and Anselm of Laon and others into the *Glossa Ordinaria* compensated for Mary's minimal presence in the Bible by interpreting verses from the Old and New Testaments as references to Christ's mother. Marian typology in the *Ordinaria* and the devotions of men such as Ambrose and the mystic Hugo of Saint Victor, who gave the Virgin the role of the bride in Solomon's Song of Songs, combined to pave the way for more extravagantly Marian glosses. In the *Biblia Maria*, attributed for a long time to Albert the Great, the Blessed Virgin was Noah's ark, the dove that flew out from it, the olive branch the dove carried, and the rainbow of God's promise. She was the holy tabernacle of Isaiah, the throne of the incarnation of the son of God and the flowering rod of Jesse. She was every good woman mentioned in the Hebrew scriptures as well as the woman of John's revelation of the Apocalypse, groaning in travail, the moon beneath her feet and a crown of stars on her head. Mary was Eve redeemed, Wisdom, Mother of God, sister of men, bride of Christ, and the eternal Beloved.

Slowly over centuries the bronze figure of the woman in the centre of Rome was supplanted by the new queen of the City of God. Her public presence was every bit as monumental as that of the woman of bronze, but far from being an unwieldy mass of alloy she was as intimate as every man's soul. The Virgin's dual function as private belonging and public presence is the key to her power. For a glimpse of her more intimate face we turn to some of the opening stanzas of Walter's *Marie Carmina*. Acting as muse, Mary has appeared before the poet as he writes, placing the pen of her praise in the poet's modestly unwilling hand. He looks to her womb for inspiration:

Pausing for a moment, I raise my trembling eyes
To where the sacred belly of the Virgin lies;
I see the swelling, but no navel[8] can devise
and I wonder what source feeds the sealed vessel's rise.

Rising, I circle round the waist's purse bulging,
desiring to know how the vessel is holding
the sacred weight without compromising
either covering or seal, or fastening.

Wondering, again wondering at this miracle,
I discover a confessional, or cubicle
and finally, see something softly spherical
and hiding deep within, the deer celestial.

I walk, turning around the belly's little mound,
scarcely aware of the perfume rising around;
so breaking forth my tears and moans abound
and seeking the Virgin's foot again I sink down.[9]

Under Walter's gaze the Virgin is immobile; he imagines her as real, but she very well could be a statue, although in a private rather than public place. Her presence is signalled by a rising perfume, but the tears and the turning and falling are Walter's. This kind of affective piety is often identified, as I have said, with the Franciscans, but, in fact, devotional practice was highly articulated in the Middle Ages by more than one order. Hugh of Saint Victor, for example, distinguishes between meditation, a sort of linear problem-solving in his view, and contemplation, a holistic embrace of the divine presence.[10] Bernard of Clairvaux, a mystical writer whose sermons on Mary and the Song of Songs Walter knew very well, was Cistercian. Another Cistercian with a similar devotional temperament was Aelred, the famous twelfth-century abbot of Rievaulx in Yorkshire, who instructed his own cloistered sister in a method for the female celibate's spiritual development.[11] Sexual renunciation allows the contemplative to identify with the Virgin Mother in her life with Christ, he wrote. Aelred urged his sister to meditate on the past – the annunciation and conception, Christ's childhood, ministry and crucifixion – allowing her mind to engage with the narrative in order to bring the story home to her own soul in its present and future life. Mary is a complex figure who allows her devotee to stand with her in a number of different relationships: as sister and daughter, and through her to Christ as sister, daughter and lover. Walter's *Marie Carmina* is a poetic variation of this threefold meditation, but, as might be expected, the fact that its author is a man complicates his relationship with Mary. She is mother and sister but also beloved, as well as the beloved of both Christ and God the Father.[12] In stanzas 13 and 14, keeping his gaze fixed on the figure of Mary, Walter begins to experience the Virgin's conception of Christ:

Mary, you speak, for rivers of honey rushing
down from your lips are sweetly trickling
and with such a surging springs of milk are gushing
that in a sweet milky flood the world is drowning.

By this honey the lord is drawn down from heaven;
with this honey suckle to the father's son is given;
once sent, to the honey right away he's taken,
a kiss of honey from the honey to awaken.[13]

The sensual, indeed openly erotic language of these stanzas is not particular to Walter's sensibility. We might say that the libido has been transferred from a physical object of desire to the divine image. Medieval contemplatives would have no difficulty with that transference; the point of contemplation is to move available energy away from the physical by redirecting it towards a spiritual end. The source of the erotic language is the Song of Solomon: 'Your lips distill nectar, my bride; honey and milk are under your tongue.'[14] Bernard meditates on the bride's kiss in his second sermon on the Songs.[15] Walter, in his *Moral Treatise*, writes: 'A kiss is not given from afar; no one in Paris can give a kiss to one in Rome ... In a kiss there is contact and a joining of faces ... The one who contemplates must join his face to the divine face.' The contemplative, according to Walter, is a passionate lover who enters the *thalamus*, the bedchamber of the bridegroom.[16]

The female contemplative renounces sex with an earthly companion because she longs for her divine lover. She seeks him, opening herself to his embrace. The male contemplative, as a virgin, often identifies with the bride who seeks the bridegroom's kisses. Or, he may make the Virgin herself his beloved.[17] Either way, his ecstatic approach to the divine presence draws past and future into a transformative present; the future union in death of soul and God is subsumed in the present union of the virgin meditator with the Virgin Mediator.

In theory at least. Those, however, who have read medieval guides to mystical practice such as the anonymous *Cloud of Unknowing*[18] may doubt that 644 quatrains of rhythmical aesclepiads qualify as ecstatic union, the poet's claim to virginity notwithstanding. Fair enough: while the Middle Ages have left us manuals for the instruction of contemplation, and masterful sermons meant to inspire contemplation, the actual practice of the contemplative is incommunicable, being by its very nature a private communion between one soul and its Beloved. Walter's *Marie Carmina*, moreover, is neither manual nor sermon nor even hymn,[19] but rather a kind of metrical exploration of the territory and its themes. Indeed, repetition, rhythm, and metre seem to draw him into places he might never have ventured without the stanzaic form, which may, perhaps, have lulled him into thinking he was safe within its strictly limited boundaries. Certainly, his prose treatise shows none of the daring, even outrageous, tinkering with scriptural narrative that he demonstrates in his last extant poem. 'Be a child with child Jesus!' the

Pseudo Bonaventure urges the 'daughter' who is the reader of his meditations on the life of Christ.[20] Although it is unlikely Walter had read the *Meditations*, in *Marie Carmina* he plays at the feet of the Virgin Mother with often childlike naiveté.

In his groundbreaking study of children's play, Jean Piaget identified two poles of ego development – accommodation of the ego to reality and assimilation of reality to the ego. Imaginative play works towards both these ends. When a child plays with a doll, for example, she identifies with it as the object of various familiar and imagined experiences drawn from family life; but she also has mastery over it as, with the doll as subject, she relates these experiences from her own perspective.[21] Female mystics of the thirteenth century actually dressed life-sized baby dolls and laid them into cradles as part of the liturgy. They sometimes clothed themselves as brides when they went to receive the Eucharist.[22] These aids to worship must have helped the women both assimilate and accommodate themselves to the spiritual content of Christian doctrine as well as the reality of daily life in convents and beguinages.

Male contemplatives, like Walter, did not, as far as we know, play with dolls. Instead, some of them used language to tame the divine and bring themselves into the intimacy of play. In stanza 221 of the *Marie Carmina* Walter has seen the Magi come with their gifts, then leave:

Let others go home to their countries, I will stay,
our little boy in his cradle gently to sway;
those who wish let them leave; I will not go away
but will cling to the cradle by night and by day.[23]

Spoken aloud the Latin lines resonate with the rhythms of Dr Seuss. There is a kind of comfort in the repetition of the single rhyme and the sing-song metre that fits like an old and well-loved blanket. But what has become of Mary? Earlier I remarked that men sometimes identified directly with the Virgin Mother. In this scene Walter assumes the Virgin's point of view, looking over her shoulder as she offers her breast to the baby:

... I stay behind to see the breast which the Virgin
offers to her tiny wee little newborn son.

The tiny babe sits in his mother's lap secure
and now with moistened lips a kiss he offers her,
a dewy kiss sweetened with intimate mixture
of saliva sprinkling its sweet melting moisture.

> The infant's tiny body Mary is turning,
> now the cheeks, the mouth, now the tiny neck kissing,
> the hand, tiny arm, chest and back of the princeling,
> the thigh, tiny leg, foot and knee of the kingling.[24]

Walter's over-the-shoulder view participates in the pleasure of both the mother kissing and the child being kissed. Allow me to argue for a moment that for Walter the Virgin has become a kind of soul-doll, figuring in his personal devotion, in his approach, that is, to God, the way a doll a child has designated as 'Mommy' figures in the imagination of a pre-adolescent girl or boy, offering the child an opportunity to play at owning the adult woman's power over the child's body. Dolls, according to Piaget, 'are a symbolic construction with multiple functions which borrows its means of expression from the family but is by its content related to the whole life of the child.'[25] If we replace Piaget's 'family' with Roman Catholicism's Holy Family we can imagine that Walter's elaborately constructed praise of Mary allows him to minister to himself according to a whole range of possible needs created by past experiences and present circumstances, even as the stanzaic form of his poetry, with its overlapping images and repetitions, draws him into the future.

Before I comment further on the nature of the reality Walter is playing with in *Marie Carmina*, it is important to look more closely at the wardrobe of images Walter has available to him in his verbal doll-play. I have characterized Mary as a Mommy doll, but we have seen that she is also a lover with honey under her tongue. In fact, in her wealth of accessory images it is tempting to compare Mary to a Barbie doll with its pre-tailored, packaged, and labelled outfits for every imaginable occasion. Many children wish they were the owners of the full range of Barbie's wardrobe; Walter, writing squarely within the tradition of Marian devotion, has instant access to all of Mary's wealth. In fact, a glance at the contents of an encyclopedia of Marian praise – once again attributed to Albertus Magnus, but now believed to be the work of a canon at the Cathedral of Rouen, Richard of St Laurent[26] – reveals how richly elaborated are the costumes that support the enormous repertoire of Mary's roles. The headings alone of the Twelve Books of the *De laudibus Beatae Marie virginis* state that the Blessed Virgin was full of grace, without sin of intercourse, without pain of childbirth, at once mother and virgin. In the first several books the author establishes the Virgin's feminine form as exemplary, much the way the ripe proportions of Barbie establish an ideal of feminine maturation for the pre-adolescent girl or boy.[27] In Book Six, Richard indicates the relationships which are possible between the meditator and his mediator – she is mother, friend, sister, beloved, daughter, betrothed, wife, widow, good woman, virgin, strong woman (*virago*), and queen. In Book Seven, he establishes the extent of her realm – she is heaven, the firmament, sun, moon, horizon, morning star, dawn, daylight, morning, and day, as well as a cloud of protection from the sun's intensity. In Books Eight through Eleven, Richard attributes to Mary a collection of outfits and accessories appropriate to a complete presence on Earth, dressing her as field and stone, fountain and sea, temple, church, library, bedroom, fortress, ship and tavern – and that's merely to hint at her quick-change artistry. Finally, in Book Twelve, we arrive at the *hortus conclusus*, Eve's garden redeemed.[28] Most of these images are biblical; the exceptions are the library and the tavern. Leaving to Boethius the development of the library as an image of interior wealth,[29] I will consider Walter's conception of Mary as tavern.

In medieval Latin *taverna* is not just any shop but specifically a shop that sells wine. Stanzas 132–42 demonstrate what Walter does with the collection of accessories labelled *Maria taverna*:

Her belly's cask Maria has consecrated;
mortals, angels and shades be inebriated;
let the poor man along with the rich be invited,
to drain wine from that cask until he is sated.

The angelic throng from the belly's cask tipples,
drunk from it too are all the catholic peoples;
alone in despising it are Jewish pit-bulls –
excellent wine! they are oenephobic cripples.

To see the tavern close is excruciating;
so damn close and yet so far my hand is shaking;
I'm nowhere near paying what it costs for slaking
thirst with the likes of the wine the Virgin's making.

Desperate now, I'm within sight of Mary's store;
I open gaping wide my throat, so dry it's sore;
gasping internally I pound the tavern door –
one little drinkypoo or a teensy trickle more![30]

Walter indulges this alcoholic grovelling for another seven stanzas. Amplification was a more popular rhetorical device in Walter's day than it is in ours. In fact, at the beginning of the thirteenth century the rhetorician Geoffrey of Vinsauf wrote: 'If you choose an amplified form, proceed first of all by this step: although the meaning is one, let it not come content with one set of apparel. Let it vary its robes and assume different raiment.'[31] The power of the Virgin, I would suggest, comes to the contemplative through precisely these varied robes, manipulated in a playful combination of ego accommodation and assimilation. To our minds, perhaps, Walter gives away more than he gets at Mary's tavern, but by carefully inscribing his craving for drunken love in metrical verse he is subordinating undisciplined desire to purposeful repetition, the key to the contemplative project. We may believe from our particular temporal lookout that he is breaking one or another rule of decorum, but in fact Walter plays fair from start to finish. Once again the game metaphor is useful here since everyone is familiar with the endless diversionary tactics of the child's imaginative invitation 'let's just say.' 'Let's just say' allows the figure who one moment ago was exchanging honeyed kisses with the godhead to adopt in the next moment the attitude of a (somewhat discouraging) patroness of an English local.

Is the aging Franciscan celibate pining after a youth spent in the pub? This would be far too simplistic an interpretation to do justice to an extraordinary passage, and we do not know enough about Walter to guess at what meaning these stanzas contain for him. We must take him at his own word, that he craves Mary's potent wine. The tradition of mystical contemplation gives him ample room to express this craving, and while the eleven tavern stanzas of *Marie Carmina* are outrageous, they are by no means outside the pale. Peter Comester (d. 1179) describes Holy Scripture as 'God's dining room, where the guests are made soberly drunk' and also refers to the 'sober drunkenness' of the mystics.[32] Walter, it may be countered, seems susceptible as a poet more to the inebriating possibilities of rhyme and metre than to the mystical pleasures of scripture. However, within the next fifty or so stanzas he recovers and embarks on a more conventional, scripture-based 'let's just say,' for a while at least.

What Walter actually writes at the start of his narrative section of the poem is 'Pono quod reuocet Deus hoc tempora,' or, in Rigg's translation: 'Let us suppose that God brings back those times.'[33] Rigg notes that the abbreviated version of the poem that survives from the fourteenth century omits this stanza:[34] can it be that Walter's near-contemporary sensed the audacity of our poet's authorial manipulation of the deity? In any case, in the process of supposing the return of those times, Walter, naturally enough, imposes on them the structures of his Franciscan theology. One of the suggestions taken up in the thirteenth-century development of Marian devotion was that the two courts of divine Justice and Mercy were separately presided over by the ruling figures of Christ and Mary respectively.[35] The enormous popularity of the Greek legend of Theophilus, translated by Paul the Deacon of Naples in the ninth century, and increasingly retold in the West of the high Middle Ages, attests to the extent to which the division appealed to the imagination of the age. As the legend has it, clerical ambition drove Theophilus to sign a pact with the devil. Nonetheless, because of his continued devotion to the Virgin, when Theophilus died and the devil came to collect on his contract, Mary ripped up the signed document and released the sinner to heaven. To put the moral of the story in Piagetian terms: Christ, as a figure of justice, gets associated with his chief executive officer, the devil; both require the ego to accommodate to the reality of divine justice. Mary dismisses the devil and his consequences, allowing the ego to assimilate divine reality to its own terms of justice. This is not to say that the rules of the Marian game are so flexible as to become meaningless. Submission to the Lady can be exacting. In an earlier sequence of *Marie Carmina* Walter writes that inside Mary's womb the whips and scourges of the Old Testament God are transformed into 'a fiddle of rejoicing.'[36] In the passage below, the whips are returned, this time to the hand of Mary:

I will if you command go down on all fours as
your donkey; roll up the child's clothing and we'll pass
on our way, flying by night without a witness
so that the wicked enemy has no notice.

I am the donkey, so onto me now transfers
the Virgin's small weight and the little one that's hers;
if the brute should falter, then, Virgin, he deserves
that you goad with your heels, give him your bloodied spurs.

Should the beast falter and under the sweet weight trip
it's up to you to lash him, to prick and to grip
with the spurs; should he kick, unwilling to gallop
then punish the wretched little ass with your whip.

I am your ass, for whatever reason, freely
you may kill me, I'm your beast and property;
if when he's meant to run the ass walks unwillingly
why not plunge the spur into its side instantly?

With your sweet right hand, if the beast goes slow
snatch up the whip; you're the mistress, with thick strokes show
the wretched creature, till with bloody sides he knows
your sacred heels, and then again repeat the blows.[37]

The whips and scourges of God's judgments inflict pain; those wielded by the Virgin dominatrix seem rather to give pleasure.[38] In the first instance, Walter represents humanity as victims of divine wrath, whereas in the second, he is the Virgin's willing accomplice.

Johann Huizinga wrote that not only does play create order, 'it is order.' Play tests a player's prowess but also 'his spiritual powers – his "fairness"; because, despite his ardent desire to win, he must still stick to the rules of the game.'[39] The game of Our Lady has only one rule, and that is total devotion. But total devotion to the mother clashes with the threefold meditation in the two places in the New Testament where Jesus himself made a point of separating from his mother, first at the age of twelve and then at his death, aged thirty-three. These will therefore be crucial scenes for Walter. Indeed, when his narration follows the Holy Family to Jerusalem at Passover only to have the boy Jesus disappear, leaving his mother frantically searching for her lost child, Walter takes Christ to court, calling on the Father to act as the judge on behalf of higher justice and, in spite of the precocious boy's pretensions to divinity, to decide in Mary's favour:

On behalf of My Lady, Lord, I make my plea:
Let the judge of mercy and piety decree
Whether, free of the slightest criminality,
A woman should endure such pain and cruelty.

He will not use words against the Word but instead calls on the expressions of the mother's suffering as supporting witnesses:

The witness trembling at the stand with anxious eyes
is mother of a thousand tears, a thousand sighs;
and if I add a hundred thousand groaning cries,
see the crowd of people, a family uprise![40]

Walter wins his case and Christ is returned to his mother, but since the court has lasted three days, scriptural integrity is unaffected. Furthermore, Walter has reinforced the story of the crucifixion by creating a little allegory for the final return of the son following his three-day separation of Mary from her son at Calvary. Still, the fact that he has arranged for the outcome on his terms, with God the father acknowledging Walter's righteous indignation on the mother's behalf, is no small accomplishment. Walter has interpreted the hard things of his faith in a way he can live with. This repetition of the scriptural narrative with the purpose of its assimilation to the ego of the narrator is an important part of imaginative play.

We see this work of the ego again later in the poem in the midst of some rather conventional verses on human vanity. Walter may have held the Franciscan lector's chair at Cambridge for a term but likely spent most of his teaching life instructing schoolboys in the lowly basics of Latin grammar. It is one thing to submit to the Celestial Queen-Mother, quite another to tolerate a fellow human being, especially a colleague with a superior teaching post. Walter's treatment of the conventional topos of the vanity of human knowledge suggests that his nose has been put out of joint on more than one occasion during the course of his professional life. In a tenth-century Coptic text of ritual magic, the Creator is called upon to 'obliterate all the power of the adversary, / and make all his power become like the power of a gnat.'[41] In dealing with his own adversary, Walter gives an ironic twist to this curse, calling on the mysteries of the gnat to obliterate the power of his adversary:

I don't want to make a speech about the stars at all,
or set forth any topic that's celestial,
I wish to play instead with the smallest of the small
and seek what to the tiny gnat is natural.

The gnat with its sting first makes its incision,
drawing waves of blood into its inner region;
you've got two days to find out what constriction,
what little pipe or fissure gives the gnat suction.

Into its guts the gnat sucking delicately
draws thick blood; you from whom highest reality
cannot be hidden, nor deepest profundity,
unfold the ways lead by this fragile entity.

You know the source that causes the earthquake's motion,
and the ebb and flow of the waves of the ocean,
what's engendered by the mineral concoction;
look how easily stumped you are by my question.

You who blabber on, your empty words so risible
about heaven's spheres and stars inummerable;
tell me, I ask you, how with barely visible
conduits the gnat can make blood drinkable.[42]

Whatever the passage may suggest about the effect of the Aristotelian translations on the thirteenth-century project of science, its tone taps an undercurrent of self-righteous peevishness tugging at Walter's long-suffering humility. The Virgin-Mother doll may stand in for the highest Queen of Heaven, but she is tethered to the emotional complexities of the ordinary human being who manipulates her.

As Walter's poem approaches the defining moment of the Christian story, we are increasingly caught up in a drama that moves beyond the terms of an individual imagination while still retaining the stamp of that individuality. Piaget has remarked 'that every symbolic game, even if it is an individual game, sooner or later becomes a performance given by the child to an imaginary companion, and that every collective symbolic game, even the most highly organized, retains something of the ineffable which characterizes the individual symbol.'[43] It is instructive to recall that Walter probably died in the last decade or so of the thirteenth century and that in 1290 all Jews were expelled from England. The reader will have noticed, earlier in the *Maria taverna* passage, Walter's disparaging reference to the 'Jewish dogs' who lack an appreciation of good wine. Walter has his quibbles with scholars; he may even view them, in his everyday struggle, as the players. Jews, however, once insiders, have ruined the game; they're what Huizinga would call spoilsports:

The spoilsport is not the same as the false player, the cheat; for the latter pretends to be playing the game and, on the face of it, still acknowledges the magic circle. It is curious to note how much more lenient society is to the cheat than to the spoilsport. This is because the spoilsport shatters the play-world itself. By withdrawing from the game he reveals the relativity and fragility of the play-world in which he had temporarily shut himself with others. He robs play of its *illusion* – a pregnant word which means literally 'in-play' (from *inlusio, illudere* or *inludere*). Therefore he must be cast out, for he threatens the existence of the play-community.[44]

This is an apt description of Walter's relationship with 'Judeus.' Walter breaks his head against his presence; Judeus is the negation, if you will, of the longed-for reunion of mother and child. Nearly 150 stanzas of the *Marie Carmina* are devoted by Walter to venting his outrage against Judas, who for him represents all Jews. What wounds him most deeply is the failure of God to strike down the torturers of Mary's child:

Why not pay the Jewish wickedness a visit?
Why not smash them to pieces, bare your teeth a bit
that such barbarity might plunge into the pit
and the Styx swallow up the ruined aggregate?[45]

But, infuriatingly, God will not deploy the forces of his creation against the Jews as he once did against their enemies in the Old Testament. Walter summons the creation to Christ's aid in a battle against the assembly of Hell:

The army of Christ turns tail on its assurance
and when the four elements, who owe allegiance,
it's said, to Christ first, deny him their assistance,
the leader goes to battle with no alliance.

The soldier is terrified and gives way to the thug;
at least, let the flea come to give Christ some plug,
the locust and stinging wasp and whatever bug
helped to loosen the grip of the Egyptian hug.[46]

The cosmic battle he longs for fails to materialize, and when what does appear before his eyes instead is the 'hateful carpenter' of the 'gruesome woodwork' of the cross, Walter can no longer control himself. He's like a fan in the stands charging the referee who's made a call against the home team:

Tormented by my zeal's impetuosity
I rush on the man with too much velocity
and with his own hatchet for his atrocity
dispatch him swiftly to the Stygian nethercity.

To the worker, too, of the hatchet's artifice
by which the cross I see was made an edifice,
inflamed, hacking his neck in two, I dismiss
both vipers, handing them down to the black abyss.[47]

Walter curses the carpenter and the artisan who made the hatchet the carpenter has used. Then he curses the tools themselves, the fire and metal of the forge, and finally, the earth:

Cursed likewise the earth which gave the iron
that poured out streams of such pestiferous poison
from which the lethal material was drawn
by him who made the hatchet making carrion.

Why did the earth throw up this deadly fever?
Why did it open up a view of foul things? Why offer
no grave to the diggers but instead proffer
poison that best lies within earth's deepest coffer?[48]

The questions Walter asks are difficult ones. Why does the earth offer a view of foul things? Why, we might ask, does a child playing with a favourite doll occasionally subject it to violence? The answer to both sets of questions lies, I think, in the double nature of play as accommodation to and assimilation of reality, as well as the double nature of the mediating image as shared container of public expectation and projected personal content. I have said that the dual potencies of Mary's private and public presence are the key to her enormous influence. The internalized image, whether child's doll or contemplative's beloved, is the exact location where self and other meet. Why this intersection should become both bedchamber and battleground is a question poets often ponder. Walter's suffering, in the meantime, is made more acute by his conviction that both halves were once united:

The race of Jews Jesus was specially content
to choose that they receive from him sweet nutriment
as from his nurse a son; look how vile their intent
now to destroy the one who gave them nourishment![49]

Walter's poetry breathes the air of anti-Semitism.[50] His devotionally inspired, poetically articulated hatred serves as a reminder that empowerment is morally neutral; the same figure that enables Walter to come to terms with his faith also permits him to turn his rage against a people for whom his own nation has designated the role of spoilsport. Just how fraught with contradictions is that role is suggested by Walter's final desperate attempt to keep mother and child together:

Perfidious Jews, take Mary with the other,
and, with welcome execution, kill the mother;
into them both, I beg, pound the nails yet further
and both son and mother crucify together.

On one single cross let the mother and son
rejoice, embracing each other in unison,
let the fluids of the dear friends' blood mingled run,
let the dead stiffen into a single junction.[51]

His plea for the Virgin's sacrifice goes unheeded; the scriptures are already written and there is no 'let's pretend' to stave off the sentence of death and separation. Walter is forced at last to resign himself to the inevitable:

Wholeness languishes and life gives up the fight,
profound clarity turns into murky night,
extinguished is the inextinguishable light;
Not Isaac but the highest crown concedes its height.[52]

The time has come for him to give up his pen. True to his contemplative model, he humbly embraces the paradoxes of the crucifixion and accepts his own mortality. Mary's unbroken body still stands above him; to her he addresses his final request:

O gate of heaven, open what's been locked away,
and when your servant's dressed in funeral array,
grant him be your footstool so that your feet you may,
one on his mouth, the other on his forehead lay.[53]

From our perspective at the far side of a century much given to psychoanalysis, we have, no doubt, some insights that were unavailable to Walter. Regardless of how we interpret his devotion, however, in working through the familiar story so thoroughly and so honestly, Walter provides us with a glimpse into the remarkable complexities of one thirteenth-century male soul. Whipped, no doubt, as a young child, and in turn the 'whip' of his small students, he rages against his experience of divine and human justice by execrating the spoilsport Jews. Not an exemplary but, in the final analysis, an unavoidably ordinary individual afflicted by all-too-human passions and disappointments, the aging Franciscan celibate stands before us, a mirror of our own cultural beginnings. Humble and arrogant by turn, Walter delights in the sensual possession of a feminine figure, a presence who is not the tawdry fallen Eve of passing pleasure but the bride of Christ, as beautiful as the rising sun and as terrible as an army. In his final stanzas the Virgin remains, like an old man's heart, as mysterious as the universe:

This work I offer to the boys to read;
may their prayers commend me in my final peace
to the boy child late from the tender womb released,
born from the father's womb before the dawning's east.

Here ignorance makes an end to the paper scrap;
here confusion of the senses makes a gap;
around you, heavenly lady, all glory wrap;
around you, lady, uncharted praises map.[54]
Amen.

NOTES

1 For the sleuth work behind this paragraph, see Rigg (1971) and Townsend (1986). I will refer to the *Ave Virgo Mater Christi* as *AV* and the *Marie Carmina* as *MC*. The translations are mine unless otherwise noted. In an attempt to capture the flavour of the original I have erred on the side of colloquialism.

2 The complete poems of Walter of Wimborne have been edited by Rigg (1978) with excellent notes and introduction. All of the poetry quoted in this article comes from this Latin edition. These phrases are from *MC*, stanzas 23 and 38, and *De Palpone*, 168. The *Marie Carmina* is in Oxford, Bodleian Library, MS Laud misc. 368, fols. 2034-216r.

3 '... cum maiestatem Romane vrbis principes visibili specie censerunt honorandam, exquisito artificio formam muliebrem, que orbem dextra continet, in eris materia fieri studuerunt. Ea perfecta in forma egregia, quidam solas [tibias] tante moli perferende inhabiles esse causati sunt. Quibus faber respondit: Eas vsquequaque sufficere donec virgo pareret, impossibilem credens virginis partum.' Kirkwood (1988, 36–7). The word *tibias* is missing from the manuscript and is supplied by the editor from the text of John of Salisbury, whose earlier telling of the story Walter is quoting. A variation of the story is told by Jacobus de Voragine in *The Golden Legend* (1993, 38–9).

4 'Quod in Christo nato impletum est, ea corruente et fracta.'

5 Smalley (1960, 50).

6 Rigg (1978, 6).

7 'Ave, uirgo gloriosa / que comentum es et glosa / scripture prophetice, / cuius glosa facit nudum / quod uelatum erat dudum / literali cortice' (*AV* 3).

8 'Neuulum,' literally 'flaw.'

9 'Cum pausam facio, trementem oculum / ad sacrum uirginis levo ventriculum; / tumorem uideo sed nullum neuulum; / mirror quo tumeat intactum uasculum. // Surgens circueo uentralem sacculum / nosse desiderans quale pondusculum / uas sacrum teneat, quod nec operculum / nec seram perdidit neque signaculum. // Miror et iterum miror miraculum; / lustrum inuenio siue cubiculum, / tandem inspiciens unum molliculum / et intus celicum latentem hinnulum. // Giro perambulo uenteris monticulum / uix fere senciens dulcem odorculum; / prorumpens igitur in luctum querulum / descendo uirginis reuisens pedulum' (*MC* 9–12).

10 Astell (1990, 78).

11 In his *Rule of Life for a Recluse* (Aelred of Rievaulx [1971]). There is a rich alternative tradition of female-authored spirituality in the twelfth and especially thirteenth centuries using Christ's body as the focus of meditation, the body typically gushing with blood rather than the Virgin's milk. For an

excellent discussion of women mystics and Christ's body see 'The Body of Christ in the Later Middle Ages,' in Bynum (1992, 79–117).
12 Even Freud sometimes has difficulty sorting out the 'object of desire' and the 'object of identification.' See, for example, his analytical contortions in 'A Case of Homosexuality in a Woman' in Freud (1979, esp. 380–6). For a discussion of the underlying difficulty of desire and identification in Freudian theory see Borch-Jacobsen (1994).
13 'Maria, loquere nam tua labia / torrentes mellios sunt distillancia / tantoque gurgite lac resudancia / quod mundus mergitur in lactis copia. // Hoc melle dominus de celo trahitur; / hoc melle filius patris allicitur; / statim ad melculum missus dirigitur / et mellis osculum a melle petitur' (*MC* 13–14).
14 Song of Solomon 4.11.
15 Bernard of Clairvaux (1952, 25–8).
16 Kirkwood (1988, 22).
17 The variations of human relationship with the divine bridegroom are, one suspects, endless. The most famous example of a woman who wedded 'the Godhead' is Margery Kempe. She recounts the experience in chapter 35 of her early fifteenth-century autobiography. Hermann Joseph (c. 1150 to 1241) was a clockmaker who, according to art historian Carolyn D. Muir (2000–1, 51–69), entered the monastery at Steinfeld (not far from Cologne) and spent most of his life there, apparently after having consummated a marriage with Mary. While it is not clear that Margery identified with Mary in her marriage with Christ, Hermann took on the name of Joseph after his wedding, suggesting he had appropriated Joseph's role.
18 Anonymous (1961).
19 Its title, assigned by Rigg and later regretted by him, comes from the first line of the poem, actually a reference to a previous work, not likely the Victorine sequence, 'Ave Virgo Mater Christi,' which does not fit the description 'carmina exametra,' but another poem that has been lost to us.
20 Pseudo Bonaventure (1961, 75). Current scholarship has moved the date of composition of the *Meditations* from the thirteenth to the fourteenth century, attributing them to John of Caulibus (see McNamer 1990). A recent Latin edition of the work is in Iohannis de Caulibus (1997).
21 Piaget (1962, 107).
22 Bynum (1992, 198).
23 'Illi repatrient, ego remaneo / et nostrum paruulum in cunis cilleo; / qui uolunt, abeant; ego non abeo, / sed cunis perdius pernox adhereo' (*MC* 220).
24 '... ego remaneo uisurus ubera / que profert paruulo uirgo puerpera. // Sedet infantulus in matris gremio / et offert osculum humecto labio, / quod quidem osculum indulcat mixtio / saliue tenuis et deguttacio. // Maria paruuli girat corpusculum, / nunc genas osculans, nunc os, nunc collulum, / manus,

brachiola, pectus, dorsiolum, / latus et crustula, pedem, geniculum' (*MC* 221, 223, 229). Rigg glosses 'crustula' as the diminutive of 'crus.' It can also be a little pastry. To give the effect of the Latin diminutives, and to save the rhyme scheme, I have introduced 'princeling' and 'kingling' into the translation of stanza 229, since 'backling' and 'kneeling' would only confuse.

25 Piaget (1962, 107).
26 Pseudo Albertus Magnus (1884). For an account of the attribution of authorship to Richard of St Laurent see Chatillon (1946).
27 There is only anecdotal evidence that boys, as much as girls, have been influenced by the Barbie figure, which, after all, is only a commercially produced plastic representation of a cultural ideal shared by men and women alike. In Walter's day the evidence that women 'played' with Jesus, men with Mary, is overwhelming. Julian of Norwich's *Showings* is an important example of the first. Bynum's (1982 and 1992) research touches on the division of devotion along gender lines.
28 Pseudo Albertus Magnus (1884, 843–9).
29 In Book 1, Prose 5 of the *Consolation,* Philosophy dismisses the prisoner's elaborately appointed library, claiming instead a place in his mind 'in qua non libros, sed id, quod libris pretium facit, librorum quondam meorum sententias collocavi' (O'Donnell 1990, 16).
30 'Maria dolium uentris iniciat, / mortales, celicos et manes debriat; / pauper cum diuite secure ueniat, / de uentris dolio quantum uult hauriat. // De uentris dolio potantur celici, / potantur etiam omnes catholici; / hoc uinam nobile Judei canici / soli despiciunt, sunt enim rustici. // Ue michi misero! Tavernam uideo / et uentris dolium, sed tamen doleo; / non enim precium condignum habeo / quo frui merear uino uirgineo. // Marie dolium dolens aspicio, / hiulcans aridas fauces aperio; / cauponam intimo pulso suspirio / ut fruar uinuli uel stillicidio' (*MC* 132–5).
31 Geoffry of Vinseuf (1967).
32 Smalley (1964, 242 n. 3).
33 Rigg (1978, 185). In the notes for the stanza at p. 221 n. 216 he writes 'I posit that God brings back those times'; i.e. 'let's pretend').
34 British Library, MS Cotton Titus A.xx, saec. 14ex., fols 171v2–175r2, which provides a version of *Marie Carmina* in 144 stanzas.
35 For a brief but useful account of this development see Graef (1963) 64. For its literary expressions, see the entry 'Four Daughters of God' in *A Dictionary of Biblical Tradition in English Literature* (Jeffry 1992, 290–1).
36 'Antiqus paruulus effectus ferulam / e manu proecit et trucem uirgulam; / sic planctus uertitur in plausus [viulam], meror in canticum, nox in dieculam' (*MC* 38). Rigg offers the lovely 'a fiddle of rejoicing' as a translation for 'in plausus viulam.'

37 'Uolo, si iubeas, asellum sternere / et paucos pueri pannos conuoluere, / et caute uolumus de nocte fugere, / ne possit impius hostis aduertere. // Ego sum asinus; mihi sarcinula / debetur uirginis cum prole paruula; / si pecus cespitat, tu uirgo uirgula / cede calcaribus, cruenta stimula. // Si pecus cespitat dulci sub onere / tuum est cedere, tuum est pungere; / si forte calcitret nolens procedere, / castiga miserum asellum uerbere. // Tuus sum asinus, ergo me libere / ut pecus proprium potes occidere; / si non uult asinus ut placet currere, / cur non uis lateri ferrum immergere? // Si pecus lentum est, dulci tu dextera / flagellum arripe crebroque uerbera / miscellam bestiam, cruenta latera / sacratis calcibus, et ictus itera' (*MC* 235, 238–41).

38 An interesting parallel to this is Jean-Jacques Rousseau's account of the development of his sexual proclivities in Book I of his *Confessions*.

39 Huizinga (1967, 10).

40 'Appello, domine, pro mea domina: / decernat pietas si debet femina / quam nulla faciunt ream peccamina / tot mala perpeti, tot cruciamina. // Testis que titubat est mater anxia / milleque lacrime, mille suspiria; / addo gemituum centena milia; / en quantus populus, quanta familia!' (*MC* 287, 292).

41 Meyer (1994, 328).

42 'Nolo de sidere sermonem facere / nec de celestibus quicquam obicere, / sed uolo paruulus in paruis ludere, / et parui culicis naturam querere. // Culex aculeo forat articulam, / in se trahiciens cruoris undulam; / queso, perhendie dic per quam canulam / uel per quam rimulam uel per quam fistulam? // Cruorem turbidum culex in uiscera / sugendo trahicit; tu quem nec supera / latere poterunt, immo nec infera, / subtilis explica ductus itinera. // Scis unde prodeat terrarum mocio, / fluctus equorei reciprocacio, / que mineralia gignat decoctio, / et ecce facilis artat te questio! // Tu qui deblateras uerbis inanibus / de celi circulis et de sideribus, / dic, queso, quomodo uix uisibilibus / cruorem attrahit culex canalibus' (*MC* 392–6).

43 Piaget (1962, 109).

44 Huizinga (1967, 11).

45 'Cur non Judaicum scelus increpitas? / Quare non dissilis, quare non oscitas / ut petat baratrum tanta crudelitas / et Stix excipiat cateruas perditas?' (*MC* 488).

46 'In fugam uertitur Christi milicia / et mundi quatuor dicta principia / que debent denegant Christo suffragia, / et dux soliuagus uadit ad prelia. // Formidant milites et cedunt furie, / saltem subueniant Christo cinomie, / brucus et ciniphes et musce uarie,/que terre fuerant onus Egipcie' (*MC* 531–2).

47 'Cum zeli crucior impaciencia, / in carpentarium ruo ui nimia, / cesumque miserum securi propria / mitto celeriter ad regna Stigia. // Fabro similiter qui securiculam / fecit, qua fieri cerno cruciculam, / accensus animo cedo ceruiculam, / utramque baratro tradens aspidulam' (*MC* 536–7).

48 'Ue terre pariter, que ferrum dederat / que tam pestiferum uirus effuderat / de

qua materiam letalem sumpserat / is qui letiferam securim fecerat! // Cur terra noxium uirus euomuit? / Cur fodientibus hiando paruit? / Cur non fossoribus sepulcrum prebuit? / Cur non profundius hoc uirus posuit?' (*MC* 540–1).

49 'Genus Judaicum peculialiter / Jesus elegerat et fouit dulciter/ut nutrix filium, et ecce qualiter / suum nutricium occidit uiliter!' (*MC* 580).

50 The racialization of the Jews was well underway in England following the Fourth Lateran Council of 1215. See Roth (1978).

51 'Judei perfidi, Mariam prendite, / cum dulci pignore matrem occidite, / eisdem, obsecro, clauis confodite / matrem et filium et crucifigite. // Mater et filius eandem habeant / crucem ut mutuo complexu gaudeant; / amici sanguinis liquores misceant, / in uno stipite defuncti rigeant' (*MC* 595, 597).

52 'Languiscit sanitas et uita moritur, / profunda claritas in noctem vertitur, / inextinguibile lumen extinguitur; / non tamen Ysaac sed uertex ceditur' (*MC* 636).

53 'O celi ianua, tu celum aperi / tuumque famulum cum datur funeri / fac tuis pedibus scabellum fieri, / os uni subice, frons detur alteri' (*MC* 639).

54 'Hoc opus pueris legendum offero; / illi me precibus commendent puero / qui sero prodiit de uentre tenero / ante luciferum de patris utero. // Hic finem cartule facit inscicia, / hic metam uendicat sensus aporia; / sit tibi, domina celorum, gloria, / sit tibi, domina, laus mete nescia. Amen' (*MC* 643–4).

8

Christ from the Head of Jupiter: An Epistemological Note on Huet's Treatment of the Virgin Birth

THOMAS LENNON

The birth of Christ from a Virgin Mother can be read as belonging to the Classical tradition of the miraculous birth of Minerva from the head of Jupiter, or of heroes like Perseus or Heracles born of mortal women but fathered by gods. This claim was made by a major thinker of the early modern period, Pierre-Daniel Huet, who was challenging the empirical approach to the virgin status of the mother of Christ. With his claim, which linked Christ's miraculous birth to a tradition supplied by pagan narratives, Huet entered the arena of intellectual debate that flourished in the age of Enlightenment. In a climate of empiricism, virginity was identified as a physiological state capable of verification, consistent with belief systems of earlier centuries when various forms of testing were applied to a virgin's claim of sexual innocence. Huet anticipates the modern anthropological and psychoanalytical approaches to truth claims by basing the truth of the virginity of Mary in accumulated theological dogma and belief.

The epistemology of virginity is an exceedingly interesting question from a historiographical perspective. How did people think they could establish virginity? An even more interesting question is what they thought they were doing by this. The status of the concept of virginity – among other concepts that were religiously charged – was dramatically altered by biblical studies in the early modern period. Prior to the higher criticism of the seventeenth century, virginity was taken to be a brute physiological fact relatively easy to verify, whose significance, even if obviously transcending the physical, was transparent. Consider the fourth-century St Ambrose, whose works on virginity were translated into French as late as 1729: 'a virgin who is not immediately recognized as such is not worthy of the name.'[1] At the end of the period discussed here, Pierre Bayle, to whom the significance of nothing was transparent and who therefore does not accept the reports of Democritus's ability to determine virginity by external signs, nonetheless devotes one of his famously long footnotes to a discussion of the topic and includes a report of the same ability in Albertus Magnus.[2]

To make the case that this epistemological complacency, its naive acceptance of virginity as physically verifiable, was first undone in the seventeenth century would require more resources than can be mounted here. But if it is at all plausible to suggest this thesis at least as a reading hypothesis, or even as a research program, then a key figure will be Pierre-Daniel Huet, whose views on the Virgin Birth construed the concept of virginity in unprecedented terms. Huet was a committed antiquarian and just as committed to the idea that the knowledge of truth depended upon some tradition. He rejected the Cartesian position that any epistemological project begins *de novo*, and in this Huet made the Classical tradition acceptable. In reading this tradition allegorically, he was anticipated to some degree by the hermetic and Neo-Platonic schools, but with Huet this epistemological approach was established with security. Without difficulty, Huet accepted the Virgin Birth but gave it – or at least invited his reader to give it – a non-physical interpretation. And he does so (necessarily, as we shall see) in a self-conscious fashion, arguing for its theological validity. In his view, previous treatments of the Virgin Birth that were heavily invested with mythological, moral, political, and other kinds of overlay rendered them theologically invalid by rooting them in the past. Huet instead brings forward the fact of a pagan tradition of miraculous births to argue for the validity of Christ's birth from a virgin. Previously, not to accept the Virgin Birth as physically true was simply to reject it as false. Because of Huet's authority as an intellectual and as a religious leader his orthodoxy was never questioned, and the influence of his novel alternative may have been considerable.

Though far from being unknown in his own time, Huet has for a number of reasons slipped into relative oblivion, so he will first need to be identified. Then, the Bible criticism that was the philosophical context for his work will be outlined, and three figures of particular importance here will be highlighted: Isaac La Peyrère, Spinoza, and Richard Simon. Finally, it will be suggested that in Huet is found the earliest attempt to understand the Virgin Birth in something like modern anthropological terms. Indeed, there will be data to suggest a proleptic reading of it in terms even of Jungian archetypes. If anything of this is at all plausible, then not only the concept of virginity, but the significance of the previous sorts of physical testing for it, will have undergone a dramatic alteration in this period. For, to repeat the main epistemological point, although Huet introduces a non-literal concept of virginity that for him had wide application in a variety of domains, he took that concept to be true of the Blessed Virgin in a way that secured the truth of the relevant Church dogma. To put it in simplest terms, the suggestion from Huet is that the truth of the Virgin Birth is not a physiological question but a theological question.

Pierre-Daniel Huet (1630–1721) was an erudite, perhaps a rather lesser Scaliger (and thus a friend and correspondent of Leibniz, himself a rather greater Scaliger). He was a polyglot, his linguistic competence including 'oriental languages,' which is to say Hebrew in addition to Greek, and his having read the Bible in the original languages twenty-four times. He was a member of the French Academy, charged along with Bossuet with the instruction of the Dauphin. Ordained in 1678, he received the Abbey of Aulnay two years later and, in 1692, was consecrated Bishop of Avranches (under which title he came most usually to be known). But health problems and the incompatibility of episcopal duties with his scholarly interests led him first to the Abbey of Fontenay and then to the Paris house of the Jesuits, his first teachers, where he spent the rest of his life. A condition for his pension there was the bequest to them of his huge library (the story has it that its weight once brought the walls down around him); when the Jesuits were expelled from France in 1763, this collection passed to the royal library, thence to the Imperial Library, and finally the National Library, all of whose stamps, in addition to Huet's *ex libris* coat of arms, have been seen by many generations of seventeenth-century scholars who have used the collection. Especially earlier in his life, he was very interested in the sciences. He founded an important academy of sciences in Caen in 1662. He was led to a study of astronomy by Huygens's work and was also interested in anatomy and chemistry, although the most notable result of his work in chemistry is a rather Paracelsan 122-hexameter poem in Latin on salt. He has been credited with the invention of the anemometer. In addition to those to be discussed here, his works include books on translation, the origin of the novel, the location of the Garden of Eden (between the junction of the Tigris and Euphrates, and the Persian Gulf), a history of trade, a certain amount of poetry, and a novel (the posthumous *Diane Castro, ou le Faux Yucab*). There is also a delightful, if not always reliable, set of memoirs.

Huet tells us in his memoirs that as a youth, before he had studied ancient philosophy, he 'belonged for several years body and soul to Cartesianism.'[3] It is not clear what changed his mind, but in time Huet came to be one of Cartesianism's bitterest and, perhaps, most effective opponents. While investigating the relation between reason and faith, he argued in a series of works a kind of skeptical fideism that saw in Descartes's attempt to arrive at absolute certainty by reason alone a threat to religion that was in bad faith in at least two senses of the expression.⁴ Very roughly, the thrust is that Descartes is an arrogant pretender, whose views if taken seriously would upset the only basis for living, which is religious faith. This opposition to Descartes is something of an irony, for Cartesian methodology may well have been the initial basis for the higher criticism that was the context for Huet's own apologetics.

Popkin traces the new Bible criticism to mid-century and the application of Descartes's method of clear and distinct ideas to the authentication and interpretation of Scripture, beginning with the work of Isaac La Peyrère, who was led to deny that the existing text was authentic, that the Bible was the framework for human history, and that Moses was the author of the Pentateuch.⁵ La Peyrère's arguments and even his new linguistic methods are here of less interest than his conclusions. For a while there had been critical debates right from the first attempts to establish canonicity, even to the point of accusations of atheism over disagreement. None had resulted in views so extreme as these. The same is true in the next decade of the works of Spinoza, whom La Peyrère may have influenced. For him, a biblical view at odds with reason – even if it was of interest historically, psychologically, philologically, and so forth – was *ipso facto* false. La Peyrère was a Calvinist who was ultimately hounded into recanting his views and converting to Catholicism; the fate of Spinoza was no better. Employing the same sorts of arguments and methods, however, the Oratorian Richard Simon in the next decade was rather more clever and enjoyed a much better fate.⁶ To be sure, he was expelled from the Oratory and his seminal *Histoire critique du Vieux Testament* (1679) was placed on the Index of Forbidden Books, but he was allowed to continue exercising his priestly offices and (more importantly here) to go on publishing his works of criticism, despite denying the Mosaic authorship of the Pentateuch, for example. Unlike Spinoza, in any case, he seems never to have admitted to heterodoxy of any sort.

One of the credentials Simon presented is of particular interest. In the preface to the *Histoire critique* he underlines his adherence to ecclesiastical tradition, its powers of validation: 'It will be shown in the pages which follow, that, if the rule of law is divorced from the rule of fact, in other words, if the Scriptures are unaccompanied by Tradition, one can be sure of scarcely anything in religion. It is in no way to derogate from the Word of God to associate with it the Tradition of the Church, since he who bids us search the Scriptures has bidden us also to betake ourselves to the Church, to whom he confided the sacred treasure.'⁷ This necessary appeal to tradition in the authentication and interpretation of Scripture was, of course, the principal argument levied against Protestantism and likely explains why Simon was accorded a measure of relative toleration by the Church. Huet's step, however, was much more radical, for he appealed to all traditions.

Huet declares in the *Alnetanae quaestiones de concordia rationis et fidei* that what is known by reason through evidence is asserted with greater certainty and strength than what is known by faith.[8] This is a rather startling declaration, for it seems to assert the very Cartesianism he was concerned to overthrow. But by 'evidence' Huet does not mean what Malebranche meant by the term, or what Descartes meant by clarity and distinctness – that is, a property of eternal truth available to individual minds divorced from history, experience, and even their own bodies – all of which are for Malebranche and Descartes impediments to the apprehension of truth. For Huet's notion of evidence we look to an earlier work, the *Demonstratio evangelica*: 'Evidence is the criterion of belief; we thus call true what seems true to the greatest number, or at least to the greatest number of the learned; the more a thing is generally believed, the more its truth is obvious ... Cicero got it right when he said, general agreement is the voice of nature.'[9] Huet doesn't draw the inference in so many words, but the upshot is that for him belief in the Virgin Birth *if true, cannot be an isolated phenomenon*, and that it is not is precisely what he attempts to show.

The *Alnetanae quaestiones* is divided into three books. In the first, Huet argues the value of reason to faith. In the third, he offers a comparison of Christian and pagan morality. The second book consists of comparisons of Christian and pagan beliefs. Some of the comparisons border on the outrageous: Orestes because of his matricide given over to the Furies is parallel to Job delivered to the demon; Jupiter's delaying the arrival of dawn so as to spend an extended night with Alcmena is parallel to Joshua's halting the sun. One of the twenty-four chapters in the second book deals with the Virgin Birth and compares this with extraordinary births in the Classical mythical tradition. He begins as follows. 'Are we now any less able to say and believe that Christ was born of a virgin than the Greeks were able to say that Minerva was born of the head of Jupiter and Bacchus from his thigh, and Orion from three fathers, Jupiter, Neptune and Mercury without any female role, that Erichthonius was born of Vulcan without mother, that Vulcan and Mars were born of Juno without father? Many were born of a mortal woman by gods and, by the same miracle, of a mortal father by goddesses.'[10] According to Huet, then, there were widespread beliefs in miraculous births that were no less credible than, and justified belief in, Christ's virgin birth.

The reception of this work was controversial. Arnauld, for one, despised it. Huet 'destroys his own religion' by showing paganism to be no less reasonable than Christianity.[11] The abbé Houtteville later showed how the argument might be stood on its head: because the pagan analogues were absurd, incredible, less than serious, not intended to be taken as true, and so forth; therefore the same is true of the Christian analogues.[12] The charge against Huet was what was called indifferentism: the choice of religion is one of indifference, for one is as good as another. Whether applicable to him or not, Huet certainly was optimistic about the possibility of reconciliation among Christian sects. 'If the parties act with sincerity, without stubbornness and self-interest, they would soon find ways to reconcile; but on both sides there are such hotheads that they censure no less strongly their own members who advocate conciliation than they do their opponents.'[13] By contrast, then, the work was favourably received by the Huguenot Menjot, even if not by all of his co-religionists (Basnage criticized the work, in the *Histoire des ouvrages des savants* for June of 1691, as based on an imagination gone out of control).

In the nineteenth century, Huet's work was still able to evoke outraged protest. Here is Joseph d'Avenel, whose text summarizes the rest of Huet's catalogue of virgin births and, not incidentally, indicates the range of his scholarship:

Frankly, because ... Alexander, Remus, Romulus, Achilles, Aratus, Hercules, Inachus, were all the fruit of the union between a god and a mortal; because antiquity gave virgins as mothers to Perseus, Homer and Plato; because the magician Simon dared to claim himself the son of a virgin; because among the Turks those whose mothers are said to remain virgins are called 'soulsons'; because Avicenna and Paracelsus dreamed that below the equator the earth or the sun give birth to men; because Ulanus among the Tartars, and Buddha and Somonocodon among the Indians, are regarded as sons of a virgin; because among the Chinese the rainbow introduces Fohi; because some Buddhist priest in Japan claims to be the son of a virgin and some exceedingly credulous men attribute the same origin to Merlin; because of all this we are able to conclude nothing in favor of the great miracle that made the Blessed Virgin the mother of Christ![14]

Huet's response to his critics was to accuse them of ignorance, prejudice, and failure to read his book. 'Unfortunately for them, Justin Martyr in two places made use of the same comparison as mine [between the Incarnation of Christ and the birth of Perseus]; these sorts of comparisons and arguments are common among the Church Fathers.'[15] Once again, Huet's point is that it is entirely legitimate to appeal to pagan sources, even mythographical ones, in order to mobilize an argument based upon *consensus gentium*, to support Christian doctrines. However seriously Huet intended this sort of argument, its significance here is the concept of virginity that he self-consciously employs in it. First, it must be understood that Huet is no *naïf*. One of the sciences in which he was most interested in his early career was anatomy, with hands-on experience in dissection.[16] Whatever his experience with human anatomy, he cannot have been ignorant about the physiology of virginity. Nor can he have been claiming that hymens in the physiological sense were miraculously preserved all over antiquity, mythical or otherwise. What, then, was the meaning that Huet attached to the concept of virginity?

The more relevant question here is what he detached from it. The question of the Virgin Birth, to take the key example, is not one to be decided on the basis of gynecological data, even if such existed, from the Middle East two millennia ago. Instead, it is a question to be examined in light of certain texts as interpreted by a certain tradition. Huet's contribution lay in his appeal to texts and traditions beyond those expected of a seventeenth-century bishop of unquestioned orthodoxy, whose very orthodoxy validated a novel concept of non-physical virginity.

NOTES

1. Ambrose (1729, 128).
2. Bayle (1701), art. 'Democritus, rem. C'.
3. Huet (1718, 35–6). I give an English translation of the influential French translation cited in all the literature, which, however, is not quite supported by the original Latin text.
4. Huet (1679, 1689, 1690, 1692, 1723).
5. Popkin, in Lennon et al. (1982, 61–81).
6. For a discussion of Simon's subversion of authority, see Hazard (1990).
7. Ibid., 189. For the law (*droit*)/fact (*fait*) distinction, see Lennon (1999, chap. 2).
8. Huet (1690, 87–9).
9. Huet (1679, preface) (unpaginated).
10. Huet (1690, 237).
11. Arnauld (1775–83, 400–2).
12. Flottes (1857, 204–6).
13. Ibid. 44–5. Only Spinoza and Toland were beyond the pale. Huet evidenced a generally latitudinarian skepticism that one thinks of in connection with La Mothe-Le Vayer, for example, who opened the gates of heaven to at least certain pagan philosophers, or Bayle, who famously found (pagan) atheism less problematic than (Christian) heresy.
14. Avenel (1853, 215–16).
15. Flottes (1857, 208).
16. Tolmer (1949).

9

'Sew and snip, and patch together a genius': Quilting a Virginal Identity in Margaret Atwood's *Alias Grace*

ANNE GEDDES BAILEY

Near the end of Margaret Atwood's *Alias Grace*, Simon Jordan dreams of a dissection he must perform for his medical examination:

> It's a woman, under the sheet; he can tell by the contours ...
>
> But under the sheet there's another sheet, and under that another one. It looks like a white muslin curtain. Then there's a black veil, and then – can it be? – a petticoat. The woman must be down there somewhere; frantically he rummages. But no; the last sheet is a bed sheet, and there's nothing under it but a bed. That, and the form of someone who's been lying here. It's still warm. (422)

Bedding – good linen sheets, second-best sheets 'cut in two and turned' (138), and thick, warm, well-crafted quilts – abounds throughout the pages of *Alias Grace*. The plethora of sheets and quilts suggests that Simon's dream of the veiled female body which lies forever hidden under layers of bedding is a crucial one to the novel as a whole. Indeed, we might argue that the image is the novel's governing metaphor, not only of the sexual and psychological enigma of Simon Jordan's patient, Grace Marks, but also of the very shape of her narrative and of the omniscient narrator's additions which frame it. Just as Simon draws away bed sheet after bed sheet in search of the woman's hidden body in this dream, the reader turns sheet after sheet of paper in hopes of uncovering the mystery at the heart of Grace Marks and her story. And, like Simon, we are ultimately frustrated in our attempt since instead of a body under the layers of narrative, we find only traces of her presence.

This approach to the novel complements Margaret Rogerson's article 'Reading the Patchworks in *Alias Grace*.' Also noting the important function of bedding in the novel, she contends that quiltmaking is the central thematic and structural metaphor of the novel. Rogerson situates the novel within the 'cultural and literary history of patchwork'[1] and shows how Atwood's novel mimics the process of quilting. By doing so, she brings into focus the ways in which quilting has long served women, in particular, as a venue for both sharing and preserving female secrets. In the case of Grace, Rogerson argues that quiltmaking 'empowers Grace to speak in language that is not universally accessible' and 'enables her to withhold her secrets from her male inquisitor ... as [she] attempts to recover her lost memories.'[2] Although quilts are often communally made and the art of quiltmaking one which most nineteenth-century women pursued, Rogerson also reminds us that the actual manifestation of any pattern is coloured, framed, and arranged by the individual quilter, and thus the meaning of any quilt is ultimately inscrutable. Likewise, the meaning of the story which Grace stitches together over the course of her conversations with Simon and the patchwork history of the novel as a whole remain frustratingly elusive. While Rogerson's article focuses on the social and feminist meanings of quilting and their implications for Grace's story, I am more interested in the metaphorical implications of Atwood's quilting framework for the psycho-sexual dimensions of Grace's identity and Simon's attempts to uncover it. Grace not only spends her days stitching various pieces of fabric together; she also pieces together her memories, a process which, like a quilt, appears to reveal her inner self but in reality re-veils it.

The search for and the inscrutability of the self are common themes in Margaret Atwood's other works as well. As Eleanor Rao notes, 'the presence of doubles, encounters between the self and other, bodily transformations and metamorphosis in Atwood's novels posit the question of identity as a recurring concern.'[3] Not surprisingly, then, *Alias Grace* returns to these concerns. When Mary Whitney suddenly speaks from the mouth of Grace Marks near the end of the novel, it seems that our heroine has subconsciously incorporated the spirit of her beloved friend into her own and is now divided between the two personalities. Literally imprisoned by her society, which judges her guilty of murder, and figuratively damned by the numerous reports of her barely suppressed criminality and uncontrolled mad outbursts, Grace, it seems, can only escape by turning within. That she would need to do so suggests the depth of her entrapment and powerlessness. Indeed, so profound is Grace's alienation from community that it appears that perhaps the depths of her own psyche are a perpetual mystery to her own conscious self. However, as Simon's terror at the absence of the female body in his dream suggests – an absence which represents his lack of control – I will argue that Grace's submerged self is not a sign of her powerlessness but rather evidence of her power to resist and transform both the political and linguistic forces which imprison her. Instead of losing control of her self, Grace purposely 'absents' her inner self – puts it under cover, so to speak – and replaces it with a carefully contrived 'self' which enables her to regain a socially acceptable public life while protecting her inner, and powerful, self from psychological dissection.

Throughout the novel, Grace's secret and elusive power is consistently connected to her avowed virginity. Although virginity is sometimes defined as antithetical to notions of agency and power, since it is denoted as a negative rather than a positive state, it is used throughout *Alias Grace* as a metaphor for both active resistance and intentional secrecy. As Simon's dream suggests, if Grace can protect the secrets of both her body and mind through a perpetual striptease of sorts, then she will endlessly frustrate Simon and her readers and succeed in protecting herself from intrusive psychic and physical penetration. And such penetration is just what Grace's voyeuristic readers want. As she brilliantly surmises:

> They don't care if I killed anyone, I could have cut dozens of throats, it's only what they admire in a soldier, they'd scarcely blink. No: was I really a paramour, is their chief concern, and they don't even know themselves whether they want the answer to be no or yes. (28)

In the 1840s, the story of Grace Marks caused a stir because of its mix of sex, violence, and politics. She was a young servant girl who reportedly acted on her sexual jealousy when she helped James McDermott to kill their employer, Thomas Kinnear, and his lover, Nancy Montgomery. In the public's estimation, it was not surprising that such a sexually lascivious woman would also commit violent crimes; a woman so loose with her body was likely out of control of her mind and behaviour as well. In addition, there was a political dimension to her alleged sexual and criminal acts. Her Tory attackers held her up as an example of what could result from the insubordination of the lower classes, while her early defenders were largely republicans. If only McDermott, her partner in crime, had claimed they were Rebels, Grace tells us, they might have been given safe haven from the Americans, rather than the death penalty from the Canadians.

By the time we meet Grace in the setting of Atwood's novel, the political implications of her story have faded. In 1859, her defenders are largely middle- and upper-class do-gooders, many of whom now harbour democratic sentiments themselves. Indeed, in their minds, her membership in the lower class adds to her innocence rather than her guilt. They cannot imagine how a girl so skillful in the domestic arts, and so apparently without guile, could possibly have been willingly involved in the murders. In the intervening sixteen years between her arrest and the present, Grace has evolved from Rebel paramour and murderess to, as Simon Jordan notes upon first seeing her, 'a nun in a cloister, a maiden in a towered dungeon ... the cornered woman' (66) – in short, a virgin. However, Grace Marks, Simon will quickly discover, is not as helpless as she sometimes appears. Shortly after first seeing her, Simon watches as the 'maiden' steps 'forward, out of the light, and the woman he'd seen the instant before was suddenly no longer there. Instead there was a different woman – straighter, taller, more self-possessed ... as if it were he, and not she, who was under scrutiny' (66–7).

When Grace begins to tell the story of her life to Simon Jordan in hopes of remembering the crucial moment of Nancy's death, he listens and the reader reads with the desire and expectation that the end will reveal the truth, or to use narratological terms, disclosure and resolution. We want to know exactly what happened that afternoon at Thomas Kinnear's farm and why Grace cannot remember her precise role in those events. At first, it seems that our curiosity is 'purely scientific' (45), as it is for Simon. However, it quickly becomes clear that Simon's academic research becomes infused with barely suppressed sexual impulses as he begins to speculate on her sexual experiences and his own fantasies of bedding and even marrying her.

The sexual nature of his professional interest unexpectedly, but not surprisingly, surfaces at the climax of Simon's examination of Grace. After reluctantly agreeing to subject Grace to hypnotism because his own talking cure has led nowhere (at least in his estimation), Simon is invited to ask the first question. '"Ask her," he says, "whether she ever had relations with James McDermott."' His query may not surprise the reader, but at first, Simon is shocked by his own question. After a moment's reflection, though, he realizes that it is 'the one thing he most wants to know' (478). Why is Grace's sexual state of such crucial importance to Simon? The most obvious answer is, of course, that he is in love with Grace. Before the hypnotism, when speculating on his feelings for her, he concludes 'that Grace Marks is the only woman he's ever met that he would wish to marry' (466). She has all the requisite qualities – 'beauty without frivolity, domesticity without dullness, and simplicity of manner, and prudence, and circumspection' (466) – and, more important, she has 'passion in [her] somewhere' (467). It is precisely the apparent subversion of her sexual passion in combination with her explicitly murderous impulses which enthralls Simon; a virginal murderess is the woman he most desires.

But why is the question of Grace's virginity of importance to the reader? The answer is that Simon's desire for Grace's subtle combination of innocence and experience parallels and underscores the very motor of *Alias Grace*'s plot. Peter Brooks's description of narrative dynamics in *Reading for the Plot* aptly explains the motor and shape of Grace's life story. According to Brooks, 'narratives both tell of desire – typically present some story of desire – and arouse and make use of desire as dynamic of signification.'[4] Grace's narrative, although full of the banal, domestic details of her childhood and youth, is fuelled by Simon's growing sexual anticipation and arousal over the course of their conversations. Foreplay, in this case, however, occurs through language rather than touch. Grace seductively reveals her psychic and physical centre through artfully crafted memories while Simon probes her with his pen. This sexual/textual dynamic between them is apparent from the beginning of the novel. In the first encounter between Simon and Grace, a conventional power imbalance exists between them, with Simon, the male analyst, attempting to direct his female patient's recovery of lost memories. When he first glimpses her in the cell and likens her to a maiden in distress, he is the one in control, 'the last-minute champion come to rescue her' (66). Familiar with such an imbalance, Grace fears that he, like many others before him, will literally 'draw her' with his pen. From the time of her arrest, she has been aware of the various versions of her character and life story in public circulation – from Mr MacKenzie's fallacious defence arguments to Mrs Moodie's melodramatic representations of Grace's madness and remorse in *Life in the Clearings* to various news reports, clipped and pasted in the Governor's Wife's scrapbook.

With Simon, however, it is not long before Grace becomes aware of how she, herself, can manipulate the pen, and by the end of that first interview, he is the one who must 'resist' (67). The pen with which Simon writes does not inscribe her with its nub end, but, rather, arouses her with its quill end. The experience is implicitly sexual, but she does not passively give into the sensation; instead, she is in full control of her inner psychological and sexual core:

But underneath ... is another feeling, a feeling of being wide-eyed awake and watchful ... And underneath that is another feeling still, a feeling like being torn open; not like a body of flesh, it is not painful as such, but like a peach; and not even torn open, but too ripe and splitting open of its own accord.
And inside the peach there's a stone. (78)

As their conversations continue, this image of the peach stone becomes as an apt metaphor for Grace's agency as a virginal narrator. While hinting at the hidden space within the flesh of Grace's body, the stone and the space it leaves inside the peach are also symbols of the impenetrable centre or empty hole in her memory which she cannot or, as I will argue, *will not* narrate. Objects, like this peach, play an important role within the novel. They repeatedly become symbols connected to or representative of Grace's body, which, as Cristie March concludes in her article 'Crimson Silks and New Potatoes: The Heteroglossic Power of the Object in Atwood's *Alias Grace*,' raises 'questions concerning who does or does not hold power over the meaning of words as they relate to the woman's body.'[5] Simon Jordan, as male doctor and scientist, presumes he will hold this power, but by focusing upon Grace's sexual response to *the pen*, not to Simon, the narrator suggests that for once the woman will be the one to control the story.

Caressed by the feather pen, Grace becomes a sophisticated storyteller. Her stories become increasingly structured by the dynamics of foreplay between herself and Simon, her narrative itself delaying and prolonging sexual excitement, making the possibility of orgasmic fulfillment at the end even more satisfying. Indeed, as Grace's narrative comes closer to its climax, so too does Simon's physical arousal. Yet, on the surface of their conversations, she pretends to an ignorance of the sexual dynamic growing between them and, rather insistently, confirms her physical chastity – a tactic which paradoxically preserves and endangers her virginity because her avowed innocence seduces Simon all the more. She often relates how various men attempt to take advantage of her, ranging from prison guards to doctors, employers, and lawyers, but in each case, she assures Simon that she rebuffs their advances and preserves her innocence. Even at the most exciting points of her tale of escape with McDermott, she is careful to slip in the details of their separate sleeping arrangements.

She is also quite prudish, sometimes refusing to continue the story if Simon has asked a question she deems 'improper.' Whenever she becomes a bit reckless and her conversation becomes at all suggestive or vulgar, she claims to be mimicking her friend's, Mary Whitney's, coarse language, rather than speaking as herself (182–3). Knowing that a woman's 'experience' can reveal itself in subtle ways, she also refuses to participate in Simon's associative language games. For instance, when he brings an apple to their meeting and asks her what thoughts it provokes, she pretends not to know its symbolic meaning. Instead, she answers by treating the apple as a mnemonic device – 'A is for Apple' – and a literal object – apples are made into apple pie. Although she knows he wants her to associate this apple with original sin, she pretends to be ignorant in order to highlight the apparent depths of her innocence. March argues that Grace's refusal to play Simon's game destabilizes the linguistic forum in which Simon wishes to conduct his examination. He wants the apple, and later potatoes, parsnips, beets, and turnips, to lead Grace down specific paths in her memory through various linguistic connections, such as 'Beet – Root Cellar – Corpses' (90). However, as March points out, 'the game of master and student, question and answer, does not *elude* [Grace]; instead *she slips out* of the relationship by refusing the game through her denial of the verbal.'6 The slippage between what Simon wants the objects to mean and what Grace says they mean further heightens the sexual tension between them. Simon and Grace's inability to come to agreement about what these particular objects mean leads to sexual frustration as Simon 'displaces [his linguistic frustration] onto Grace's body'7 and 'invests the objects between them with ... her inaccessibility.'8 Thus, although Simon, as examiner, seems to be in control of these associative games which he expects will lead him into the heart of her memories, Grace, as artful *mis*interpreter, uses these games to prevent him access and create the appearance of chastity.

Taking care to emphasize her sexual innocence, on the one hand, she also notices that dreams excite Simon more than any other part of her story, and so, on the other hand, she begins to fill her narration with thinly veiled dreams of her repressed sexual desires. It is a clever strategy, because these dreams once again hint at her sexual experience while not confirming it – after all, they are only dreams. As a result, just at the point where Grace seems to be most open, since she is revealing the secrets of her dreams, she is simultaneously most inscrutable. Although her narrative appears to be an honest account – which would mean that the dreams were really just dreams – Simon cannot be sure:

I do not know whether to view myself as an unwitting dupe, or, what is worse, a self-deluded fool; but even these doubts may be an illusion, and I may all along have been dealing with a woman so transparently innocent that in my over-subtlety I did not have the wit to recognize it. (506)

Simon's inability to read Grace with any certainty increasingly falters as she prolongs the story. In contrast, her control of the narrative becomes even more skillful. She embellishes with details, making her narrative 'as interesting as [she] can, and rich in incident, as a sort of return gift to him' (291). She begins to rehearse what she will say to him next. Although she may secretly question the reliability of her own memories, these insecurities are completely subverted by the time of her telling, which is always delivered in an unselfconscious but confident tone.

Significantly, in spite of Simon's growing desire, it is precisely this surface simplicity and clarity which prevent any actual assault upon Grace's virginity. Through her various rhetorical strategies, Grace frustrates Simon's desire for knowledge, which results in a corresponding chasteness in their relations. He cannot 'know' her, in other words, until he is certain of knowing whether or not she is a murderess and a paramour. In contrast, Simon has no difficulty giving in to the sexual advances of Rachel, his landlady. His physical penetration of Rachel parallels what he presumes to be his full knowledge of her psychological state as well. Throughout his time with her, he creates a sort of case study, enumerating and detailing her feelings, motivations, weaknesses, and repressed desires. He knows their affair will end soon since 'he knows he's reaching the end of the repertoire; the end of what Rachel can offer; the end of her' (488). Grace's repertoire, on the other hand, seems to have no end. Through her artful linguistic seduction, she continually arouses and refuses the consummation of his desires and in doing so, creates and preserves her sexual and textual virginity, which in turns generates further desire. As is implied by Brooks's theory of narrative, Grace's defence of both her sexual and criminal innocence, like Scheherazade's defence of her life, is the act of narration itself. All she needs to do is to continue the story and keep him guessing – did she or didn't she? With the absence of certainty in Grace's narration comes a successful guarantee of her innocence and virginity. As Simon relates to his friend,

> thus far she has manifested a composure that a duchess might envy. I have never known any woman to be so thoroughly self-contained ... She 'sits on a cushion and sews a fine seam,' cool as a cucumber and with her mouth primmed up like a governess's, and I lean my elbows on the table across from her, cudgelling my brains, and trying in vain to open her up like an oyster. Although she converses in what seems a frank enough manner, she manages to tell me as little as possible, or as little as possible of what I want to learn. (152)

As they come closer to the mystery at the heart of her story – those few precious moments on the day of the murders – Simon 'can't seem to keep track of the pieces' (346) and starts to lose control of his own thoughts and body. He begins to dream Grace's dreams and perform her subconscious desires. Whereas Grace claims to resist Thomas Kinnear, Simon passively begins the affair with Rachel. While Grace refuses to speak of gravesites and cellars – thoughts he continually attempts to elicit from her – he begins digging gigantic and apparently useless holes in Rachel's backyard. As Grace remembers herself caught up in the murderous schemes of McDermott, Simon finds himself embroiled in Rachel's melodramatic wish for her husband's death. However, the parallels between his current experience and Grace's past escape Simon; all he knows is that he has learned 'nothing' conclusively about Grace and so cannot conclude either his scientific report or act on his love for Grace. Eventually Simon's frustration overwhelms him. As his indiscreet question during Grace's hypnotism indicates, the line between his intellectual and sexual interest is openly blurred and he can no longer pretend to a solely professional interest in her case.

Following Simon's lead, readers are also drawn into the sexual dynamic of the text. While Simon longs to penetrate Grace's untouched sexual core, we read with a slightly different emphasis – after all Grace is only a character – but with a similar intent; we read in order to deflower the virginal text, to consummate, through the act of interpretation, our sexually charged textual desires. At first, it seems that we will succeed where Simon has failed because Grace is more frank with us, and as is demonstrated by my previous discussion, we are privy to her growing artistry. When Simon asks her intrusive questions or attempts to elicit certain responses through associative games and gifts, she allows us access to her private thoughts while she remains mute or frustratingly inarticulate with Simon. We hear reports of dreams that never reach Simon's ears. However, just before the crucial moment of the narrative, Grace's apparent frankness becomes as murky for us as it is for Simon. As she prepares to tell Simon about the day of the killings, she begins by emphasizing the insecurity of her memory and then rehearses her material for the reader in a series of questions.

Did he say, I saw you outside at night, in your nightgown, in the moonlight? Did he say, Who were you looking for? Was it a man? Did he say, I pay good wages but I want good service in return? Did he say, do not worry, I will not tell your mistress, it will be our secret? Did he say, You are a good girl?
He might have said that. Or I might have been asleep.
Did she say, Don't think I don't know what you've been up to? Did she say, I will pay you your wages on Saturday and then you can be gone out of here, and that will be the end of it and good riddance?
Yes, she did say that.
Was I crouching behind the kitchen door after that, crying? Did he take me in his arms? Did I let him do it? Did he say Grace, why are you crying? Did I say I wished she was dead?
Oh no. Surely I did not say that. Or not out loud. And I did not really wish her dead. I only wished her elsewhere, which was the same thing she wished for me.
Did I push him away? Did he say I will soon make you think better of me? Did he say I will tell you a secret if you promise to keep it? And if you do not, your life will not be worth a straw.
It might have happened. (351–2)

This passage, which might let the reader into Grace's secret memory, is frustratingly inscrutable. Significantly, the only definitive statement is spoken by Nancy Montgomery, which suggests that Grace has no need to raise doubts about her relationship with another woman. However, in order to keep the reader guessing about her own sexual and criminal innocence, she obscures the other voices, all of which are male. Indeed, to whom does the pronoun 'he' refer throughout this passage? To the lawyers at the trial, to Kinnear, to McDermott, or to all three at different moments? Are these questions asked at the trial by lawyers or by Kinnear and/or McDermott at the time of the events? If the former, then Grace's memory of the event is certainly mediated by what she has heard from others, but if the latter, then she seems to have access to the very memories she claims not to have. Most important, are these rhetorical questions posed by Grace to confuse her reader, or is she simply rehearsing the questions she truly cannot answer? Precisely at the moment when readers most earnestly seek textual resolution, Grace suddenly refuses us entry into her private, 'true voice' (351) and preserves her text's virginity, just as she protects her body's purity from Simon's covert advances. She is manipulating not only Simon's desires but those of the reader as well.

The question of how much Grace manipulates the story becomes even more intriguing and baffling at the climax of Simon's examination of his subject. As I have already mentioned, at this point in the story, Simon's analysis of Grace is completely stalled. In despair, he agrees to allow Dr Jerome DuPont to hypnotize Grace. Once she is hypnotized, the spirit of her dead friend, Mary Whitney, is heard, apparently speaking through Grace's body. It is a shocking scene for a number of reasons – not only because Simon openly confesses his sexual interest in his patient, but also because Mary is everything Grace is not. She is vulgar, loud, and aggressively sexual. Whereas Grace subtly manipulates the sexual tension between herself and Simon, when Mary hears Simon's surprising and improper question, she accuses Simon outright of illicit sexual desires and calls Lydia, his young admirer, a slut. Mary also freely admits her own sexual and criminal guilt – describing with relish the strangulation of Nancy. The small group in attendance – Grace's greatest defenders – feel betrayed and humiliated, as Mary mocks them, suggesting that they have only deluded themselves.

Yet the most fascinating effect of this scene is that although it resolves the mystery – Grace *is* guilty – there is no interpretive resolution for either Simon, Grace's other defenders, or the reader. Why not? Because the appearance of Mary Whitney suddenly throws Grace's selfhood, and thus her agency and culpability, into question. We are not sure what precisely we have witnessed. Have Dr Jerome DuPont and Grace conspired to trick the audience? Or, as the spiritualists might argue, has the spirit or soul of Mary Whitney actually entered Grace's body and used it to commit immoral and criminal acts? Or is a psychiatric explanation more plausible? Has Grace split herself into two, incorporating Mary's personality into her own as a way of coping with the trauma of Mary's death, and then through this second personality, repressed her own violent and sexual actions and desires? Or, and this is the theory I prefer, is Grace Marks actually Mary Whitney? Has Mary embodied an alias and constructed a completely new self – one which will redeem her, bring her 'grace,' and in doing so, make her innocent and virginal once again?

At first glance this last theory seems impossible. After all, according to Grace, she and Mary were once two distinct girls, serving together in the household of Mrs Alderman Parkinson. Grace movingly relates the fate of her friend, who dies a bloody and painful death after having an abortion. Grace's apparently sincere retelling of these troubling events touches Simon, but he has to admit that 'the only witness who could corroborate her testimony ... would be Mary Whitney herself, and she is not available' (215–16). Nor, he discovers later, are there any potential witnesses from the Parkinson household, since it disintegrated a number of years ago. When he finally finds Mary Whitney's gravesite, it offers no clues either in support of or against Grace's version of events:

> But this stone is only that: a stone. For one thing, it has no dates on it, and the Mary Whitney buried beneath it may not have any connection with Grace Marks at all ...
> Nothing has been proved. But nothing has been disproved either. (466)

This stone without dates or familial detail is similar to the peach stone which lies within the flesh of Grace's story. It potentially contains all but reveals nothing. We are only left with theories. Perhaps the gravestone marks the burial of some other Mary Whitney – a mother or grandmother. Without birth and death dates, the stone tells us nothing definitely.

There are several clues in the narrative that allow for the possibility that Grace and Mary are not, in fact, two distinct young women. I will relate two of the most convincing. First, in her story Grace claims she did not witness Mary's abortion; she only saw the doctor greet Mary and take her into the other room. Yet, when another doctor dressed in a black coat arrives to measure Grace's skull in the Governor's parlour over sixteen years later, it is not until the doctor reaches into his bag with his gloved hand that Grace becomes hysterical:

> And then I see his hand, a hand like a glove, a glove stuffed with raw meat, his hand plunging into the open mouth of his leather bag. It comes out glinting, and I know I have seen a hand like that before; and then I lift my head and stare him straight in the eye, and my heart clenches and kicks out inside me, and then I begin to scream.

Because it's the same doctor, the same one, the very same black-coated doctor with his bagful of shining knives. (31)

Her extreme response suggests that Grace, as Mary, did not simply witness the effects of the abortion but actually had the abortion herself and during her recovery afterwards reinvented herself as Grace.

Second, the only person who appears in both Grace's memories and the present time of the narrative who could actually corroborate the separate existence of Mary and Grace is Jeremiah the pedlar, who himself adopts various aliases throughout his life. Jeremiah's relationship to Grace is an intriguing one. The first time he meets her, he quietly whispers to her, 'You are one of us' (180) and thereafter always claims an intimacy which belies the actual length of contact between them. They always understand each other immediately, often through the smallest of gestures and subtlest of looks. In the one lengthy conversation they have, which occurs after Mary's apparent death when Grace is already at Kinnear's farm, Jeremiah proposes that Grace run away with him and become his partner in a mesmerism act. The very fact that he should make this suggestion to her hints that Grace is an accomplished con artist of a sort already, or at least as Jeremiah says, she 'ha[s] the talent for it' (318). Perhaps it is a change of name which induces Jeremiah's presumptuousness? Perhaps, having met Mary before, he knows that she is now posing as Grace Marks. Although she refuses his offer to work (and sleep) with him (with a remarkable lack of distress at the impertinence of it), Grace and Jeremiah thereafter agree to keep each other's secrets.

While Grace always makes it clear to her reader precisely what secret Jeremiah needs kept, the same is not so for herself. What could it be? That her real name is Mary Whitney? In the climactic scene, as we see Jeremiah and Grace working together, we have good reason to question whether she is actually hypnotized by Jeremiah. When Grace is first introduced to Jeremiah as Dr Jerome DuPont, he 'made a pact with [her] under [the others'] very eyes' (365) but what pact? Not to tell anyone that he is not really Dr DuPont? Or that they would together perpetrate a fraud on the others? This ambiguity becomes even more unclear later in the novel when Grace writes Jeremiah a letter. In the first two-thirds of the letter, Grace writes from the perspective of ignorance; she really does not seem to know what happened while she was hypnotized and cannot understand why the others now react to her as they do. However, near the end of the letter, Grace's supposed ignorance becomes questionable when she writes:

The other thing I would like to know is, why did you want to help me? Was it as a challenge, and to outwit the others, as with the smuggling you used to do; or was it out of affection and fellow-feeling? You said once we were of the same sort, and I have often pondered over that. (511–12)

The fact that Grace knows that Jeremiah 'outwits' the others suggests that the climactic scene in the library was an act, performed together by the two of them.

The possibility of 'Grace Marks' being the alias for Mary Whitney – one which is also suggested by the title of the novel – may detract from her actual physical and criminal innocence, but it adds another dimension to her agency, both in terms of the construction of her narration and, most important, her manipulation of the sexual dimensions of her narrative. Her alias, in other words, highlights the crucial connection developed in *Alias Grace* between virginity and agency. If we accept that Grace is actually Mary Whitney, we can see how imperative it is that she reform not only her behaviour but also her sexual identity if she is to survive her disastrous affair with her employer's son, George Parkinson. Having given in to the seductions of George, Mary, as Agnes and Mrs Parkinson clearly indicate, is 'lost.' He refuses to acknowledge and marry her, leaving her little choice but to have an abortion if she is to retain her place in the community. If she were to remain pregnant, Mary would no longer have control of her sexual secrets, and with that loss, so Atwood's novel suggests, would come a corresponding inability to control the telling of her own life story. According to Amanda Anderson's research on fallen women in Victorian society, Mary would have been perceived 'as lacking the autonomy and coherence of the normative ... subject';[9] in other words, she would no longer have a subject position from which to author her own autobiography. Anderson contends that the fallen woman's lack of autonomy was evident not only in her inability to resist seduction, but, more importantly, in her failure to sustain a separate, distinct selfhood in the face of various economic, social, or environmental forces. The fallen woman was not only morally weak, she was also socially determined, a person who 'lack[ed] any transformative capacity' and 'power to alter her fate.'[10] By hiding away the truth about her sexual fall under the more powerful cultural 'secret' of virginity, Mary is able to maintain this transformative power. She reinvents herself and her virginity, not only *finding* 'grace' but actually *conceiving of and creating* a form of 'grace' which will make her a visible, autonomous person once again. Through 'Grace Marks' Mary regains the purity implied by her own namesake and, as Simon notes, becomes as impenetrable as the Virgin Mary:

As she stitches away at her sewing, outwardly calm as a marble Madonna, she is all the while exerting her passive stubborn strength against him ... Her strongest prison is of *her own* construction. (435; my italics)

With the construction of 'Grace,' we can see how Mary is able to keep her admirers and defenders guessing while at the same time actually achieving political and social revenge. She kills Nancy Montgomery and Thomas Kinnear, both of whom deserved to die in Mary's mind – Nancy because she was about to receive the social and financial security that Mary had been denied and Kinnear because he, as a Tory, was indirectly responsible for her family's losses in the Rebellions and her parents' subsequent deaths. Indeed, after the murders, Mary apparently believes that she is no longer in need of her alias and gives her own name after she and James McDermott cross the border and register at a hotel. As Mary falls asleep in America, she thinks of the action of the lake's waves:

And it was as if my own footsteps were being erased behind ... all traces of me, smoothed over and rubbed away as if they had never been, like polishing the black tarnish from the silver, or drawing your hand across dry sand.

On the edge of sleep I thought: It's as if I never existed, because no trace of me remains, I have left no *marks*. And that way I cannot be followed.

It is almost the same as being innocent. (411–12; my italics)

Mary's words here are interesting, especially since she claims to have been innocent all along. These thoughts seem to confirm the opposite, that she has, in fact, helped James McDermott kill Thomas Kinnear and Nancy Montgomery, but that in doing so, she has revenged the sins perpetrated against her family and herself. That night, 'Grace' dreams of Mary and is about to be reunited with, I would argue, herself when a knock is heard at her hotel door. As the police come to arrest her, Mary discovers she is in need of her alias 'Grace' once again and cleverly claims to have used the name 'Mary Whitney' as an alias for Grace.

By the time we reach the climax of the novel and are witness to Mary's emergence, she has so destabilized our ability to interpret who she is that we cannot know with certainty what is happening. When Mary announces to Grace's defenders that 'I am not lying! ... I am beyond lying! I no longer need to lie!' (481), she is quite right. She can be truthful or deceitful and we will not be able to know the difference and the effect will be the same – in our minds, 'Grace' will emerge as innocent, virginal, 'calm,' and 'dutiful' (483). This is precisely what happens. In spite of witnessing Mary's shocking emergence, Reverend Verringer, along with other supporters, argue that poor Grace is the victim of a rare psychiatric disorder and so cannot be held responsible for her actions. In his final report, Verringer argues for Grace's innocence even while acknowledging 'Mary's' guilt. Thanks to his efforts, Grace is finally released from prison and reintegrated into society successfully. That his arguments fool the parole board, however, should not be grounds enough for us to accept them. To concede that Verringer's interpretation of events is the most plausible would mean that Grace is truly unable to control or know her own self or story and that the crucial connection between virginity, power, and narration, which I have argued the novel subtly weaves, would be lost.

If, instead, we are convinced that Mary has brilliantly created her alias Grace, then we can read the ending of the novel as a carefully orchestrated realization of everything Mary has desired. Her alias 'Grace' receives clemency, marries the farmer Mary planned on finding in her youth, and climbs up the social ladder. She lives in America, under the kind of republican democracy her parents died working for in Canada. With Simon, she also succeeds in wreaking revenge upon the medical profession. His inability to 'know' Grace not only creates sexual confusion within Simon but rocks his very sense of self. As his professional experiment with Grace fails, Simon admits to his friend that he almost suffers a nervous breakdown, and like a conventional 'fallen woman,' he lacks agency and becomes determined by forces external to his self. His only defence is to flee. In doing so, Simon literally ends up losing himself – a head injury sustained during the American Civil War causes the loss of his adult memories. Like Grace, he now has a hole in his story, but unlike Mary, he has no power to transform himself, only the memory of Grace to perplex him. She, in other words, succeeds in preventing him access to her physical and psychic centre and in doing so refuses him the ability to 'write' her. Instead, she takes that power for herself and defies not only moral and social judgment but economic and class determinants as well.

Grace, of course, is also not the only narrator playing with the materials of her life. Running parallel to Grace's rhetorical flourishes and sleights of hand are those of the omniscient narrator, who, like Grace, preserves the text's 'virginity' by ensuring our inability to get to the interpretative centre of the novel. Just as Grace teases Simon with the possibility of future consummation of their relationship, the omniscient narrator simultaneously adds to the outside readers' confusion while also suggesting that our confusion will ultimately be resolved.

In order to explore the role of this narrator let me return to my opening metaphor: the quilt as metaphor for the novel itself, as both interpretable pattern and impenetrable cover. As Rogerson has carefully shown in her article, the motif of the quilt is everywhere present in the pages of the novel, most obviously displayed in the section titles and illustrations. These quilts highlight how Grace's sexual innocence or experience underpins her public history and her private story; indeed, the novel repeatedly illustrates how all women's sexuality is crucial to their social position and value. As Grace tells us, quilts illustrate this position and value. Not only does quilting allow women to demonstrate their unique talents and their community with one another, it also indicates their sexual experience. Married women are allowed to display certain patterns, such as the Tree of Paradise, while unmarried women must hide them away until they have a marriage bed to cover. Quilts can also reveal whether a woman is an acceptable member of society. While Grace is welcomed into the Governor's house daily and asked to sew hundreds of quilting squares on her own because of her exceptional needlework, she is also painfully aware that she cannot be included in the larger community of a quilting bee, due to her criminal and sexual past as well as her class.

Although denied one of her own, Grace often contemplates various quilts' symbolic value. As a young servant girl, she notices that quilts waving on the line look like flags, an observation she thinks about later as she sews during her long incarceration:

why is it that women have chosen to sew such flags, and then to lay them on the tops of beds? For they make the bed the most noticeable thing in a room. And then I thought, it's for a warning. Because you may think a bed is a peaceful thing, Sir, and to you it may mean rest and comfort and a good night's sleep. But it isn't so for everyone; and there are many dangerous things that may take place in a bed. (186)

Her comments, of course, seem a thinly veiled reference to the traumatic events in Grace's life – Mary's 'death,' Kinnear's murder – both of which take place in bed. However, they also point to more general notions of female subjection illustrated in the novel; while, for men, beds are cozy, desirable places, for women, they are the site of wanted and unwanted sexual encounters and all their consequences – labour, childbirth, and, often, death. For women, the quilt is a way of communicating and also covering what cannot be said aloud, serving as an ambiguous sign for what occurs in secret. In contrast, as Simon's dream recounted at the beginning of this article suggests, for men the quilt is a prelude to disclosure, a final veil they need only peel back before the female body will finally be exposed and made ready for them.

The omniscient narrator highlights the dual function of quilts by giving each section of her text the name of a quilt pattern. These patterns, at first, seem to function as signs, as 'flags.' Their presence seems to imply that if we look carefully enough at the various fragments and pieces in the quilt of this novel, a definitive pattern will finally emerge. Indeed, Grace, in her narrative, also claims to have learned this lesson:

Then something came clear to me which I used to wonder about. There is a quilt pattern called Lady of the Lake, which I thought was named for the poem; but I could never find any lady in the pattern, nor any lake. But now I saw that the boat was named for the poem, and the quilt was named for the boat; because it was a pinwheel design, which must have stood for the paddle going around. And I thought that things did make sense, and have a design to them, if you only pondered them long enough. (409)

Although Grace is finally enlightened as to the source and meaning of the Lady of the Lake pattern, the pattern itself highlights the layers of references and meanings embedded within the quilt. Significantly, Grace's discovery demonstrates that while the quilt may allude to the story of the Lady of the Lake, it also stops short of it; instead of portraying the fate of the lady, the quilt is a representation of a boat named for the poem. So the quilt hints at and covers over the story simultaneously. Similarly, *Alias Grace* is full of the traces of Grace Marks, hinting at the possibility of our knowing the truth about her while never fulfilling this promise.

As Simon shifts through the various details of Grace's life, we sort through both her life story and the various other versions of that story provided to us by the omniscient narrator. We read trial transcripts, letters from doctors and lawyers, conversations between Simon and Mr MacKenzie, and so forth, all with the aim and hope that a coherent portrait of Grace will finally emerge from the patchwork of narratives, reports, and letters. However, while the presence of the quilt patterns elicits such expectations, they also, paradoxically, highlight how the pattern can shift and repeatedly defy our attempts to define it. Indeed, as Grace makes clear at the end of the novel, one cannot fully interpret or understand the pattern without knowing the one who sews it. And if the sewer finally eludes us, then so too does interpretation.

All of this begs the question: who precisely is sewing the textual 'quilt' known as Grace Marks? The answer is complex. Even though Simon believes when he first meets Grace that 'her story is over. The main story, that is: the thing that has defined her,' Grace starts the story over again while 'threading the needle' (104). Later when he is completely perplexed by Grace, Simon wonders if 'you [could] sew and snip, and patch together a genius' (217). Throughout the novel, Grace sews as she talks and she does precisely this – she brilliantly pieces together an alias that others will interpret as innocent and virginal. However, until Mary surfaces at the hypnotism, we believe that Grace is gradually exposing her lost, inner self rather than artfully concealing herself under a textual quilt. By giving Grace space to tell her own (albeit fictional) life story – the opportunity to pattern her own life – the omniscient narrator suggests that the 'real' Grace Marks is not, in fact, constituted by the various texts which have been written about her (both in her day and since then) – that she, instead, escapes all textual attempts to define her, just as she frustrates Simon's (and other men's) attempts to deflower her. The first indication of a gap between the Grace who is already written and the 'I' who narrates comes early in the novel:

I think of all the things that have been written about me – that I am an inhuman female demon, that I am an innocent victim of a blackguard forced against my will and in danger of my own life, that I was too ignorant to know how to act and that to hang me would be judicial murder, that I am fond of animals, that I am very handsome with a brilliant complexion, that I have blue eyes, that I have green eyes, that I have auburn hair and also brown hair, that I am tall and also not above the average height, that I am well and decently dressed, that I robbed a dead woman to appear so, that I am brisk and smart about my work, that I am of a sullen disposition with a quarrelsome temper, that I have the appearance of a person rather above my humble station, that I am a good girl with a pliable nature and no harm is told of me, that I am cunning and devious, that I am soft in the head and little better than an idiot. And I wonder, how can I be all of these different things at once? (23)

The very fact that Grace is conscious of the different versions of her in public circulation suggests a gap between those 'selves' and the 'self' which lies hidden within, and the autobiographical tale which follows illustrates how this 'real' Grace incorporates and exceeds these versions. Until the climactic scene in the Governor's parlour, the whole novel seems to be moving towards the revelation of what Grace refers to as her 'true voice' (351). With Mary's appearance, however, the narrative pattern which has slowly been emerging over the course of the novel is abruptly changed. We suddenly realize that, like Simon and all of the others in Grace's circle, we have actually been shown the quilt – an artfully patterned cover – rather than the body underneath.

Grace may be clever, but she is also only a character, and so we might argue that Margaret Atwood, as author, is the master quilter. Yet, much of the content of her novel calls her authority into question. Many of the bits and pieces within the novel are not fictional; they are copied from other historical and literary resources authored by others, such as Susanna Moodie, Mr MacKenzie, and others. To cloud the issue further, though, many of these sources also have indeterminate origins. As Atwood tells us in her Afterword, 'Moodie's retelling of the murder is a third-hand account' (556), and as MacKenzie tells us within the novel, Moodie's account was, in turn, influenced by her readings of Dickens. However, the very presence of these other accounts, which have an existence outside of *Alias Grace*, undermine Atwood's authority over her own text and remind the reader that Grace Marks is not wholly an invention of Atwood's imagination. Significantly, it is Atwood herself who underscores her own lack of authority by including an Afterword which both emphasizes the historical accuracy of her novel and raises doubts about such supposed 'accuracy.' The Afterword has the paradoxical effect of illustrating how Atwood is confined and dictated by a story which is not initially her own while also revealing how the prior story is ripe for her artful manipulation. Like a quilter, she has a pattern to follow, but she can adapt it, within bounds, as well.[11]

In addition, Atwood's Afterword reveals how she is not simply the author of 'Grace Marks' but the reader of her as well. The 'Grace' which emerges on the pages of *Alias Grace* is as much the product of Atwood's reading as she is a product of Atwood's writing. Like the readers in and of *Alias Grace*, Atwood, for all the patchwork she does, ultimately admits defeat in her pursuit of the 'real' Grace Marks. As she writes, 'the true character of the historical Grace Marks remains an enigma' (558). Likewise, the inner core of the fictional Grace Marks remains frustratingly and tantalizingly untouchable. Fittingly, the novel ends with Grace sewing a Tree of Paradise quilt for herself. A quilt only married women can display, Grace's Tree of Paradise publicly marks her apparently new sexual state; she is unexpectedly pregnant as well, another soon-to-be public sign of her sexual experience. Yet, as much as the quilt suggests the successful penetration of Grace, it also seals the secrets of the past and so both reveals and covers her hidden self. This quilt may appear to be conventional, she writes Simon, but she will sew into the pattern her own secret variations, which will be visible and meaningful only to her. It is true; although she tells Simon (and us) how her quilt will be different, she refuses to interpret those differences, and the quilt becomes yet another of Grace's ingenuously crafted masks.

NOTES

1 Rogerson (1998, 5).
2 Ibid. 6.
3 Rao (1993, 41–2). See Mycak's study (1996) for a critical overview of this issue.
4 Brooks (1984, 37).
5 March (1997, 80).
6 March (1997, 75).
7 Ibid. 79.
8 Ibid. 80.
9 Anderson (1993, 1).
10 Ibid. 65.

11 In *In Search of* Alias Grace (1997), Atwood discusses the process of writing this novel: 'I devised the following set of guidelines for myself: when there was a solid fact, I could not alter it: long as I might to have Grace witness McDermott's execution, it could not be done, because, worse luck, she was already in the penitentiary on that day. Also, every major element in the book had to be suggested by something in the writing about Grace and the times, however dubious such writing might be; but in the parts left unexplained – the gaps left unfilled – I was free to invent' (35).

WORKS CITED

Abbot, Elizabeth. 1999. *The History of Celibacy*. Toronto: Harper Collins.
Aelred of Rievaulx. 1971. 'The Threefold Meditation.' In *Treatises: The Pastoral Prayer*. Spencer: Cistercian Publications.
Altman, Charles F. 1975. 'Two Types of Opposition and the Structure of Latin Saints' Lives.' *Medievalia et Humanistica*, n.s., 6: 1–11.
Ambrose. 1729. *Les oeuvres de St. Ambrose sur la virginite ... traduites ... avec notes, & une dissertation preliminaire sur les vierges, par le reverend pere de Bonrecueil, pretre de l'oratoire*. Paris.
Anderson, Amanda. 1993. *Tainted Souls and Painted Faces: The Rhetoric of Fallenness in Victorian Culture*. Ithaca, NY: Cornell University Press.
Anonymous. 1477. *Passio Sanctorum Gallicani Hilarinini. Item sanctorum Iohannis et Pauli martirum (BHL 3236)*, Boninus Mombritius, *Sanctuarium seu vitae sanctorum*. Milan, 1477; 2nd ed. Paris: Fontemoing 1910.
Anonymous. 1961. *The Cloud of Unknowing and Other Works*. Translated by Clifton Wolters. London: Penguin.
Armstrong, David, and Ann Ellis Hanson. 1986. 'Vox Virginis.' *Bulletin of the Institute of Classical Studies* 33: 97–100.
Arnauld, Antoine. 1775–83. *Works*. Lausanne: Simon, J. and C. Jourdain, 1893.
Arthur, Marylin B. 1984. 'Early Greece: The Origins of the Western Attitude toward Women.' *Arethusa* 6: 7–58. Reprinted in John Peradotto and J.P. Sullivan, eds, *Women in the Ancient World: The Arethusa Papers*. Albany: State University of New York Press, 7–58.
– 1982. 'Cultural Strategies in Hesiod's Theogony: Law, Family, Society,' *Arethusa* 15: 63–82.
Astell, Ann W. 1990. *The Song of Songs in the Middle Ages*. Ithaca: Cornell University Press.
Atwood, Margaret. 1997. *In Search of* Alias Grace: *On Writing Canadian Historical Fiction*. Ottawa: University of Ottawa Press.

– 1996. *Alias Grace*. Toronto: McClelland and Stewart.
Austin, J.L. 1962. *How to Do Things with Words*. Cambridge: Harvard University Press.
Avagianou, Aphrodite. 1991. *Sacred Marriage in the Rituals of Greek Religion*. Bern and New York: Peter Lang.
Avenel, Joseph d'. 1853. *Histoire de la vie et des ouvrages de Daniel Huet*. Mortain Lebel.
Bächtold-Stäubli, H., and E. Hoffmann-Krayer, eds. 1987. *Handwörterbuch des Deutschen Aberglaubens* 5. Berlin: Walter de Gruyter.
Bagnall, Roger S. et al., eds. 2001. *Checklist of Editions of Greek and Latin Papyri, Ostraca and Tablets* (= *BASP* Supplement 9). Oakville, CT: Oxbow.
Bagnall, Roger S., and Bruce W. Frier. 1994. *The Demography of Roman Egypt*. Cambridge: Cambridge University Press.
Baier-Futterer, Ilse. 1936. *Die Bildwerke der Romanik und Gotik Katalog des Schweizerischen Landesmuseums*. Zurich: Kartoniert.
Bakewell, G. 1997. 'Metoikia in the Supplices of Aeschylus.' *Classical Antiquity* 16.2: 209–28.
Bamberger, Joan. 1974. 'The Myth of Matriarchy: Why Men Rule In Primitive Society.' In *Woman, Culture and Society*, edited by Michelle Zimbalist Rosaldo and Louise Lamphere, 263–80. Stanford, CA: Stanford University Press.
Bartholmess, Christian. 1850. *Huet, Eveque d'Avranche et le Scepticisme Théologique*. Paris.
Bauman, Richard A. 1992. *Women and Politics in Ancient Rome*. London and New York: Routledge.
Bayle, Pierre. 1701. *Dictionnaire Historique et Critique*, 2nd ed. Paris.
Beard, Mary. 1995. 'Re-reading (Vestal) Virginity.' In *Women in Antiquity: New Assessments*, edited by Richard Hawley and Barbara Levick, 166–77. New York and London: Routledge.
– 1980. 'The Sexual Status of Vestal Virgins.' *Journal of Roman Studies* 70: 12–27.
Beard, Mary, John North, and Simon Price. 1998. *Religions of Rome*. Vol. 1: *A History*. Cambridge: Cambridge University Press.
Beaumont, Lesley. 1998. 'Born Old and Never Young? Femininity, Childhood and the Goddesses of Ancient Greece.' In *The Sacred and the Feminine in Ancient Greece*, edited by Sue Blundell and Margaret Williamson, 71–95. London: Routledge.
Beidelman, T.O. 1963. 'Witchcraft and Sorcery in Ukaguru.' In *Witchcraft and Sorcery in East Africa*, edited by John Middleton and E.H. Winter, 57–98. London: Praeger.
Bell, James Harle, John Richard von Sturmer, and Rodney Needhamm, trans. 1991. *Lexikon der Kunst*, Leipzig: Seemann.

Benko, Stephen. 1993. *The Virgin Goddess: Studies in the Pagan and Christian Roots of Mariology.* Leiden: Brill.

Bernard of Clairvaux. 1952. *Sermons on the Song of Songs.* London: A.R. Mowbray and Co.

Bidez, Joseph, and Günther Christian Hansen, eds. 1995. Socrates, *Historia Ecclesiastica 7.32, Sozomenus Kirchengeschicte,* 2nd ed. Berlin: Akademie-Verlag.

Blok, Josine H. 2001. 'Virtual Voices: Towards a Choreography of Women's Speech in Classical Athens.' In *Making Silence Speak: Women's Voices in Greek Liter-ature and Society,* edited by A. Lardinois and L. McClure, 95–116. Princeton: Princeton University Press.

Blundell, Sue. 1998. 'Marriage and the Maiden. Narratives on the Parthenon.' In *The Sacred and the Feminine in Ancient Greece,* edited by Sue Blundell and Margaret Williamson, 47–70. London: Routledge.

– 1995. *Women in Ancient Greece.* Cambridge, MA: Harvard University Press.

Borch-Jacobsen, Mikkel. 1994. 'The Oedipus Problem in Freud and Lacan.' *Critical Inquiry* (Winter): 267–82.

Bosing, Walter, and Hieronymus Bosch. 1987. *Zwischen Himmel und Hoelle.* Cologne: Taschen.

Bouillier, Francisque. 1970. *Histoire de la Philosophie Cartésienne.* Vol. 1, ch. 28. Geneva: Slatkine Reprints (1868).

Bown, Demi. 1995. *Encyclopedia of Herbs and Their Uses.* London: DK Publishing.

Brandes, Stanley H. 1987. 'Reflections on Honour and Shame in the Mediterranean.' In *Honor and Shame and the Unity of the Mediterranean,* edited by David D. Gilmore, 121–34. Washington, DC: American Anthropological Association.

– 1980. *Metaphors of Masculinity.* Philadelphia: University of Pennsylvania Press.

Brasington, Bruce C. 1992. 'Non imitanda sed veneranda: The Dilemma of Sacred Precedent in Twelfth-Century Canon Law.' *Viator* 23: 135–52.

Brelich, Angelo. 1949. *Vesta.* Zurich: Rhein-Verl.

Bremmer, Jan. 1983. 'Scapegoat Rituals in Ancient Greece.' *Harvard Studies in Classical Philology* 87: 299–320.

Briggs, Robin. 1996. *Witches and Neighbors: The Social and Cultural Context of European Witchcraft.* New York: Viking.

Briquel, Dominique. 1984. 'Forms de mise à mort dans la Rome primitive.' In *Du Châtiment dans la cite: Supplices corporels et peine de mort dans le monde antique. CEFR* 79: 225–40.

Brooks, Peter. 1984. *Reading for the Plot: Design and Intention in Narrative.* New York: Knopf.

Brown, A.L. 1977. 'Eteocles and the Chorus in the *Seven against Thebes.*' *Phoenix* 31: 300–18.
Brubaker, Leslie. 1997. 'Memories of Helena: Patterns in Imperial Female Matronage in the Fourth and Fifth Centuries.' In *Women, Men and Eunuchs: Gender in Byzantium*, edited by L. James, 52–75. London: Routledge.
Brucker, Jakob. 1743. *Historia Critica Philosophiae.* Vol. 4, pt. 1. Leipzig: Literis et Impensis, Bernhard Christoph Breitkopf, 552–74.
Buckland, W.W. 1908. *Roman Law of Slavery.* Cambridge: University of Cambridge Press.
Bullough, V.L. 1974. 'Transvestites in the Middle Ages.' *American Journal of Archaeology* 79.6: 1381–94.
Burkert, Walter. 1985. *Greek Religion: Archaic and Classical.* Translated by John Raffan. Oxford: Basil Blackwell.
– 1983. *Homo Necans.* Berkeley and Los Angeles: University of California Press.
– 1979. *Structure and History in Greek Mythology and Ritual.* Sather Classical Lectures 47. Berkeley: University of California Press.
Burkhard, Arthur. 1932. *Hans Burgkmair der Ältere.* Berlin: Klinkhardt and Biermann.
Burrus, Virginia. 1991. 'The Heretical Woman as Symbol in Alexander, Athanasius, Epiphanius, and Jerome.' *Harvard Theological Review* 84: 229–48.
Büttner, F.O. 1983. *Imitatio Pietatis: Motive der Christlichen Ikonographie als Modelle der Verähnlichung.* Berlin: Mann Verlag.
Buzzati, Dino. 1966. *L'opera completa di Bosch.* Milan: Rizzoli.
Bynum, Caroline Walker. 1992. *Fragmentation and Redemption: Essays on Gender and the Human Body in Medieval Religion.* New York: Zone Books.
– 1982. *Jesus as Mother.* Berkeley and Los Angeles: University of California Press.
Calame, C. 1997. *Choruses of Young Women in Ancient Greece: Their Morphology, Religious Role, and Social Function.* Translated from the French edition (1977) by D. Collins and J. Orion. Lanham: Rowman and Littlefield.
Caldwell, R.S. 1973. 'The Misogyny of Eteocles.' *Arethusa* 6: 197–228.
Campbell, D.A. 1982. *Greek Lyric I.* London and Cambridge: Heinemann and Harvard University Press.
Cantarella, Eva. 1987. *Pandora's Daughters: The Role and Status of Women in Greek and Roman Antiquity.* Translated by Maureen B. Fant. Baltimore: Johns Hopkins University Press.
– 1976. 'Adulterio, omicidio legittimo e causa d'onore in diritto romano,' In *Studi sull'omicidio in diritto greco e romano*, 162–204. Milan: A. Giuffre.
Catalogue of the Kunsthistorisches Museum Vienna, The Secular and Ecclesiastical Treasuries, Illustrated Guide. Vienna, 1991.
Chatillon, Jean. 1946. 'L'heritage littéraire de Richard de St Laurent.' *Revue du Moyen Age Latin* 2: 148–66.

Chevalier, Andrew. 1996. *The Encyclopedia of Medicinal Plants*. New York: DK Publishing.

Clark, Elizabeth A. 1990. 'Patrons not Priests: Gender and Power in Late Ancient Christianity.' *Gender and History* 2: 253–73.

Clay, Jenny Strauss. 1984. 'The Hecate of the *Theogony*.' *Greek, Roman and Byzantine Studies* 25: 24–38.

Cohen, David. 1991. 'The Augustan Law on Adultery: The Social and Cultural Context.' In *The Family in Italy from Antiquity to the Present*, edited by David I. Kertzer and Richard P. Saller, 109–26. New Haven, CT: Yale University Press.

Cooper, Kate. 1998. 'Contesting the Nativity: Wives, Virgins, and Pulcheria's imitatio Mariae.' *Scottish Journal of Religious Studies* 19: 31–43.

– 1996. *The Virgin and the Bride: Idealized Womanhood in Late Antiquity*. Cambridge and London: Harvard University Press.

– and Julia Hillner, eds. forthcoming. *Religion, Dynasty, and Patronage in a Christian Capital, 300–900*. Cambridge: Cambridge University Press.

Cornell, Tim. 1981. 'Some Observations on the "Crimen Incesti."' *Le délit religieux dans la cité antique. Collection de l'École française de Rome* 48: 27–37.

Cowie, Elizabeth. 1978. 'Woman as Sign.' *m/f* 1: 49–63.

Crossley, Michelle L. 2000. *Introduction to Narrative Psychology: Self, Trauma, and the Construction of Meaning*. Buckingham and Philadelphia: Open University Press.

Culham, Phyllis. 1982. 'The Lex Oppia.' *Latomus* 41: 786–93.

Culler, Jonathan. 1982. *On Deconstruction: Theory and Criticism after Structuralism*. Ithaca, NY: Cornell University Press.

Curran, John R. 2000. *Pagan City and Christian Capital Rome in the Fourth Century*. Oxford: Oxford University Press.

Currie, Sarah. 1998. 'Poisonous Women and Unnatural History in Roman Culture.' In *Parchments of Gender: Deciphering the Bodies of Antiquity*, edited by Maria Wyke, 147–67. Oxford: Oxford University Press.

Daly, Mary. 1968. *The Church and the Second Sex*. New York: Harper and Row.

Davis, John. 1977. *People of the Mediterranean: An Essay in Comparative Social Anthropology*. London: Routledge and Kegan Paul.

Dean-Jones, Lesley. 1994. *Women's Bodies in Classical Greek Science*. Oxford: Clarendon Press.

de Caulibus, Iohannis. 1997. *Meditationes Vitae Christi*. Corpus Christianorum Continuatio Mediaevalis. Vol. 153. Edited by M. Stallings-Taney. Brepols: Turnhout. Original, 14th century.

Dessau, Hermann. 1954. *Inscriptiones Latinae selectae*, 2nd ed. Berlin: Weidmann.

Dexter, Miriam Robbins. 1985. 'Indo-European Reflection of Virginity and Autonomy.' *Mankind Quarterly* 26.1–2: 57–74.

Dillon, Mathew. 2002. *Girls and Women in Classical Greek Religion.* London: Routledge.

Dixon, Suzanne. 1992. *The Roman Family.* Baltimore: Johns Hopkins University Press.

Douglas, Mary. 1970. *Natural Symbols.* London: Barrie and Rockliff.

– 1966. *Purity and Danger.* Middlesex: Penguin Books.

Dowden, K. 1989. *Death and the Maiden: Girls' Initiation Rites in Greek Mythology.* London: Routledge.

Dumézil, George. 1970. *Archaic Roman Religion.* 2 vols. Translated from the French edition (1966) by Philip Krapp. Chicago: University of Chicago Press.

Dumouchel, Paul, ed. 1988. *Violence and Truth: On the Work of René Girard.* Stanford, CA: Stanford University Press.

Dupront, A. 1930. *Pierre-Daniel Huet et l'Exegèse Comparatiste au XVIIe Siècle.* Paris: E. Leroux.

Durkheim, Emile. 1915. *The Elementary Forms of the Religious Life.* Repr. New York: Free Press, 1965.

Edwards, Catherine. 1993. *The Politics of Immorality in Ancient Rome.* Cambridge: Cambridge University Press.

Eliade, Mircea. 1961. *Myths, Dreams, and Mysteries.* New York: Harper.

– 1954. *The Myth of the Eternal Return.* New York: Pantheon.

Epstein, S. 1967. 'A Sociological Analysis of Witch Beliefs in a Mysore Village.' In *Magic, Witchcraft and Curing,* edited by John H. Middleton, 135–54. Garden City, NY: Natural History Press.

Falk, Tilman. 1946. *Studien zum Leben und Werk des Augsburger Malers.* Munich: Bruckmann.

Fallers, Lloyd, and Margaret C. Fallers. 1976. 'Sex Roles in Edremit.' In *Mediterranean Family Structures,* edited by J.G. Peristiany, 243–60. Cambridge: Cambridge University Press.

Fantham, Elaine, Helen Peet Foley, Natalie Boymel Kampen, Sarah B. Pomeroy, and H. Alan Shapiro. 1994. *Women in the Classical World.* Oxford: Oxford University Press.

Faraone, Christopher. 1992. *Talismans and Trojan Horses: Guardian Statues in Ancient Greek Myth and Ritual.* Oxford: Oxford University Press.

Fillitz, Hermann. 1964. *Die Schatzkammer in Wien.* Vienna: Schroll.

Flemming, Rebecca, and Ann Ellis Hanson. 1998. 'Hippocrates' *Peri Parthenion* (*Diseases of Young Girls*): Text and Translation.' *Early Science and Medicine* 3: 241–52.

Flottes, abbé J.-B. 1857. *Etude sur Daniel Huet, éveque d'Avranches.* Montpellier: Seguin.

Forge, Anthony. 1970. 'Prestige, Influence, and Sorcery.' In *Witchcraft Confessions and Accusations,* edited by Mary Douglas, 257–75. New York: Tavistock Publications.

Foucault, Michel. 1986. *The History of Sexuality*. Vol. 3: *The Care of the Self.* Translated from the French edition (1984) by Robert Hurley. New York and Toronto: Random House.
– 1985. *The History of Sexuality*. Vol. 2: *The Use of Pleasure*. Trans-lated from the French edition (1984) by Robert Hurley. New York: Random House.
Fowler, Warde. 1922. *The Religious Experience of the Roman People*. London: Macmillan.
Franchot, J. 1994. *Roads to Rome: The Antebellum Protestant Encounter with Catholicism*. Berkeley: University of California Press.
Fraschetti, Angelo. 1984. 'La sepoltura delle Vestali e la Città.' *Du Châtiment dans la Cité: Supplices Corporels et Peine de Mort dans le Monde Antique. Collection de l'École française de Rome* 79: 97–128.
– 1981. 'Le Sepolture Rituali del Foro Boario.' *Le Délit Religieux. Collection de l'École française de Rome* 48: 51–115.
Frazer, J.G. 1921. *Apollodorus. The Library.* Vols. 1 and 2. London: Heinemann and Cambridge: Harvard University Press.
– ed. 1911. *The Golden Bough*, 3rd ed. Vol. 1. London: Macmillan.
Fredriksen, Paula. 1986. 'Paul and Augustine: Conversion Narratives, Orthodox Traditions, and the Retrospective Self.' *Journal of Theological Studies* 37: 3–34.
Freud, Sigmund. 1979. 'The Psychogenesis of a Case of Homosexuality in a Woman.' In *Sigmund Freud: Case Histories*. Penguin Freud Library, vol. 9, 369–400. London: Penguin.
Friesen, Ilse E. 2001. *The Female Crucifix: Images of St. Wilgefortis since the Middle Ages*. Waterloo, ON: Wilfrid Laurier University Press.
– 1998. *Frau am Kreuz: Die Hl. Kümmernis in Tirol*. Exhibition cata-logue, Museum Stift Stams and Telfs. Tyrol: Hörtenbergdruck.
Friis-Johansen, F., and E.W. Whittle, eds and comm. 1980. *Aeschylus the Suppliants*, 3vv. Leiden: Brill.
Gagé, Jean. 1963. *Matronalia*. Brussels: Latomus.
Gallini, Clara. 1970. *Protesta e integrazione nella Roma antiqua*. Bari: Laterza.
Gamble, Harry Y. 1995. *Books and Readers in the Early Church: A History of Early Christian Texts*. New Haven, CT: Yale University Press.
Gardner, Jane F. 1986. *Women in Roman Law and Society*. London: Croom Helm.
Geoffrey of Vinseuf. 1967. *Poetria Nova*. Translated by Margaret F. Nims. Toronto: Pontifical Institute for Medieval Studies.
Gibson, Walter S. 1973. *Hieronymus Bosch*. New York: Praeger.
Gilmore, David D., ed. 1987. *Honor and Shame and the Unity of the Mediterranean*. Washington, DC: American Anthropological Association.
Giovannini, Maureen J. 1987. 'Female Chastity Codes in the Circum-Mediterranean: Comparative Perspectives.' In *Honor and Shame and the Unity of the Mediterra-nean*, edited by David D. Gilmore, 61–74. Washington, DC: American Anthropo-logical Association.

– 1981. 'Woman: A Dominant Symbol within the Cultural System of a Sicilian Town.' *Man* 16: 408–26.
Girard, René. 1986. *The Scapegoat*. Translated by Yvonne Freccero. Baltimore: Johns Hopkins University Press.
– 1977. *Violence and the Sacred*. Baltimore: Johns Hopkins University Press.
Gluckman, Max. 1956. *Custom and Conflict in Africa*. Oxford: Blackwell.
Golsan, Richard. 1993. 'An Interview with René Girard.' In *René Girard and Myth: An Introduction*, 129–49. New York: Garland Publishing.
– ed. 1990. 'René Girard and Western Literature,' *Special Issue of Helios* 17.1.
Grace, Sherrill. 1994. 'Gender as Genre: Atwood's Autobiographical "I."' In *Margaret Atwood: Writing and Subjectivity*, edited by Colin Nicholson, 189–203. New York: St Martin's.
Graef, Hilda. 1963. 'The Devotion to Our Lady.' In *Twentieth Century Encyclopedia of Catholicism*. Section 4: *The Means of Redemption*, edited by Henri Daniel-Rops. Vol. 45. New York: Hawthorn Books.
Grensemann, Hermann. 1982. *Hippokratische Gynäkologie. Die Gynäkologischen Texte des Autors C nach den Pseudohippokratischen Schriften* De Muliebribus I, II und De Sterilibus. Wiesbaden: Steiner.
Groden, S.Q. 1966. *The Poems of Sappho*. Indianapolis, New York: Bobbs-Merrill.
Gruen, Erich S. 1990. *Studies in Greek Culture and Roman Policy*. Leiden: Brill.
– 1968. *Roman Politics and the Criminal Courts, 149–78 B.C.* Cambridge: Harvard University Press.
Guarino, Antonio. 1943. 'Studi sull' "*incestum*."' *ZRG* 63: 175–267.
Guellouz, Suzanne, ed. 1994. *Pierre-Daniel Huet (1630–1721): Actes du Colloque de Caen (1993)*. Paris: Biblio 17.
Gugitz, Gustav. 1985. *Fest- und Brauchtumskalender für Österreich, Süddeutschland und die Schweiz*. Linz: Hollinek.
Guizzi, Francesco. 1968. *Aspetti Giuridici del Sacerdozio Romano: Il Sacerdozio di Vesta*. Naples: Jovene.
Hallett, Judith P. 1989. 'Women as *Same* and *Other* in the Classical Roman Elite.' *Helios* 16: 59–78.
– 1984. *Fathers and Daughters in Roman Society*. Princeton: Princeton University Press.
Halperin, David M., John J. Winkler, and Froma I. Zeitlin, eds. 1990. *Before Sexuality: The Construction of Erotic Experience in the Ancient Greek World*. Princeton: Princeton University Press.
Hamburger, Jeffrey F. 1997. *Nuns as Artists: The Visual Culture of a Medieval Convent*. Berkeley: University of California Press.
Hamerton-Kelly, Robert G. 1987. *Violent Origins*. Stanford: Stanford University Press.
Hanson, A.E. 2004. 'A Long-Lived "Quick-Birther" (*okytokion*).' In *Naissance et petite enfance dans l'Antiquité, Actes du colloque de Fribourg, 28 novembre–1er*

décembre 2001, edited by V. Dasen, 265–80. Fribourg, and Göttingen: Academic Press and Vandenhoeck and Ruprecht (*Orbis Biblicus et Orientalis*, vol. 203).
– 2000. 'Widows Too Young in Their Widowhood.' In *I, Claudia*. Vol. 2: *Women in Roman Art and Society*, edited by D.E.E. Kleiner and S.B. Matheson, 149–65. Austin: University of Texas Press.
– 1999. 'A Hair on Her Liver Has Been Lacerated ...' In *Aspetti della Terapia Nel Corpus Hippocraticum. Atti del IXe Colloque International Hippocratique*, edited by Ivan Garofalo, Alessandro Lami, Daniela Manetti, and Amneris Roselli, 235–54. Florence: Olschki.
– 1998a. 'Talking Recipes in the Gynaecological Texts of the *Hippocratic Corpus*.' In *Parchments of Gender: Deciphering the Body in Antiquity*, edited by Maria Wyke, 71–94. Oxford: Clarendon Press.
– 1998b. 'Galen: Author and Critic.' In *Editing Texts / Texte Edieren* (*Aporemata* 2), edited by Glenn W. Most, 22–53. Göttingen: Vandenhoeck and Ruprecht.
– 1995. 'Uterine Amulets and Greek Uterine Medicine.' *Medicina nei secoli*. 7: 281–99.
– 1992. 'Conception, Gestation, and the Origin of Female Nature in the *Corpus Hippocraticum*.' *Helios* 19: 31–71.
– 1990. 'The Medical-Writers' Woman.' In *Before Sexuality. The Construction of Erotic Experience in the Ancient World*, edited by David M. Halperin, John J. Winkler and Froma I. Zeitlin, 309–38. Princeton: Princeton University Press.
– 1989. 'Diseases of Women in the Epidemics.' In *Die Hippokratischen Epidemien: Theorie-Praxis-Tradition* (*Sudhoffs Archiv*, Beiheft 27), edited by Gerhard Baader and Rolf Winau, 38–51. Stuttgart: Steiner.
– 1975. 'Hippocrates: Diseases of Women I.' *Signs* 1: 567–84.
Hanson, Ann Ellis, and Monica H. Green. 1994. 'Soranus of Ephesus: *Methodicorum princeps*.' In *Aufstieg und Niedergang der Römischen Welt* II 37.2, edited by W. Haase, 968–1075. Berlin: de Gruyter.
Harding, Susan F. 1987. 'Convicted by the Holy Spirit: The Rhetoric of Fundamental Baptist Conversion.' *American Ethnologist* 14: 167–81.
Harper, E.B. 1969. 'Fear and the Status of Women.' *Southwestern Journal of Anthropology* 25: 81–95.
Hastrup, Kirsten. 1978. 'The Semantics of Biology: Virginity.' In *Defining Females: The Nature of Women in Society*, edited by Shirley Ardener, 49–65. New York: Wiley.
Haussherr, Reiner. 1962. 'Das Imervardkreuz und der Volto-Santo-Typ.' *Zeitschrift für Kunstwissenschaft* 16: 129–70.
Hazard, Paul. 1990. *The European Mind: The Critical Years. 1680–1715*. Translated by J. Lewis May. New York: Fordham University Press. Originally published as *La crise de la conscience européenne*. Paris, 1935.
Herington, C.J. 1955. *Athena Parthenos and Athena Polias: A Study in the Religion of Periclean Athens*. Manchester: Manchester University Press.

Herrmann, Claudine. 1964. *Le role judiciaire et politique des femmes sous la République Romaine*. Brussels: Collection Latomus.
Holmes, Lowell D. 1987. *Quest for the Real Samoa: The Mead/Freeman Controversy and Beyond*. South Hadley, MA: Bergin & Garvey.
Holum, Kenneth. 1982. *Theodosian Empresses, Women, and Imperial Dominion in Late Antiquity*. Berkeley: University of California Press.
Hommel, Hildebrecht. 1972. 'Vesta und die Frühromische Religion.' *Aufstieg und Neidergang des Römisches Welt* 1.2: 397–420.
Huet, P.-D. 1996. *Nouveaux mémoires pour servir à l'histoire du cartésianisme*. Edited by Claudine Poulouin. Rezé: Séquences. (First published 1692).
– 1974. *Traité philosophique de la foiblesse de le'esprit de l'homme*. Hildesheim: Georg Olms. (First published Amsterdam, 1723).
– 1971. *Censura philosophiae cartesianae*. Hildesheim: Georg Olms. (First published Paris, 1689).
– 1853. *Mémoires*. Translated by Ch. Nisart. Paris.
– 1810. *Memoirs*. Translated by John Aiken. 2 vols. London.
– 1722. *Huetiana, ou pensées diverses de M. Huet*. Edited by Joseph d'Olivet. Paris.
– 1718. *Commentarius de rebus ad eum pertinentibus*. The Hague.
– 1691. *Traité de la situation du paradis terrestre*. Paris.
– 1690. *Alnetanae quaestiones de concordia rationis et fidei*. Caen, Paris.
– 1679. *Demonstratio evangelica*. Paris.
– 1668. *Origenis commentaria in Sacras Scripturas*. Rouen.
– 1661. *De interpretatione*. Paris.
Huizinga, Johann. 1967. *Homo ludens*. Paris.
Hummel, Christine. 1999. *Das Kind und Seine Krankheiten in der Griechischen Medizin. Von Aretaios bis Johannes Aktuarios*. Frankfurt: Lang.
Hunter Wilson, Monica. 1970. 'Witch Beliefs and Social Structure.' In *Witchcraft and Sorcery: Selected Readings*, edited by Max Marwick, 252–63. Harmondsworth: Penguin.
Iohannis de Caulibus. 1997. *Meditationes Vitae Christi*. Corpus Christianorum Continuatio Mediaevalis. Vol. 153. Edited by M. Stallings-Taney. Turnhout: Breopols.
Irigaray, Luce. 1985a. *This Sex Which Is Not One*. Translated by Catherine Porter and Carolyn Burke. Ithaca, NY: Cornell University Press.
– 1985b. 'Women on the Market' ('La Marché des Femmes'). Reprinted in *The Logic of the Gift: Towards an Ethic of Generosity*, edited by Alan D. Schrift, 174–89. Translated by Catherine Porter and Carolyn Burke. New York: Routledge, 1997.
Jacobus de Voragine. 1993. *The Golden Legend: Readings on the Saints*. 2 vols. Translated by William Granger Ryan. Princeton: Princeton University Press.
Jeffry, David Lyle, ed. 1992. *A Dictionary of Biblical Tradition in English Literature*. Grand Rapids, MI: William B. Eerdmans.

John of Salisbury. 1909. *Policraticus*. In *Episcopi Candensis Policratici*, edited by C.J. Wood. Oxford: Clarendon Press.

Johnston, Sarah Iles. 1999. *Restless Dead: Encounters between the Living and the Dead in Ancient Greece*. Berkeley: University of California Press.

– 1990. *Hekate Soteira. A Study of Hekate's Roles in the Chaldean Oracles and Related Literature*. Edited by American Classical Studies. Vol. 21. Atlanta, GA: Scholars Press.

Joly, Robert, ed. 1970. *Hippocrate XI*. Paris: Les Belles Lettres.

Jones, A.H.M., J.R. Martindale, and J. Morris. 1971. *The Prosopography of the Later Roman Empire*. Vol. 1. Cambridge: Cambridge University Press.

Jouanna, Jacques, ed. 2000. *Hippocrate IV. Épidémies V et VII*. Paris: Les Belles Lettres.

Just, Roger. 1989. *Women in Athenian Law and Life*. New York: Routledge.

Kajanto, Iiro. 1977. *L'onomastique latine*. Paris: Centre national de la recherche scientifique.

– 1972. 'Women's Praenomina Reconsidered.' *Arctos*, n.s., 7: 13–30.

Kelly, J.N.D. 1977. *Early Christian Doctrines*, 5th ed. London: Adam and Charles Black.

Kempe, Margery. 1940. *The Book of Margery Kempe*. Edited by Sanford B. Meech. Annotations by H.E. Allen. Vol. EETS. o.s. 212. London: Oxford University Press.

Kempis, Thomas à. 1974. *The Imitation of Christ*. Translated by Betty I. Knott from the original Latin, 1471–72. London: Fontana Books.

Kerenyi, K. 1978. *Die Jungfrau und die Mutter der griechischen Religion. Eine Studie Über Pallas Athene*, Zürich: Rhein-Verlag.

King, Helen. 2004. *Disease of Virgins: Green Sickness, Chlorosis, and the Problems of Puberty*. London and New York: Routledge.

– 1998. *Hippocrates' Woman: Reading the Female Body in Ancient Greece*. London and New York: Routledge.

– 1993. 'Bound to Bleed: Artemis and Greek Women.' In *Images of Women in Antiquity*, edited by Averil Cameron and Amélie Kuhrt, 109–27. London and New York: Routledge.

Kirk, G.S. 1974. *The Nature of Greek Myths*. Cambridge: Cambridge University Press.

Kirkwood, Anna D. 1988. 'The *Tractatus Moralis Super Quatuor Elementa* of Walter of Wimborne: An Edition of Selected Portions.' Dissertation, University of Toronto.

Klindienst, Patricia Joplin. 1991. 'The Voice of the Shuttle Is Ours.' In *Rape and Representation*, edited by Lynn A. Higgins and Brenda R. Silver, 35–64. New York: Columbia University Press.

Koch, Carl. 1960. *Religio: Studien zu Kult und Glauben der Römer*. Nürnberg: H. Carl.

– 1958. 'Vesta.' *Pauly-Wissowa, Real-encyclopädie der klassischen Altertumswissenschaft* 2.16 (8A2): 1717–76.
Kramer, Samuel. 1969. *Sacred Marriage Rite.* Bloomington: Indiana University Press.
Kraus, Theodor. 1960. *Hekate: Studien zu Wesen und Bild des Göttin in Kleinasien und Griechenland.* Heidelberg: Carl Winter Universitätsverlag.
Larson, J. 1995) *Greek Heroine Cults.* Madison: University of Wisconsin.
Lefkowitz, Mary R. 1996. 'Women in the Panathenaia and Other Festivals.' In *Worshipping Athena: Panathenaia and Parthenon,* edited by Jennifer Neils, 78–91. Madison: University of Wisconsin Press.
– 1986. *Women in Greek Myth.* London: Duckworth.
Leithe-Jasper, Manfred, and Rudolf Distelberger. 1982. *Kunsthistorisches Museum Wien.* Volume 1. *Schatzkammer und Sammlung für Plastik und Kunstgewerbe.* Munich: Beck.
Lennon, Thomas M. 1999. *Reading Bayle.* Toronto: University of Toronto Press.
Lennon, Thomas M., J.M. Nicholas, and J.W. Davis. 1982. *Problems of Cartesianism.* Kingston and Montreal: McGill-Queen's University Press.
Lerner, Gerda. 1986. *The Creation of Patriarchy.* Oxford: Oxford University Press.
Levine, Nancy E. 1982. 'Belief and Explanation in Nyinba Women's Witchcraft.' *Man* 17: 259–74.
Lévi-Strauss, Claude. 1969. *The Elementary Structures of Kinship.* French original 1949. London: Eyre & Spottiswoode.
Linfert, Carl. 1970. *Hieronymus Bosch.* Cologne: Du Mont.
Lissarrague, François. 1995. 'Women, Boxes, Containers: Some Signs and Metaphors.' In *Pandora. Women in Classical Greece,* edited by Ellen D. Reeder, 91–100. Baltimore: Walters Art Gallery.
Lonie, Iain M. 1981. *The Hippocratic Treatises 'On Generation,' 'On the Nature of the Child,' 'Diseases IV.'* Berlin and New York: de Gruyter.
Loofs, Friedrich. 1905. *Nestoriana.* Halle a.S.: Niemeyer.
Loraux, Nicole. 1993. *The Children of Athena. Athenian Ideas about Citizenship and the Division between the Sexes.* Translated by Caroline Levine. Princeton: Princeton University Press.
– 1992. 'What Is a Goddess?' In *A History of Women,* edited by Pauline Schmitt Pantel, 11–44. Volume 1. Cambridge and London: Harvard University Press.
Lyons, Deborah. 1997. *Gender and Immortality: Heroines in Ancient Greek Myth and Cult.* Princeton: Princeton University Press.
MacBain, Bruce. 1982. *Prodigy and Expiation: A Study in Religion and Politics in Republican Rome.* Brussels: Latomus.
MacLachlan, Bonnie. 2002. 'The Ungendering of Aphrodite.' *Bulletin of the American School of Oriental Research* 325: 369–83.
Maia Neto, Jose. 1997. 'Academic Skepticism in Early Modern Philosophy.' *Journal of the History of Ideas* 58: 199–220.

Malbreil, G. 1991. 'Descartes Censuré par Huet.' *Revue philosophique*: 311–28.
– 1985. 'Les droits de la raison et de la foi, la dissociation de la raison, la métamorphose de la foi, selon Pierre Daniel Huet.' *XVII siècle* 147: 119–33.
March, Cristie. 1997. 'Crimson Silks and New Potatoes: The Heteroglossic Power of the Object in Atwood's *Alias Grace*.' *Studies in Canadian Literature* 22.2: 66–82.
Marrow, James H. 1989. *The Golden Age of Dutch Manuscript Painting*. Stuttgart: Belser.
Marshall, Bruce A. 1985. *A Historical Commentary on Asconius*. Columbia: University of Missouri Press.
Marwick, Max, ed. 1970. *Witchcraft and Sorcery: Selected Readings*. Harmondsworth: Penguin.
Massimi. 1985. 'Vérité et Histoire chez P.-D. Huet.' *XVIIe siècle* 147: 167–8.
Mathews, Thomas F. 1993. 'Christ Chameleon.' In *The Clash of Gods: A Reinterpretation of Early Christian Art*, 115–41. Princeton: Princeton University Press.
Mauss, Marcel. 1972. *A General Theory of Magic*. Translated by Robert Brain. French original 1902–3. London: Routledge and K. Paul.
Mayer, Philip. 1970. 'Witches.' In *Witchcraft and Sorcery: Selected Readings*, edited by Max Marwick, 45–64. Harmondsworth: Penguin.
McClure, Laura. 1999. *Spoken Like a Woman: Speech and Gender in Athenian Drama*. Princeton: Princeton University Press.
McKenna, Andrew J. 1992. *Violence and Difference: Girard, Derrida, and Deconstruction*. Urbana: University of Illinois Press.
McKenna, Antony. 1985. 'Pascal et Huet.' *XVIIe siècle* 147: 135–42.
McNamer, Sarah. 1990. 'Further Evidence for the Date of the Pseudo-Bonaventuran Meditationes Vitae Christi.' *Franciscan Studies* 50: 235–61.
Mead, Margaret. 1928. *Coming of Age in Samoa: A Psychological Study of Primitive Youth for Western Civilization*. New York: Morrow.
Mernissi, Fatima. 1975. *Beyond the Veil: Male-Female Dynamics in a Modern Muslim Society*. Cambridge: Schenkman.
Meyer, Jerry D. 1997. 'Profane and Sacred: Religious Imagery and Prophetic Expression in Postmodern Art.' *Journal of the American Academy of Religion* 65.1: 19–46.
Meyer, Marvin. 1994. 'A Coptic Book of Ritual Power From Heidelberg.' In *Ancient Christian Magic: Coptic Texts of Ritual Power*, edited by Marvin Meyer and Richard Smith, 323–41. San Francisco: Harper San Francisco.
Middleton, John, and E.H. Winter, eds. 1963. *Witchcraft and Sorcery in East Africa*. London: Praeger.
Milton, John. 1957. 'Comus.' In *John Milton, Complete Poems and Major Prose*, edited by Y. Hughes Merrit, 89–114. Indianapolis & New York: The Odyssey Press.
Mirecki, P., and M. Meyer, eds. 2002. *Magic and Ritual in the Ancient World*. Leiden: Brill.

Mommsen, Theodore. 1899. *Römisches Strafrecht*. Leipzig: Duncker und Humblot.
– 1887. *Römisches Staatsrecht*, 3rd ed. 3 vols. Leipzig: S. Hirzel.
Monaco, Lucia. 1984. '*Veneficia matronarum*: Magia, medizina e repressione.' In *Sodalitas: Scritti in onore di Antonio Guarino*, 5: 2013–24. Naples: Jovene.
Monk, M. 1836. *The Awful Disclosures of Maria Monk, or The Hidden Secrets of a Nun's Life in a Convent Exposed*. Manchester: Milner Press.
Morgan, M. Gwyn. 1974. 'Priests and Physical Fitness: A Note on Roman Religion.' *Classical Quarterly* 24: 137–41.
Morin, Germain. 1928. 'Rainaud l'ermite et Ives de Chartres. Un épisode de la crise du cénobitisme au XIe–XIie siècle.' *Revue Bénédictine* 40: 384–474.
Muir, Carolyn Diskant. 2000–1. 'Art and Religion in Seventeenth-Century Antwerp: Van Dyck's *Mystic Marriage of the Blessed Hermann-Joseph*.' *Simiolus* 28: 51–69.
Mulvey, Laura. 1975. 'Visual Pleasure and Narrative Cinema.' *Screen* 16: 6–18.
Münzer, F. 1923. 'Servilia,' *Pauly-Wissowa, Real-encyclopädie der Klassischen Altertumswissenschaft* 2A: 1721.
Mustakallio, K. 1992. 'The "crimen incesti" of the Vestal Virgins and the Prodigious Pestilence.' In *Crudelitas: The Politics of Cruelty in the Ancient and Medieval World*, edited by T. Viljamaa, A. Timonen, and C. Kritzel. Krems, 56–63. Krems: Medium Aevum Quotidianum.
Mycak, Sonia. 1996. *In Search of the Split Subject: Psychoanalysis, Phenomenology, and the Novels of Margaret Atwood*. Toronto: ECW.
Nelmes, Jill. 1999. *An Introduction to Film Studies*. 2nd ed. London: Routledge.
Newman, Barbara. 1995. *From Virile Woman to WomanChrist: Studies in Medieval Religion and Literature*. Philadelphia: University of Pennsylvania Press.
Nock, Arthur Darby. 1972. *Essays on Religion and the Ancient World*. 2 vols. Cambridge, MA: Harvard University Press.
Noy, David. 1991. 'Wicked Stepmothers in Roman Society and Imagination.' *Journal of Family History* 16: 345–63.
Nutton, Vivian. 1995. 'Roman Medicine 250 BC to AD 200.' In *The Western Medical Tradition: 800 BC to AD 1800*, edited by L.I. Conrad et al., 39–70. Cambridge: Cambridge University Press.
O'Donnell, James J., ed. 1990. *Boethius, Consolatio Philosophiae*. 3 vols. Bryn Mawr: Bryn Mawr Commentaries.
Ogilvie, R.M. 1965. *A Commentary on Livy I–V*. Oxford: Oxford University Press.
Ortner, Sherry B. 1978. 'The Virgin and the State.' *Feminist Studies* 4.3: 19–35.
Paganini, Gianni. 1991. *Scepsi Moderna*. Cosenza: Busento.
Page, Denys. 1955. *Sappho and Alcaeus: An Introduction to the Study of Ancient Lesbian Poetry*. Oxford: Oxford University Press.
Pailler, Jean-Marie. 1990. 'Les Bacchanales: Une affaire de famille.' In *Parenté et*

stratégies familiales dans l'antiquité romaine. Actes de la table ronde des 2–4 octobre 1986, Paris. CEFR 129: 77–83.
— 1988. *Bacchanalia: La repression de 186 av. J.-C. a Rome et en Italie.* Rome: École française de Rome.
Palmer, R.E.A. 1974. 'Roman Shrines of Female Chastity from the Caste Struggle to the Papacy of Innocent I.' *Rivista Storica dell' Antichà* 4: 122–59.
Panofsky, Erwin. 1923. 'Das Braunschweiger Domkruzifix und das "Volto Santo" zu Lucca.' *Festschrift für Adolph Goldschmidt zum 60 Geburtstag am 15 Januar 1923*, 37–44. Leipzig: Seemann.
Parker, Holt N. 1998. 'Loyal Slaves and Loyal Wives: The Crisis of the Outsider-within and Roman *exemplum* Literature.' In *Women and Slaves in Greco-Roman Culture*, edited by Sandra Joshel and Sheila Murnaghan, 52–73. New York: Routledge.
Patterson, Cynthia B. 1998. *The Family in Greek History.* Cambridge and London: Harvard University Press.
Pelikan, Jaroslav. 1996. *Mary through the Centuries: Her Place in the History of Culture.* New Haven, CT: Yale University Press.
Pelissier, Léon-G. 1889. *A Travers les Papiers de Huet.* Paris.
Penglase, Charles. 1994. *Greek Myths and Mesopotamia: Parallels and Influence in the Homeric Hymns and Hesiod.* London and New York: Routledge.
Peristiany, John G., ed. 1965. *Honour and Shame: The Values of Mediterranean Society.* London: Weidenfeld and Nicolson.
Piaget, Jean. 1962. *Play, Dreams and Imitation in Childhood.* Translated by C. Galtegno and F.M. Hodson. New York: Norton.
Pitt-Rivers, Julian. 1977. *The Fate of Shechem or the Politics of Sex: Essays in the Anthropology of the Mediterranean.* Cambridge: Cambridge University Press.
Podlecki, A.J. 1972. 'The Aeschylean Chorus as Dramatic Persona.' In *Studi Classici in Onore di Quintino Cataudella*, 187–204. Catania: Università di Catania.
Pomeroy, Sarah. 1997. *Families in Classical and Hellenistic Greece.* Oxford and New York: Oxford University Press.
— 1995. 'Women's Identity and the Family in the Classical *Polis*.' In *Women in Antiquity: New Assessments*, edited by Richard Hawley and Barbara Levick, 111–21. London and New York: Routledge.
— 1976. 'The Relationship of the Married Woman to Her Blood Relatives in Rome.' *Ancient Society* 7: 225–6.
— 1975. *Goddesses, Whores, Wives, and Slaves.* New York: Schocken Books.
Popkin, R. 1991. 'Bishop Pierre-Daniel Huet's Remarks on Malebranche.' In *Nicolas Malebranche: His Philosophical Critics and Successors*, edited by S. Brown, 10–21. Assen: Van Gorcum.
— 1982. 'Cartesianism and Bible Criticism.' In *Problems of Cartesianism*, edited by

Thomas M. Lennon, John H. Nicholas, and John W. Davis, 61–81. Kingston and Montreal: McGill-Queen's University Press.
– 1959. 'The Manuscript Papers of Bishop Pierre-Daniel Huet.' *Yearbook of the American Philosophical Society*: 449–53.
Porte, Danielle. 1984. 'Les Enterrements Expiatories à Rome.' *Revue de Philologie* 58: 233–43.
Price, Theodora Hadzisteliou. 1978. *Kourotrophos: Cults and Representations of the Greek Nursing Deities*. Brill: Leiden.
Prins, Y. 1991. 'The Power of the Speech Act: Aeschylus' Furies and Their Binding Song.' *Arethusa* 24.2.
Pseudo Albertus Magnus. 1884. 'De Laudibus Beatae Mariae Virginis.' In *Opera Omnia*, edited by A. Borgnet. Paris.
Pseudo Bonaventure. 1961. *Meditations on the Life of Christ: An Illustrated Manuscript of the Fourteenth Century (Ms.Ital. 115, Paris Bibl.Nat)*, edited by I.R. and R.B. Green. Princeton: Princeton University Press.
Purcell, Nicholas. 1986. 'Livia and the Womanhood of Rome.' *Proceedings of the Cambridge Philological Society* 32: 78–105.
Radcliffe-Brown, A.R. 1979. 'Taboo.' In *Reader in Comparative Religion*, edited by W.A. Lessa and E.Z. Vogt, 46–56. 4th ed. New York: Harper & Row.
Radke, Gerhard. 1975. 'Vesta.' *Der Kleine Pauly: Lexikon der Antike* 5: 1127–9.
– 1972. 'Acca Larentia und die fratres Arvales.' *Aufstieg und Niedergang der romischen Welt* 1.2: 421–41.
– 1965. *Die Götter Altitaliens*. Münster: Aschendorff.
Rao, Eleanor. 1993. *Strategies for Identity: The Fiction of Margaret Atwood*. New York: P. Lang.
Rawson, Elizabeth. 1991. 'Religion and Politics in the Late Second Century B.C. at Rome.' In *Roman Culture and Society: The Collected Papers of Elizabeth Rawson*, edited by Fergus Millar. Oxford: Clarendon Press. Orig. publ. 1974.
Reay, Marie. 1959. *The Kuma: Freedom and Conformity in the New Guinea Highlands*. Melbourne: Melbourne University Press.
Reeder, Ellen D. 1995. *Pandora: Women in Classical Greece*. Princeton: Princeton University Press.
Reineke, Martha J. 1997. *Sacrificed Lives: Kristeva on Women and Violence*. Bloomington: Indiana University Press.
Richlin, Amy. 1981. 'Approaches to the Sources on Adultery at Rome.' *Women's Studies* 8.1–2: 225–50. Reprinted in *Reflections of Women in Antiquity*, edited by Helene P. Foley, 379–404. New York: Gordon and Breach.
Riddle, John M. 1992. *Contraception and Abortion from the Ancient World to the Renaissance*. Cambridge: Harvard University Press.
Rigg, A.G., ed. 1978. *The Poems of Walter of Wimborne*. Toronto: Pontifical Institute for Medieval Studies.

– 1971. 'Walter of Wimborne, O.F.M.: An Anglo-Latin Poet of the Thirteenth Century.' *Medieval Studies* 33: 371–8.
Robertson, Noel. 1996. 'Athena's Shrines and Festivals.' In *Worshipping Athena. Panathenaia and Parthenon*, edited by Jennifer Neils, 27–77. Madison: University of Wisconsin Press.
Robson, J.E. 1997. 'Bestiality and Bestial Rape in Greek Myth.' In *Rape in Antiquity: Sexual Violence in the Greek and Roman Worlds*, edited by S. Deacy and K. Pierce, 65–96. London: Duckworth.
Rodis-Lewis, Geneviève. 1985. 'Huet Lecteur de Malebranche.' *Le XVIIe siècle* 37: 169–89.
Rogerson, Margaret. 1998. 'Reading the Patchworks in *Alias Grace*.' *Journal of Commonwealth Literature* 33.1: 5–22.
Rosaldo, Michelle Zimbalist. 1974. 'A Theoretical Overview.' In *Woman, Culture, and Society*, edited by Michelle Zimbalist Rosaldo and Louise Lamphere, 17–42. Stanford, CA: Stanford University Press.
Rose, H.J. 1970. 'Vesta.' *Oxford Classical Dictionary*. 2nd ed. Oxford: Clarendon Press.
– 1926. 'De Virginibus Vestalibus.' *Mnemosyne*, n.s., 54: 440–8.
Roth, Cecil. 1978. *A History of the Jews in England*, 3rd ed. Oxford: Clarendon Press.
Rotondi, Giovanni. 1912. *Leges publicae populi romani*. Milan: Società Editrice Libraria.
Rousselle, Robert. 1989. 'Persons in Livy's Account of the Bacchic Persecution.' In *Studies in Latin Literature and Roman History* 5, edited by Carl Deroux, 55–65. Brussels: Latomus.
Rubin, Gail. 1975. 'The Traffic in Women: Notes on the "Political Economy" of Sex.' In *Toward an Anthropology of Women*, edited by R.R. Reiger, 157–210. New York: Monthly Review Press.
Rüpke, Jorg. 2001. *Die Religion der Römer: eine Einführung*. München: C.H. Beck.
Saller, Richard P. 1994. *Patriarchy, Property and Death in the Roman Family*. Cambridge: Cambridge University Press.
Salisbury, Joyce. 1991. *Church Fathers, Independent Virgins*. New York: Verso Books.
Santoro L'Hoir, Francesca S. 1992. *The Rhetoric of Gender Terms: 'Man,' 'Woman,' and the Portrayal of Character in Latin Prose*. *Mnemosyne* suppl. 120. Leiden: Brill.
Sarbin, T. 1986. 'The Narrative as a Root Metaphor for Psychology.' In *Narrative Psychology*, edited by T. Sarbin, 3–21. New York: Praeger.
Schaps, D.M. 1998. 'What Was Free about a Free Athenian Woman?' *Transactions of the American Philological Association* 128: 161–88.
Schneider, Jane. 1971. 'Of Vigilance and Virgins.' *Ethnology* 9: 1–24.

Schneider, Jane, and Peter Schneider. 1976. *Culture and Political Economy in Western Sicily.* New York: Academic Press.

Schnürer, Gustav, and Joseph Ritz. 1934. *Sankt Kümmernis und Volto Santo.* Düsseldorf: Schwann.

Schreiber, Georg. 1937. *Deutsche Bauernfrömmigkeit, Forschungen zur Volkskunde* 29. Düsseldorf: Schwann.

Scodel, Ruth. 1996. '*Domôn Agalma*: Virgin Sacrifice and Aesthetic Object.' *Transactions of the American Philological Association* 126: 111–28.

Scott, Wm. C. 1984. *Musical Design in Aeschylean Theatre.* Hanover and London: University Press of New England.

Seaford, R. 1988. 'The Eleventh Ode of Bacchylides: Hera, Artemis, and the Absence of Dionysos.' *Journal of Hellenic Studies* 88: 118–36.

Serwint, Nancy. 1993. 'The Female Athletic Costume at the Heraia and Prenuptial Initiation Rites.' *American Journal of Philology* 97: 403–22.

Shankman, Paul. 1996. 'History of Samoan Sexual Conduct and the Mead-Freeman Controversy.' *American Anthropologist* 98: 555–67.

Shinners, John, ed. 1997. *Medieval Popular Religion. 1000–1500: A Reader.* Peterborough, ON: Broadview Press.

Sissa, Giulia. 1990a. *Greek Virginity.* Vol. 3. of *Revealing Antiquity.* Translated by Arthur Goldhammer. Edited by G.W. Bowersock. Cambridge: Harvard University Press.

– 1990b. 'Maidenhood without Maidenhead: The Female Body in Ancient Greece.' In *Before Sexuality: The Construction of Erotic Experience in the Ancient World,* edited by David M. Halperin, John J. Winkler, and Froma I. Zeitlin, 339–64. Princeton: Princeton University Press.

Smalley, Beryl. 1964. *The Study of the Bible in the Middle Ages.* Notre Dame: University of Notre Dame Press.

– 1960. *English Friars and Antiquity in the Early Fourteenth Century.* New York: Barnes and Noble.

Smith, Wesley D. 1979. *The Hippocratic Tradition.* Ithaca, NY: Cornell University Press.

Solmsen, F. 1937. 'The Erinys in Aischylos' *Septem.*' *Transactions of the American Philological Association* 68: 197–211.

Sommerstein, A., ed. and comm. 1989. *Aeschylus: Eumenides.* Cambridge: Cambridge University Press.

Sourvinou-Inwood, C. 1988. *Studies in Girls' Transitions: Aspects of the Arkteia and Age Representation in Attic Iconography.* Athens: Kardamitsa.

Staber, Joseph. 1955. *Volksfrömmigkeit und Wallfahrtswesen des späten Mittelalters im Bistum Freising.* Munich.

Staples, Ariadne. 1998. *From Good Goddess to Vestal Virgins: Sex and Category in Roman Religion.* London and New York: Routledge.

Stehle, Eva. 1990. 'Sappho's Gaze: Fantasies of a Goddess and Young Man.' *differences* 2.1: 88–125.
– 2005. 'Prayer and Curse in Aeschylus' *Seven against Thebes.*' *Classical Philology* 100: 101–22.
Strathern, Marilyn. 1988. *The Gender of the Gift*. Berkeley: University of California Press.
Swartz, K. 1941. 'Der Vestakult und seine Herkunft.' PhD diss., Heidelberg, 1941.
Tambiah, Stanley Jeyaraja. 1985. *Culture, Thought and Social Action*. Cambridge, MA: Harvard University Press.
Thalmann, W. 1978. *Dramatic Art in Aeschylus'* Seven against Thebes. New Haven: Yale University Press.
Thurston, Herbert, and Donald Attwater. 1956. *Butler's Lives of the Saints*. London: Burn and Oates.
Tolmer, Abbé Leon. 1949. *Pierre-Daniel Huet: Humaniste-Physicien*. Bayeux: Colas.
Townsend, David. 1986. 'Robert Grosseteste and Walter of Wimborne.' *Medium Aevum* 55: 113–17.
Treggiari, Susan. 1991. *Roman Marriage: Iusti Coniuges from the Time of Cicero to the Time of Ulpian*. Oxford: Oxford University Press.
Turner, Victor. 1985. 'Symbols in African Ritual.' In *Magic, Witchcraft, and Religion*, edited by A.C. Lehmann and J.E. Myers, 55–63. Palo Alto, CA: Mayfield.
– 1974. *Dramas, Fields, and Metaphors: Symbolic Action in Human Society*. Ithaca, NY: Cornell University Press.
– 1969. *The Ritual Process: Structure and Anti-Structure*. Chicago: Aldine.
Tyrrell, Wm. Blake. 1984. *Amazons: A Study in Athenian Mythmaking*. Baltimore: John Hopkins University Press.
Vauchez, André. 1991. 'Saints admirables et saints imitables: les fonctions de l'hagiographie ont-elles changé aux derniers siècles du moyen-âge?' In *Les fonctions des saints dans le monde occidental (IIIe– XIIIe siècle)*, 161–72. Rome: École Française de Rome.
Vernant, Jean-Pierre. 1983. 'Hestia-Hermes: The Religious Expression of Space and Movement in Ancient Greece.' In *Myth and Thought among the Greeks*, edited by Jean-Pierre Vernant and translated by Janet Lloyd, 127–75. London/Boston: Routledge and Keagan Paul.
– 1991. 'Mortals and Immortals: The Body of the Divine.' In *Collected Essays*, edited by Froma I. Zeitlin, 27–49. Princeton: Princeton University Press.
Versnel, H.S. 1976. 'Two Types of Roman *Devotio*.' *Mnemosyne* 29: 365–410.
Volterra, Edoardo. 1948. 'Il preteso tribunale domestico in diritto romano.' *Rivista italiana per le scienze giuridiche* 2: 103–53.
von Schlosser, Julius. 1912. *Der Burgunder Paramentenschatz des Ordens des Goldenen Vliesses*. Vienna: Schroll.

von Staden, Heinrich. 1989. *Herophilus: The Art of Medicine in Early Alexandria*. Cambridge: Cambridge University Press.

Walker Bynum, Caroline. 1982. *Jesus as Mother: Studies in the Spirituality of the High and Middle Ages*. Berkeley: University of California Press.

Warner, Marina. 1981. *Joan of Arc: The Image Of Female Heroism*. New York: Knopf.

– 1976. *Alone of All Her Sex: The Myth and the Cult of the Virgin Mary*. London: Weidenfeld and Nicolson.

Watson, Patricia A. 1995. *Ancient Stepmothers: Myth, Misogyny and Reality*. Mnemosyne suppl. 143. Leiden: Brill.

West, M.L., ed. and comm. 1966. *Hesiod. Theogony*. Oxford: Oxford University Press.

Wiedemann, T.E.J. 1987. *Slavery: Greece and Rome*. New Surveys in the Classics No. 19. Oxford: Oxford University Press.

Wilamowitz-Moellendorf, Ulrich von. 1931. *Der Glaube der Hellenen*. 2 vols. Berlin: Weidmann'sche Buchhandlung.

Winter, E.H. 1963. 'The Enemy Within: Amba Witchcraft and Sociological Theory.' In *Witchcraft and Sorcery in East Africa*, edited by John Middleton and E.H. Winter, 277–99. London: Praeger.

Wissowa, Georg. 1925. 'Vesta.' In *Ausführliches Lexikon der Griechischen und Römischen Mythologie*, vol. 6, edited by W.H. Roscher, 247–53. Leipzig: B.G. Teubner.

– 1923–4. 'Vestalinnen Frevel.' *Archiv für Religionswissenschaft* 22: 201–24.

– 1912. *Religion und Kultus der Römer*, 2nd ed. München: C.H. Beck.

Young, Frances M. 1983. *From Nicaea to Chalcedon: A Guide to the Literature and Its Background*. London: SCM Press.

Zeitlin, F. 1992. 'The Politics of Eros in the Danaid Trilogy of Aeschylus.' In *Innovations of Antiquity*, edited by R. Hexter and D. Selden. New York: Routledge.

Ziegler, Konrat. 1957. *Vitae parallelae, Romulus*. Leipzig: Teubner.

INDEX

Abbott, Elizabeth, 3
abstinence, 6, 68
adamatos, 14, 19, 25
aedes Vestae, 71, 89n16
Aemilia, 74, 87, 94n94, 94n96, 95n101
Aeschylus, 7, 9, 19, 23n33, 24, 26, 27, 34, 35, 36, 61n6, 92; *Eumenides*, 7, 19, 20, 23n33, 24, 25, 33, 34, 61n6; *Oresteia*, 33, 92; *Prometheus Bound*, 25; *Seven against Thebes*, 7, 24, 25, 27, 28, 31, 35; *Suppliant Women*, 7, 24, 25, 31, 33, 35
agency, 6, 20, 34, 102, 110, 111, 112, 158, 160, 165, 168, 170
Agnodike, midwife, 19
almah, 7
Amazons, 16–17, 36
amenorrhea, 11, 42, 43, 44, 48, 55, 62n27
Anastasia, 107–8
androgyny, 9, 17
Aphrodite, 4, 12n7, 13, 15, 20, 21n7, 117; bearded, 117; transgendered, 12
Apocryphal Acts, 10
Arkteia, 26
armour, virgin's, 9, 11, 17, 19, 23n34
Arrephoroi, 22n21, 26
Artemis, 4, 7, 8, 13–19, 21n10, 22n13, 26, 48, 89n12, 95; Brauronia, 15, 26, 89n12; virgin goddess, 15, 105
ascetics, asceticism, 5, 9, 10, 109, 120
Atalanta, 16
Athena, 4, 7, 8, 9, 11, 13, 14, 15, 16, 17, 18, 19, 20, 21n8, 22n19, 22n21, 22n25, 23n31, 23n33, 26, 27, 34–5, 44, 72, 89n12
Augustine, 110, 115n38
Aurelia Severa, 88, 94n96
autonomy, 4, 5, 7, 8, 13, 14, 20, 21n6, 168

Bayle, Pierre, 150, 155n2, 155n13
Beard, Mary, 66, 68, 73, 88nn6–7, 89n10, 89n13, 89n15, 90n40, 91n53, 95n108, 96n112, 98n138
Bernard of Clairvaux, 131, 132, 145n15
bisexual power, 12n7, 119
boundaries, 17, 31, 70, 79, 80, 82, 96n112, 132
bride(s), 4, 9, 20, 21n13, 44–5, 55, 57, 65n54, 84, 118, 130, 132, 133, 143; of Christ, 143

Calame, Claude, 29, 36n2, 37n13
Callisto, 15, 21n12, 25
celibate, 5, 8, 9, 10, 13, 15, 143

chastity/unchastity, 5, 8, 9, 10, 19, 22n20, 66, 68, 69, 70, 79, 80, 83, 84, 86, 88, 94n97, 161, 162
choregos, 27, 29, 31, 32, 34, 35, 37n9, 38n17
Christ, 4, 10, 102, 103, 104, 107, 108, 116, 117, 118, 119, 122, 123, 125, 126, 128, 130, 131, 133, 134, 136, 137, 138, 140, 141, 142, 143, 145n11, 145n17, 145n19, 149, 150, 153, 154; body of, 134, 144, 145n11, 145n17, 145n19; bride of, 130, 143; crucified, 10, 116, 119; human, 103; imitating, 107, 108; mother of, 4, 128, 130, 131, 133, 134, 138, 139, 140, 142, 149, 154; virgin birth of, 107, 129, 149, 150, 153, 154
Claudia Quinta, 84, 87
Clodia Laeta, 88
cloister/cloistered, 8, 9, 131, 159
Clytemnestra, 24, 27, 33, 34, 38n23
Constantia, 100, 112, 113n2
Constantina, 112, 113n2
Cornelia, 74, 75, 87, 92n70, 94n94
crucifix, 116, 117, 118, 119, 120, 122
crucifixion, 103, 124, 125, 126n4, 126n8, 131, 138, 143
curse, 28, 30, 31, 34, 35, 37n12, 38n16, 139, 141
Cyril, 103, 104, 105

Daly, Mary, 101, 113n3
Danaids, 18, 24, 26, 31–3, 34, 38n19, 39n30
Daphne, 16, 22n14
defloration, 46, 49, 55, 56, 62n26
Demeter, 4, 19
devotio, 8, 81, 82–3, 97n127
devotion(s)/devotional, 107, 123, 125, 126, 126n8, 128–34, 136–8, 143, 146n27

discipline/disciplined, 40, 73, 74, 83, 97n132
divine, 4, 7, 13, 14, 17, 20, 35, 86, 101, 103, 104, 107, 112, 131, 132, 133, 136, 143, 145n17; bridegroom, 100, 145n17; constructs, 13, 14; family, 14; feminine, 101, 103; justice, 136, 137, 143; lover, 132; motherhood, 14; *parthenos*, 17; presence, 131, 132; virgin, 7, 14, 20; wrath, 86, 138
divinity, 6, 9, 15, 102, 103, 119, 138; androgynous, 119; kourotrophic, 15
dolls, 6, 133–4, 140, 142
Domitian, 74, 75, 87
Douglas, Mary, 7, 11n4, 66, 70, 90n33, 93n93, 96n112
dreams, 88n8, 154, 156, 157, 158, 162, 163, 164, 169, 171

Electra, 24
Elizabeth I, 5, 7
emancipatio, 73, 99n145
embodiment, virgins as, 9, 20, 37n11, 67, 68–9, 72–3, 85, 118, 119, 166
Empress, 104, 105, 106, 109; Helena, 106; Pulcheria, 104, 105, 106, 109
enigma, 11, 156, 174
epikleros, 14
Erichthonius, 15, 19, 21n8, 153
Erinyes, 23n33, 24, 33–5, 36n1, 38nn22–3, 38nn22–3, 39n27, 39n30
Eudoxia, 105, 114n17
Euripides, 18, 21n11, 24, 36, 93n82; *Bacchae*, 93n82; *Helen*, 18; *Hippolytus*, 21n11
Europa, 36n3
Eusebius, 106, 114n23, 124, 125

Fabia, 87, 91n50
faith, 75, 80, 109, 128, 138, 142, 151–3
fasting, 11, 46

father/fathering, 9, 16, 17, 20, 24, 27, 30, 31, 32, 33, 57, 71, 72, 73, 80, 84, 85, 91n50, 94n100, 95n108, 98n145, 102, 103, 109, 117, 128, 131, 132, 138, 143, 149, 153, 154
Fathers, Church, 109, 154
fecundity, virginal, 8, 16, 18, 19, 20, 26, 35; latent, 26; potential, 16, 18
fertility, 12n7, 18, 19, 23n30, 31, 36, 40, 71, 96n118, 118, 119
Floronia, 84, 86, 93n94, 96n111
Fortuna Muliebris, cult of, 83, 86
Foucault, Michel, 23n40, 64n42
Franchot, Jenny, 8, 9, 11n5
freedom, 9, 71, 115n38
Furies, 33–4, 153

Gaius, 90n38, 91n47, 91n52, 95n107
Galen, 53, 54–8, 60n1, 63n33, 64n40–1, 64n43, 65n50, 65n56
Gallicanus, Passion of, 100, 101
gaze, male, 16, 17, 41, 110, 131
gender, 9, 10, 11, 21n7, 22n22, 40, 54, 55, 60n4, 89n13, 101, 102, 104, 106, 110, 119, 120, 123, 125, 146n27
gendered, 5, 7, 9, 12n7, 17, 54
genderless, 40–9, 57
Gilbertus Angelicus, 57, 58, 65n55
Giovaninni, Maureen J., 90n30, 90n32
Girard, René, 66, 74, 75, 76, 77, 78, 81, 82, 85, 92nn61–4, 92nn66–7, 92n72, 92n74, 93nn78–9, 93n81, 93n85, 93n88, 93n91, 96n116, 97n122, 97n125, 97n131
goddess(es), 4, 9, 11, 13–21, 21n7, 35, 153
godhead, 136, 145n17
gods, 12n7, 13, 14, 28, 29, 30, 32, 33, 36n3, 77, 80, 82, 83, 95n103, 124, 149, 153; bisexual, 12n7
guardianship, 13, 26, 31, 37n7

gyne, 13, 18, 40, 43, 45, 46, 49, 50, 56, 61n16

Handbook for Gregoria, 107, 108, 111
hearth, 9, 13, 19, 20, 23n37, 69, 89n16
heaven/heavenly, 77, 100, 107, 109, 112, 132, 135, 137, 139, 140, 143, 155n13; Queen of, 112, 140
Hecate, 7, 14, 21n4, 21n6
Helena, Empress, 106
Hera, 4, 14, 17, 18, 19, 21n12, 22nn28–9
Heraia, 17
heresy, 113n10, 155n13
hermaphrodite, 81
heroines, 4, 10, 111, 115n45, 157
Herophilus, 53, 54, 64n45
Hesiod, 14, 16, 20, 26, 92n63; *Theogony*, 14
Hestia, 7, 8, 13, 14, 20, 23nn37–9
hieros gamos, 18
Hippocrates, 36n4, 53, 58, 59, 60n2, 63n33, 64nn40–1
Hippocratic: *Aphorisms*, 41, 51, 53, 59; *Diseases IV*, 47, 59; *Diseases of Women I*, 42–3, 47, 50, 59; *Diseases of Young Girls*, 44, 46–7, 49, 52, 59; *Eight Months' Child*, 40, 59; *Epidemics*, 42, 49–53, 58, 59, 63; *Nature of the Child*, 41, 42, 44, 47, 59; *Superfetation*, 44, 46, 49, 50, 52, 60
Homer, 44, 92n63, 154; *Iliad*, 44; *Odyssey*, 44
Homeric Hymn to Aphrodite, 13, 20, 21n7
Horatia, 79, 94n100
household, 9, 19–20, 35, 40, 57, 67, 68, 69, 89n15, 112, 166
Huet, Daniel, 6, 149–55, 155nn3–4, 155nn8–10, 155n13
hymen, 48, 56, 63n29, 155

Hypermnestra, 33
hysteria, 26, 36n4, 78

icon, 5, 6, 101, 106, 111, 112, 129
iconography, 125
Ignatius, Bishop, 104, 108, 113n13
imitatio, 6, 106–9, 115n35, 115n38
impiety, 94n97, 95n103
impregnable, 82
incarnate/incarnation, 9, 27, 38n25, 72–4, 82–3, 102–3, 107–8, 130, 154
incest, 76, 80, 83, 96n118
incestum, 77–83, 86, 87, 88, 92, 93n87, 94n94, 95n101, 96n111, 96n118
independence, 5, 7, 13, 14, 18
innocence, 44, 45, 57, 68, 87, 88, 118, 149, 158, 161, 162, 163, 164, 168, 169, 170; sexual, 44, 45, 57, 149, 162, 170
inscrutable, 157, 162, 164
intact, 4, 5, 7, 8, 68, 70, 73
intercession, 100, 106, 112, 120
intercourse, 20, 26, 37n8, 42–4, 46, 48–9, 54, 58, 68, 79, 87, 134
inviolability, 11, 67, 71
Io, 16, 22n14, 26, 31, 32
Iphigenia, 37n6

Jesus, 5, 100, 101, 103, 104, 112, 132, 138, 142, 146n27; docetic, 104; historical, 103; intercessor, 112
Jews, 140–3, 148n50
Joan of Arc, 5, 9, 10–11, 23n34
Julian the Apostate, 56, 100, 112

kanephoroi, 16, 17, 26, 89n12
korai, 25, 36n1
kourotrophos, 15, 21n10
kyrios, 13, 26, 27, 31, 37n7

language, 27, 30–2, 34, 37n12, 38n16, 62n24, 110–12, 132, 133, 151, 157, 160, 161; of virgin choruses, 27, 30, 31, 32, 34
laws, 21n13, 71, 72, 77, 79–80, 84, 86, 91n49, 92n69, 95nn103, 108, 128, 144n8, 152, 155n7; magical, 71, 77; Roman, 72, 79–80, 84, 86, 92n69, 95n103, 95n108; sacred, 21n13
legal, 9, 25, 27, 31, 37n7, 66, 71, 72–3, 79–80, 91n50, 91n54, 115n38
legal entities, 37n7
legal precedent, 115n38
legal status, 9, 37n7, 66, 72–3, 79–80, 91n50; ambiguous, 79; unique, 66, 72
legends, 10, 19, 36, 93n86, 117, 120, 122, 124, 126n4, 136, 137, 144n3
Liberata, 117, 119, 121, 122, 125, 127n18
Licinia, 84, 87, 91n50, 95n101, 96n118
liminal, 7, 11, 14, 16, 44, 85
love, 3, 4, 16, 21n12, 74, 100, 109, 125, 136, 159, 163
lovers, 5, 15, 21n7, 87, 88, 90n32, 131, 132, 134, 158

Macrina, 19
Madhavi, 4, 5
madness, 26, 47
Madonna, 178
Madonna, la, 70, 72, 168
magic, 8, 67, 71, 83, 85, 139, 140; contagious, 71; imitative, 71; sympathetic, 67, 83, 85
magical, 34, 66, 71, 72, 74, 76, 77, 81, 82, 85
maidens, 7, 9, 16, 24–30, 32, 40, 44, 159–60; choruses, 9, 24–30; sacrifice, 74
Marcia, 87, 95n101, 96n118
margins/marginal, 7, 24, 75, 76, 77, 84, 85, 91n46, 93n82, 117

Marian: devotion, 129, 134, 136; imagery, 129; piety, 101, 129
Mariology, 104, 105
marriage, 3, 8, 14, 16, 17, 18, 19, 20, 21n3, 22n27, 23n30, 25, 26, 27, 32, 33, 35, 36, 36n2, 36n4, 44, 47, 53, 58, 61n17, 65n54, 66, 68, 71, 84–5, 87, 88, 90n32, 97n132, 98n145, 105, 117–18, 145n17, 171; age for, 53, 66; avoided, 117; bonds, 33; *manus*, 97n132, 98n145; resistance to, 23n30, 117; sacred marriage ritual, 18, 22n27; unconstrained by, 16
martyrdom, 100, 107–8, 111, 125
martyrs, 4, 9, 100, 101, 104, 107–9, 111, 113n1, 114nn29, 114nn32–3, 118, 125, 127n18, 154
Mary, Virgin, 4, 5–7, 11, 18, 100–6, 107, 109, 111, 112–13, 114n24, 116, 119, 125, 128–31, 133–8, 140, 142, 143, 145n17, 146n27, 149; autonomy of, 5; belief in, 149; expression of the Divine Feminine, 101; intercessor, 100, 112; sexual purity of, 5; as *Theotokos*, 101–6, 129; virginal body of, 6; virgin birth of, 6
Mary Magdalene, 102, 123
masculine females, 9, 16, 17, 33, 35, 49, 73, 91n54, 117
maternal, 5, 6, 15, 19, 21n8
matrons, 68, 83–6, 105, 108
McClure, Laura, 35, 37n10, 38n22, 38n24, 39n29
medieval, 6, 10, 110, 111, 115n38, 117, 118, 120, 124, 126n4, 126n6, 132, 135
metaphor, 23n34, 23n37, 36n2, 61n13, 69, 71, 107, 116, 136, 156–8, 160, 170
miasma, 32, 80
Middle Ages, 116–17, 122, 125, 126, 126n8, 127n10, 128, 129, 131
Minerva, 149, 153

misogyny, 83, 101–2, 116
Monk, Maria, 9, 11n6
Mulvey, Laura, 110, 115nn40–1
mystics, 133, 136, 145n11
myth/mythical/mythological, 4, 8, 14, 15, 16, 17, 20, 21n3, 24, 25, 26, 31, 36, 36n3, 37n8, 38n17, 67, 74, 76, 79, 89n8, 92n56, 94n97, 119, 150, 153, 155

Nausicaa, 44
Nestorius, 102–6, 113nn9–10, 114n17
nubile, 3, 5, 10, 13, 16, 18, 26, 27, 44, 58
nuns, 8, 9, 159
nymphe, 45

oath, 13, 15, 97n128
omens, 77, 83
Opimia, 84, 86, 93n94, 94n96, 96n111
Oppia, 77, 78, 86, 93n87, 94n94
orthodoxy, 150, 155
Ovid, 16, 22n18, 85, 90n31

pagan, paganism, 58, 100, 103, 107, 112, 113n10, 149, 150, 153, 154, 155n13
paides, 41
Palladium, 69, 73
Panathenaic festival, 17, 19, 22n21, 26
parthenios, 37n8, 63n29
parthenos, partheneia, 7, 11, 13–18, 20–1, 21n2, 21n12, 23n38, 25–7, 37n8, 40–58, 60n2, 61n16, 62n20, 63nn28–9, 63n32
Passion of Gallicanus, 100, 101, 112
patria potestas, 73, 91n44, 98n145
patriarchal/patriarchy, 4, 7, 8, 14, 16, 20, 33, 53, 85, 111, 119
Pausanias, 15, 16, 18
penetrate/penetration, 16, 17, 20, 43, 46, 48, 56, 69, 70, 79, 80, 82, 85, 158, 163, 174

Penthesileia, 16
peplos, 18, 22n21, 26, 37n6
pharmakos, 8, 75, 82, 83
Piaget, Jean, 6, 133–4, 137, 140, 145n21, 146n25, 147n43
piety, 10, 101, 106, 113, 118, 125, 129, 131, 138
Pindar, 29, 61n18
Plebeian Chastity, cult of, 84, 86
Pliny, 69, 71, 75, 81, 86, 87, 92n59, 92n71, 92n73, 94n94, 94n101, 97n125
Plutarch, 26, 66, 68, 81, 82, 84
Plynteria, 18
poisoning, 83–5, 86, 87, 97n131, 98n139, 132, 99n149
polis, 25, 27, 31, 34–6, 39n30
polluting/pollution, 20, 32, 34, 74, 80, 81, 96n112
pomerium, 69, 82, 97n126
Pomponia Rufina, 88, 94n96
Pontifex Maximus, 66, 69, 71, 73, 76, 80, 83, 90n27
Postumia, 86, 94n96
potency, virginal, 4, 7, 14, 25, 31; renewed, 4
Potnia Therôn, 17
power, 3–8, 10, 12n7, 14–20, 21n6, 24, 26, 28, 31–6, 69, 71, 73, 76, 78, 101, 102, 109, 111, 119, 130, 134, 136, 138, 139, 157–8, 160, 161, 168, 170; bisexual, 12n7, 119; generative, 19; magical, 76; Roman, 69, 73; spiritual, 101, 138; supernatural, 109; virginal, 4–8, 10, 14–21, 26, 28, 31–6, 69, 71, 73, 119, 123, 130, 136
prayer, 27–30, 32–3, 37n7, 38n16, 100, 112, 123, 143; virgins', 27–30, 100, 112; women's, 37n7
pregnancy, 26, 42–3, 47, 49, 55

priestess, 5, 15, 66, 69, 76, 89n21
privileges, 14, 37n7, 73, 91n54; Vestals', 73, 91n54
prodigium/prodigy, 8, 69, 77, 80–3, 86, 93n87, 95n111, 96nn111, 115
puberty, 18, 25, 40–3, 46, 48, 60n3, 61n9; rites, 18, 25
Publilia, 84, 87, 98n142
Pulcheria, Empress, 104–6, 109, 113, 114n17
punishment, 28, 74, 80, 83, 85, 96n118, 97n129, 128; of Vestals, 74, 80, 83, 96n118, 97n129; of wives, 85
purity, 5, 18, 68, 165, 168; and fertility, 18; sexual, 5, 68
Puttana, la, 70, 79

rape, 8, 28, 30, 33, 36n3, 79, 80, 88, 94n97, 120, 126n1; as metaphor, 28, 30
resistance, 8, 16, 23n30, 56, 158; of the virgin, 8, 16, 23n30
Rome, 5, 8, 53–4, 57, 66–71, 73–5, 77, 78, 82, 83, 84, 89n13, 89nn15–16, 93n84, 93n86, 96n118, 128, 130, 132; survival dependent upon virgins, 5, 8, 69, 71, 73, 74, 82; Vestal Virgins as symbols of, 68, 69, 70, 71, 73, 78, 82, 83, 89n16
Rossetti, Dante Gabriel, 11

sacrifice, 15, 22n13, 29, 74–5, 77, 78, 80–6, 87, 96n118, 97n126, 108, 112, 114n24, 124, 142; of martyrs, 108; of Vestals, 74–5, 77–8, 80, 81, 82, 83, 84, 86, 87, 96n118, 97n126
St Agnes, 100, 112, 124
St Julia, 124, 125
St Kümmernis, 117–20, 122, 126n8
St Ontkommer, 10, 117, 119, 123–5

St Uncumber, 117, 119
St Victor, 129–31
St Wilgefortis, 10, 116–19, 121, 122, 124, 125, 127n18; bearded female, 10
saints, 18, 100, 101, 106, 109, 110, 116–20, 123–5, 126n8; transvestite, 117; virgin, 18, 100, 117, 118, 119, 124
Sappho, 16, 37n9, 44–5, 63n32
scapegoat, 8, 74, 97n132
sexual attraction of the virgin, 16
sexual enigma, 156
sexual identity, 6, 16, 17, 157, 163, 168
sexual impurity, 67, 80
sexual independence, 7, 9, 11, 14, 16, 20, 23n38
sexual potency, through virginity, 4, 8, 15, 17, 18
sexual purity, 5, 6, 18, 20, 68, 149
sexual renunciation, 3, 4, 7, 74, 118, 129, 131
sexual status, 8, 9, 68; ambiguous, 8, 9
Sissa, Giulia, 7, 11n2, 23n38, 37n8, 63n29, 65n49
Sommerstein, Alan, 36n1, 38n23, 38n26, 39n27
Sophia, 102
Sophocles, 24, 25, 36, 95n108; female choruses of, 24, 36
Soranus, 54–7, 64n45, 64n48, 65n49
speech, 7, 27, 29–35, 37n10, 38n25, 50, 61n6, 139; female, dangerous, 7, 31–3, 34, 37n10; female, taming, 27, 29, 31, 33, 37n10
Staples, Ariadne, 23n39, 66, 68, 88n2, 88n6, 89n14, 90n38, 90n41, 91n43, 91n48, 91n50, 91n54, 93n90, 95n109, 96n114, 96n118, 97n123
status, 6, 8, 9, 25–7, 49, 53, 66, 72–3, 75, 76, 77, 79, 82, 89n8, 91n48, 91n50,
93n82, 96n113, 111, 126n6, 130, 149; Vestals' legal status, 9, 66, 68, 72–3, 77, 79; virginal, 6, 8, 13, 15, 20, 25–7, 49, 53, 91n50, 149
Strega, la, 70, 79
suspicion, 8, 79, 91n46, 101, 102
Syrinx, 16, 22n14

taming, 11, 25, 27, 34
Tarpeia, 79, 85, 94n100, 97n126
Tertullian, 108, 114n28
Thecla, 19
Theophilus, 136–7
transvestism, 9, 18, 117, 126n6
Tuccia, 86, 94n96, 96n111
Turner, Victor, 71, 88n4, 90n34, 92n66, 96n113

unchastity, of Vestals, 69, 74, 79–80, 94n94, 94n97
undefiled bodies, 66
unpenetrated, 69, 70, 82, 85
unpossessed, 9
untamed, 14, 25, 35
Ursuline convent, 9, 11

venerated/veneration, 5, 18, 109, 115n38, 116, 117, 119, 122
Venus, 84, 86, 87, 119; bearded, 119; *Obsequens*, 84, 86; *Verticordia*, 84, 86, 87
Vergine, la, 70, 72, 79
virginal, 5–11, 13, 18, 20, 23n39, 26, 35, 49, 159, 160, 166, 169, 172; autonomy, 5; body, 5, 6, 8, 11, 23n39, 49; energy, 8; fecundity, 16, 18, 19, 20; heroines, 10
Vita Macrinae, 23n36, 58
Volto Santo, 116–18, 120, 122, 126n4, 126n8

Warner, Marina, 11, 12n9, 101, 111, 113n4
weakness, 40, 60n4, 70, 79, 88n3, 93n82, 124, 163; perceived female, 40, 60n4, 70, 79, 88n3, 93n82
weaving, 9, 11, 17, 22n20–1, 22n26

well-dressing, 18
widows, 7, 42, 44, 68, 86, 107, 135
wild/wildness, 8, 14, 16, 17, 25, 28, 33, 35, 36
witches/witchcraft, 21n6, 66, 70, 77–9, 80, 82, 83, 84, 85, 93n92, 98n141

PHOENIX SUPPLEMENTARY VOLUMES

1 *Studies in Honour of Gilbert Norwood*   edited by Mary E. White
2 *Arbiter of Elegance: A Study of the Life and Works of C. Petronius*   Gilbert Bagnani
3 *Sophocles the Playwright*   S.M. Adams
4 *A Greek Critic: Demetrius on Style*   G.M.A. Grube
5 *Coastal Demes of Attika: A Study of the Policy of Kleisthenes*   C.W.J. Eliot
6 *Eros and Psyche: Studies in Plato, Plotinus, and Origen*   John M. Rist
7 *Pythagoras and Early Pythagoreanism*   J.A. Philip
8 *Plato's Psychology*   T.M. Robinson
9 *Greek Fortifications*   F.E. Winter
10 *Comparative Studies in Republican Latin Imagery*   Elaine Fantham
11 *The Orators in Cicero's 'Brutus': Prosopography and Chronology*   G.V. Sumner
12 *'Caput' and Colonate: Towards a History of Late Roman Taxation*   Walter Goffart
13 *A Concordance to the Works of Ammianus Marcellinus*   Geoffrey Archbold
14 *Fallax opus: Poet and Reader in the Elegies of Propertius*   John Warden
15 *Pindar's 'Olympian One': A Commentary*   Douglas E. Gerber
16 *Greek and Roman Mechanical Water-Lifting Devices: The History of a Technology*   John Peter Oleson

17 *The Manuscript Tradition of Propertius*   James L. Butrica

18 Parmenides of Elea *Fragments: A Text and Translation with an Introduction*   edited by David Gallop

19 *The Phonological Interpretation of Ancient Greek: A Pandialectal Analysis*   Vít Bubeník

20 *Studies in the Textual Tradition of Terence*   John N. Grant

21 *The Nature of Early Greek Lyric: Three Preliminary Studies*   R.L. Fowler

22 Heraclitus *Fragments: A Text and Translation with a Commentary*   edited by T.M. Robinson

23 *The Historical Method of Herodotus*   Donald Lateiner

24 *Near Eastern Royalty and Rome, 100–30 BC*   Richard D. Sullivan

25 *The Mind of Aristotle: A Study in Philosophical Growth*   John M. Rist

26 *Trials in the Late Roman Republic, 149 BC to 50 BC*   Michael Alexander

27 *Monumental Tombs of the Hellenistic Age: A Study of Selected Tombs from the Pre-Classical to the Early Imperial Era*   Janos Fedak

28 *The Local Magistrates of Roman Spain*   Leonard A. Curchin

29 Empedocles *The Poem of Empedocles: A Text and Translation with an Introduction*   edited by Brad Inwood

30 Xenophanes of Colophon *Fragments: A Text and Translation with a Commentary*   J.H. Lesher

31 *Festivals and Legends: The Formation of Greek Cities in the Light of Public Ritual*   Noel Robertson

32 *Reading and Variant in Petronius: Studies in the French Humanists and Their Manuscript Sources*   Wade Richardson

33 *The Excavations of San Giovanni di Ruoti, Volume 1: The Villas and Their Environment*   Alastair M. Small and Robert J. Buck

34 *Catullus Edited with a Textual and Interpretative Commentary*   D.F.S. Thomson

35 *The Excavations of San Giovanni di Ruoti, Volume 2: The Small Finds*   C.J. Simpson, with contributions by R. Reece and J.J. Rossiter

36 *The Atomists: Leucippus and Democritus Fragments: A Text and Translation with a Commentary*   C.C.W. Taylor

37 *Imagination of a Monarchy: Studies in Ptolemaic Propaganda*   R.A. Hazzard

38 *Aristotle's Theory of the Unity of Science*   Malcolm Wilson

39 Empedocles *The Poem of Empedocles: A Text and Translation with an Introduction, Revised edition*   edited by Brad Inwood

40 *The Excavations of San Giovanni di Ruoti, Volume 3: The Faunal and Plant Remains*   M.R. MacKinnon, with contributions by A. Eastham, S.G. Monckton, D.S. Reese, and D.G. Steele

41 *Justin and Pompeius Trogus: A Study of the Language of Justin's 'Epitome' of Trogus* J.C. Yardley

42 *Studies in Hellenistic Architecture*   F.E. Winter

43 *Mortuary Landscapes of North Africa*   edited by David L. Stone and Lea M. Stirling

44 *Virginity Revisited: Configurations of the Unpossessed Body*   edited by Bonnie MacLachlan and Judith Fletcher